Beyond the Gat

MW00626736

Noel Tyl in the "Introduction" . . .

For millennia, the outer three planets were not there in horoscopes. Imagine how astrologers felt when they were simply unable to explain from the measurements at hand that which was overwhelming? Misery and failure were easy perhaps: Saturn. But glory? Transcendence? Genius? Inspiration, vision, ecstacy? World perspectives, even in a smaller world; power; revolutionary change?

Jeff Jawer in "The Discoveries of Uranus, Neptune and Pluto" . . .

The moment of any beginning is an appropriate one. This is true for individuals, as well as for planets, plants or puppy dogs.

Mary E. Shea in "Making Choices with the Outer Planet Transit" . . .

The complexity of a Uranus, Neptune, or Pluto transit implies dilemma. It may be impossible to be right or wrong. But it is important that you learn. This you will do, willing or not.

Joanne Wickenburg in "Bringing the Outer Planets Down to Earth" . . .

Have you ever committed to a relationship with someone who turned out to be very different from what you originally believed? Have you ever fooled yourself in other ways and wondered later how you could have been so naive? All of these experiences are normal modus operandi for Uranus, Neptune and Pluto.

Jayj Jacobs in "Relating Through the Outer Planets" . . .

Uranus in the 8th House expects sex always to be exciting and won't settle for Yankee pot roast. It needs fancy French sauces and nouvelle cuisine but will also grab a burger on a bun or a taco on the run, with a friend or two.

Capel N. McCutcheon in "Personal Expression of Archetypal Aspects" ..

The Bible states that "The Heavens declare the glory of God!" The dance steps of the Archetypal Aspects of these great planets signal to us the changes that are to be made within our world and ourselves.

Jeff Green in "Trauma and the Outer Planets" . . .

The breakdown (Uranus) and dissolution (Neptune) of societal beliefs and values (Saturn/Capricorn), i.e. the American Dream, have begun to generate an ever-increasing collective futility, depression, anxiety angst, and hopelessness that have potentially far-reaching socio/political/economic implications to radically (Uranus) alter "the system" as currently structured.

Jeff Jawer in "The Outer Planets and the Inner Spirit" . . .

Beyond the gates of Saturn lie liberation and madness, inspiration and folly, illumination and death. Each step beyond the known is fraught with danger and opportunity, simultaneously a journey away from and toward the self. This is the story of the outer planets, each of which takes us to higher levels of consciousness and new possibilities of experience.

To Write to the Authors

If you wish to contact the author or would like more information about this book, please write to the author in care of Llewellyn Worldwide and we will forward your request. Both the authors and publisher appreciate hearing from you and learning of your enjoyment of this book and how it has helped you. Llewellyn Worldwide cannot guarantee that every letter written to the authors can be answered, but all will be forwarded. Please write to:

THE LLEWELLYN NEW TIMES
P.O. Box 64383-389, St. Paul, MN 55164-0383, U.S.A.
Please enclose a self-addressed, stamped envelope for reply, or $1.00 to cover costs.
If outside U.S.A. enclose international postal reply coupons.

Free Catalog from Llewellyn

For more than 90 years, Llewellyn has brought its readers knowledge in the fields of metaphysics and human potential. Learn about the newest books in spiritual guidance, natural healing, astrology, occult philosophy and more. Enjoy book reviews, new age articles, a calendar of events, plus current advertised products and services. To get your free copy of the New Times, send your name and address to:

THE LLEWELLYN NEW TIMES
P.O. Box 64383-389, St. Paul, MN 55164-0383, U.S.A.

Llewellyn's New World Astrology Series
Book 10

How to Personalize the Outer Planets

The Astrology of Uranus, Neptune, and Pluto

Edited by Noel Tyl

1992
Llewellyn Publications
St. Paul, Minnesota, U.S.A. 55164-0383

FIRST EDITION

Cover Painting: Hrana Janto

Library of Congress Cataloging-in-Publication Data

How to personalize the outer planets : the astrology of Uranus, Neptune, and Pluto / edited by Noel Tyl.
    p. cm. -- (Llewellyn's new world astrology series)
    ISBN 0-87542-389-2
    1. Uranus (Planet) — Miscellanea. 2. Neptune (Planet) — Miscellanea. 2. Pluto (Planet) — Miscellanea. 4. Planets — Miscellanea. 5. Astrology. I. Tyl, Noel, 1936–. II. Series.
BF1724.2.U7H68 1992
133.5′3--dc20   92-20271
                                                CIP

Llewellyn Publications
A Division of Llewellyn Worldwide, Ltd.
P.O. Box 64383, St. Paul, MN 55164-0383

THE NEW WORLD ASTROLOGY SERIES

This series is designed to give all people who are interested and involved in astrology the latest information on a variety of subjects. Llewellyn has given much thought to the prevailing trends and to the topics that would be most important to our readers.

Future books will include such topics as management of crisis, dimensions of consciousness, astrology and past lives, and many other subjects of interest to a wide range of people. This project has evolved because of the lack of information on these subjects and because we wanted to offer our readers the viewpoints of the best experts in each field in one volume.

We anticipate publishing approximately four books per year on varying topics and updating previous editions when new material becomes available. We know this series will fill a gap in your astrological library. We look for only the best writers and article topics when planning the new books and appreciate any feedback from our readers on subjects you would like to see covered.

Llewellyn's New World Astrology Series will be a welcome addition to the novice, student and professional alike. It will provide introductory as well as advanced information on all the topics listed above—and more.

Enjoy, and feel free to write to Llewellyn with your suggestions or comments.

Other Books in This Series

Forthcoming

Contents

Noel Tyl

For over 20 years, Noel Tyl has been one of the most prominent astrologers in the Western world. His 17 textbooks, built around the 12-volume *Principles and Practice of Astrology*, were extraordinarily popular throughout the 1970s, teaching astrology with new and practical sensitivity to modern psychotherapeutic methodology.

At the same time, Noel presented lectures and seminars throughout the United States, appearing in practically every metropolitan area and on well over 100 radio and televison shows. Additionally, he founded and edited the legendary *Astrology Now* magazine.

His book, *Holistic Astrology: The Analysis of Inner and Outer Environments*, distributed by Llewellyn Publications, has been translated into German and Italian. His international lectures are very popular throughout Denmark, Norway, Germany, and Switzerland where for the first three World Congresses of Astrology he was a keynote speaker.

Most recently, Noel wrote *Prediction in Astrology* (Llewellyn Publications), a master volume of technique and practice, and edited Book 9 of the Llewellyn New World Astrology Series, *How to Use Vocational Astrology*.

Noel is a graduate of Harvard University with a degree in psychology, and lives in McLean, VA.

Introduction

When The Three
Were Not There

Noel Tyl

When we reach into the past, we use our eyes, our vision. Beyond reading old texts for former thoughts, beyond looking at art to see beauty in the eyes of older times, we look at the world around us— the mountains, canyons, deserts, seas—and we say, "this is what they saw too!" This shared vision helps us identify with the presence of life before our times. Through this identification, we are able to conjecture and appreciate perceptions and values of life long ago.

Yet, it is *not* so in the astrological view, in which terms our skies today are different. The heavens long ago were indeed clearer and cleaner, therefore brighter and more animated, but before Galileo's invention of the telescope (1608) astrologers could only see as far as their natural vision would allow. In some cases, this was prodigious: the Danish astronomer/astrologer Tycho Brahe (1546–1601) was able to catalogue 777 fixed stars by *line of sight*. (Kepler published these star positions three years after Brahe's death.)

But no one saw Uranus, Neptune, and Pluto. No astrologer throughout history, before the discovery of these outer planets, saw in the heavens, in horoscopes, what we see today. This is a daunting realization for us when we seek to identify with the past, with those astrologically codified life-values of long ago. Every time we look at a horoscope from prediscovery times, we either search for these planets that are not there to "fill out" analysis, or we thrust them into the horoscope from our enlightened point in time to complete the picture.

In the eternal scheme of our astrology, we are not beyond a blink or two of our eyes with regard to understanding Uranus; maybe one blink for Neptune; and with Pluto, we are still opening them. The textbooks that fashioned the modern era of astrology were largely born of research conducted at the turn of this century, just post-Neptune and pre-Pluto. Alan Leo, in his *Art of Synthesis* —still a fine book for today's astrology—was appropriately experimental with his thoughts about Uranus and mystical about Neptune. Leo died in 1918, and later editions of this book post-Pluto carry a publisher's note, probably written when Pluto was about nine years old for us, that suggests discoverer Lowell's confusion with already postulated asteroids and assorted esoterica, which usually accompany any state of unknowing.

Out of this insecurity in our post-discovery, modern time grew an idea that, when the outer planets were not known, they were, in effect, not in human consciousness. The symbolisms could not contribute significantly to horoscopes of the past. I suggest that two things were behind this view: the new bodies were awesome discoveries apparently put under the aegis of that day's cognoscenti (a typical view of the turn-of-the-century esoteric movement; when, actually, had a new planet been discovered before anyway?) and the fact that we did not yet know how to measure the positions of these outer planets way back when. What we were not sure of and could not easily use could not be valuable earlier, when "we" knew less. What we didn't know simply had not existed!

Times change, and since eyes *have* blinked twice and are opening wide again, what we know about these giant symbolisms tells us differently: those planets *were* in the heavens, they *did* manifest in the lives of individuals, and they are essential for our understanding of horoscopes of the past. When we do *not* include the outer planets in pre-discovery horoscopes, we are talking *less* about astrology and *more* simply about what astrologers saw.

To prove our case, the argument comes down to meanings, clearly and simply; the life given to our planetary symbols at any time in history.

The outer planets symbolize concepts in terms of our observations since their discovery and our inspired understanding. It is that way with *all* the symbols of astrology: they come into development, are touched by the inspired perception of astrologers, and change over time *by keeping pace with the times*. For example, Anthony Louis, in his landmark study, *Horary Astrology* (Llewellyn Publications 1991), points out the intriguing derivation and change of the sign Libra: "Libra came to symbolize marriage because the husband and wife are jointed together in the yoke of matrimony(!)" Louis refers back to the Greek astrologer Stephanus in 621 A.D. who stated that "rising Libra brings servitude to all men," punning the Greek word for Libra, which really means "yoke."

The glyph for Libra, looking like the scales of justice—another change of concept—or the beltline region and lower back area—still another dimension—originally depicted a yoke that was placed around the necks of oxen. It had that meaning then, thanks to the inspiration of Stephanus. Louis continues: "Only in modern times is marriage seen as the egalitarian relationship symbolized by the balanced scale of Libra. In English, the word 'yokefellow' still refers to a partner or a spouse (yokemate)."

We reverse that process when we apply our modern meanings of the three modern planets back into times that were. Will this be meaningful? How can we be sure that it is or isn't? Today, we can get pretty specific about these outer planets, thanks to the inspiration of our modern-day observers; do the symbolisms reflecting our observations now intrude upon the sensibilities of times long ago or, indeed, illuminate them?

For example, Uranian concepts of individuation, eccentricity, and adventuresomeness would be awkward within the societal structures of most of past history, except in the lives of singularly special people, as we shall see. But we can simplify meanings in order to fit in better in old horoscopes. Maybe for Uranus, we can just add the concept of "intensity" or "invention" and leave it at that.

But we must contend with a horoscope-selection bias within this process: we do not see the horoscopes of average people from times long ago, the ones who simply were more or less intense and no one really caring on the farm or in the stableyard. What we do see are the horoscopes of people who made history. Perhaps they *needed* the outer planets—perhaps as we know those planets today in *our* inspiration.

Then we can ask, if Uranus, Neptune, and Pluto *had been* discovered in earlier times, what meanings would they have been given then and what refinements and change would those meanings have undergone to reach us now in modern times? Would our behaviors reflect these planets *differently* than they do now?

We are skirting the concept of whether our astrology conditions our life or whether our life creates our astrology. The safe answer is that it is astrologers, through their observation and inspiration, who give symbols meaning, and any tie-in with the everlastingly evolving imprimatur of time is either semantically fortuitous or indeed just as it should be. Astrologers are the instrument of their astrology. Without astrologers, there *is* no astrology.

Measurements for the Famous

If we study famous horoscopes from the past, we *can* get comfortable with the idea that the famous did indeed need the outer planets, that our inspired understandings of the outer planets are so far so good. Every astrologer has studied many horoscopes of people of our day who live out only a portion of their horoscopic potential; every astrologer knows that the more of the horoscope that is fulfilled, the more prominent is the human being. I often recall Aristotle's simple definition of greatness as "the fulfillment of potential!"

We are looking at highly evolved individuals (Uranus), all of whom had special vision (Neptune), to establish new perspectives (Pluto) and make history happen. It is almost to be anticipated that Martin Luther King's Pluto related to his Midheaven by opposition (he was born pre-Pluto); that Elisabeth Kubler-Ross' Pluto was tightly conjunct her Cancer Sun (born pre-Pluto). Ross is the pioneer of humane programs the world over for the management of death and care for the dying in hospitals.

We can gain great confidence with our modern meanings when we see Neptune conjunct Sun-Venus and Jupiter opposed Pluto in the horoscope of pre-Neptune, pre-Pluto Paul Cezanne (also with Uranus conjunct the Moon); when we see Pluto conjunct Moon-Venus and Neptune rising in the horoscope of pre-Pluto, pre-Neptune Auguste Renoir (also with Uranus conjunct Mercury).

Let us study a famous person's horoscope carefully in detail, first *without* the outer planets and then *with* them. This male is recognized throughout the world as one of the great geniuses of all time. There simply is no doubt of his status, and, thanks to biographies and research study by other astrologers, there is great security about his birthtime.

This horoscope is almost too simple to believe: the triple conjunction of Saturn-Sun-Mercury is trine to the Midheaven. Yes, this is very strong creativity, what with the Aquarian emphasis, the Air Sign trine, with Saturn in its own sign(s), i.e., Aquarius, and in a House with Capricorn on the cusp. This 5th House projection is definitely solid creativity, especially with Mercury ruling the Mid-heaven and the Ascendant. But, as well, we could expect some "heaviness" here, perhaps even chronic illness or worry, with Saturn conjoining the Sun, ruler of the 12th.

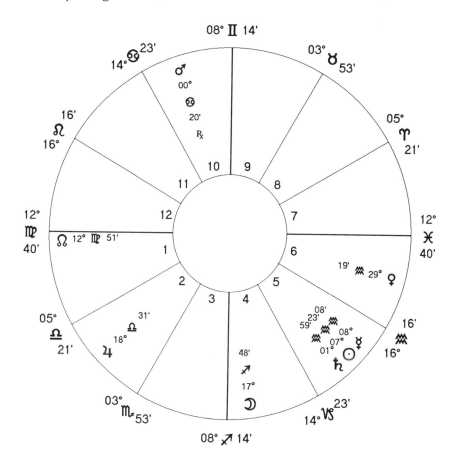

At this point, we must remember that, without the outer planets, astrologers had to load a lot of significance onto the planets they had. Saturn was *really* the end of the line. Saturn was the great grounder, the great "malefic." Medical care in older days barely existed. In this horoscope, the astrologer would have to see and study the potential for health difficulty, fear of and confrontation with death. Indeed, the astrologer would feel some amelioration of these portents because of Saturn's double dignity, if you will, ruling Aquarius and being in Capricorn's House.

Venus is trine to Mars, the only planet above the horizon, and Mars is retrograde. Again this is an aspect of professional creativity, especially involving the work Houses 6 and 10, and we also could anticipate a pleasant, even playful personality, with lots of popular acceptance from this aspect. The 18th century astrologer would anticipate emotional sensitivity here as well. The popularity dimension would be reinforced by Jupiter in Libra, ruling the 7th House of the public, sextile to the Moon in Jupiter's exuberant sign of Sagittarius.

Jupiter, ruling the 4th, sextile the Moon in the 4th suggests one parent being very supportive of the native's need to be heard, need to have impact (Moon in Sagittarius). The big trine to the Midheaven from the 5th House suggests the other parent's support. The fortified 2nd House shows excellent self-worth feelings, even to the point of self-aggrandizement. That's really all there is in this horoscope.

There is no square. There is no opposition. Where is the drive? Mars is retrograde. If we did not know that this is the horoscope of one of the most famous people who ever lived, we would be sorely pressed to see anything but a creative life—probably in the arts as a communicator (the Venus and Mercury dimensions)—going along swimingly, with only bad health or depression as extra baggage. Is this horoscope really genius? Even *after* the fact of our knowing it is? Our instincts tell us *something is missing*.

Wolfgang Amadeus Mozart *needed* the outer planets. They were there and his life used them, if you will; they were illuminated *through* his life. Why, we do not know. There were other children born close to that time in Salzburg, just as there were other babes given life in Bethlehem that night long ago. Astrology and astrologers confront this miracle often, and always that confrontation tells us what we do not know and defines what keeps all of us human.

As soon as the outer planets are introduced, however, the horoscope becomes special, extraordinarily special: Uranus is conjunct the Descendant, square the Midheaven, and square the exact conjunction of Pluto and the Moon in the 4th House (Mutable signs, angularity, and squares: indicators of sensitivity, reaction, and inspiration that take on enormous force). Neptune is opposed the 5th House triple conjunction and is sextile the Midheaven. Good Lord in Heaven, if I may, is there any doubt of musical creativity?!

The Lunar Nodal axis conjunct the horizon *and* Uranus is another extremely strong emphasis of public projection and the maternal influence.

Whew! The power from seeing the outer planets! The presence of such consummate potential is overwhelming, now and when I stood at the doorway to the room where Mozart was born and looked at the walls: "this is what they saw too, that night long ago."

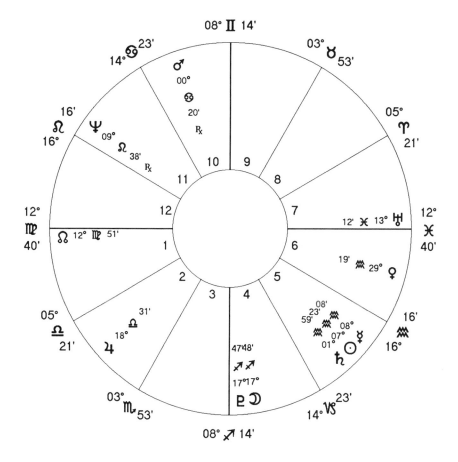

Mozart
Jan. 27, 1756, 8 p.m. LMT
Salzburg, Austria
13E00 47N45
Placides Houses
Source: Biographies and *American Book of Charts* by Lois Rodden,
ACS Publications, Inc., San Diego, CA, 1980

Some corroboration for the deductions we have made:

- Mozart's father, Leopold (Jupiter), was an outstanding violinist and composer in his own right. He was extremely supportive of young Wolfgang (sextile with Pluto-Moon), acting as mentor and stage-father and tour manager, beginning when the child was three. Mozart began composing at the age of four, and at six was with his father on a grand concert tour throughout Germany, France, Holland, and England, including command performances at the Imperial Palace in Vienna. Mozart performed as violinist, harpsichordist, organist, at the clavier, as composer and improviser, accompanying symphony orchestras, transposing music upon demand ... even playing the clavier with a sheet covering the keys to show his incredible dexterity. [Mercury emphasis by aspect and rulership of Ascendant and Midheaven].

- Mozart is described as extremely sensitive and affectionate by nature and, early on, extremely devoted to his father. But the young man started to gather steam (Uranus, if you will), and his father admonished him slightly in a letter:

  "In everything you are impulsive and hasty. Your character is now quite different from what it was when you were a child and a boy. Then you were inclined to be serious rather than childish, and when you were seated at the keyboard or otherwise occupied with music, no one dared make the slightest jest. Your face was so grave and you had such a pensive, old-before-your-years look that many forecast that you would die young." {Saturn giving way to Uranus.]

- Mozart had a wide circle of friends of all social classes. He was very sensitive to their feelings. [Moon rules XI.]

- Mozart had a great friendship with Haydn, 24 years his senior and very well-established as a brilliant composer. In 1785, when Mozart was 29 years old [Saturn return], Haydn told Leopold Mozart: "I declare to you before God as a man of honor, that your son is the greatest composer that I know, either personally or by reputation; he has taste, and beyond that the most consummate knowledge of the art of composition.

Mozart dedicated six string quartets to Haydn, and sources

agree, "the musical language of these quartets was at that time so radical and daring [Uranus] that virtually none of Mozart's contemporaries was capable of appreciating them."

- At the same time of his Saturn return, Mozart became very ill and began to worry about death. He began to ponder religious problems and in the end became a Freemason.

Leopold died in 1787, and in his last letters to his father, Mozart wrote, "Never do I go to bed without thinking that, young as I am, I may not see the dawn . . . Since it is the true end and aim of our lives, I have for the last two years worked toward an intimacy with death, mankind's best and truest friend, so that he holds for me no terror, but only tranquillity and comfort."

Sources say that Mozart's preoccupation with thoughts about death arose from his "constant ill-health." [Saturn conjunct Sun, ruler of the 12th.]

Additionally, Mozart carried the burden of the continual illness of his wife, which began to jeopardize his already precarious financial situation. [Mozart's 12th House is his wife's 6th within this horoscope; his 6th, ruled by Uranus square the Moon, is her 12th.]

At the very end of his life, without stopping his prodigious productivity, Mozart was seized by fits of depression [Saturn] and suffered attacks of dizziness, vomiting, and fainting. Sources point out that Mozart was "obsessed by the idea that he had been poisoned." [Neptune]

- Mozart died on December 5, 1791, while completing the Requiem, his Mass for the Dead. [Solar Arc Saturn was 5' of arc from exact square to his natal Midheaven.]

Mozart composed 24 operas, 41 symphonies, 23 piano concertos, 5 violin concertos, 10 other concertos, an incredible number of piano pieces, 19 Masses, many Choral Motets, many songs and serenades, and some 100 Chamber pieces. His music is still played and revered constantly throughout the turn of time, throughout the world. He died at the age of 35 years and 10 months.

This dramatic example illustrates the four points of this discussion. First: People who make history appear to "need" the outer planets to fulfill their lot. In the *World of Music, An Illustrated Encyclopedia* (Abradale Press, NY 1963), from which many of the quotes above were taken, there is cited an intriguing comment by one Robert Pitrou:

"The birth of ideas and their elaboration were probably unconscious [to Mozart]. His mind was constantly creating, without ever a break. When he came to the third stage—to committing to paper— he used to give his ideas at one stroke the very form he was aiming at." How else could Mozart's horoscope show this all-pervasive inspiration and creativity except through Neptune, its opposition with the overwhelming 5th House triple conjunction and its sextile with the Midheaven? Just the Neptune opposition with Mercury alone, ruler of the Ascendant and Midheaven, would begin to tell the story and certainly would suggest music within the creativity profile. But within the grand structure that we do see incorporating the outer planets, this Neptune *is* the unconscious, it *is* the music of this genius, it *is* his full awareness of and oneness with art.

Second: Our modern day understandings, our meanings for the outer planets, *are* valid for times past, enriching the special lives we meet. This is a credit to the inspiration astrologers have had for the last 200 years since the discovery of Uranus, for the last 150 years since the discovery of Neptune, and for about 60 years since Pluto. In fact, the magical way our meanings for any symbol in astrology evolve suggests that meanings in use in the lifestream are *always* valid: they are not contrived or imagined, they *emerge* through constant refinement and observation.

Third: We are reminded that fulfilling more of the horoscope helps to fulfill potentials and achieve greatness. This does not mean that to be great one must touch the world; it means that the person doing a job the best way possible, caring for family and society the best way possible, and fulfilling goals and dreams, is close to fulfilling potentials. One can be great without being illustrious.

And yet, with regard to the outer planets, those who *are* illustrious in reality seem also to have horoscopes that are remarkable in measurements.

And Fourth: There is an extraordinarily high incidence of *angularity* involving at least one of the three outer planets in the horoscopes of the illustrious, old or modern. Angularity seems most important first, then conjunctions, and then squares. These observations begin to tell the story.

In *The Astro*Carto*Graphy Book of Maps* by Jim Lewis and Ariel Guttman (Llewellyn Publications, St. Paul MN 1989), there are horoscopes of famous people, almost all of them reliably timed. The horoscopes are divided into sections. In the "Activists" section, there are nine cases, for example, and only two do not have an outer planet angular. Among 27 "Politicians," there are only six exceptions.

Among nine "Musicians and Artists," there is only one exception, and that person (Sir Rudolph Bing) was not a musician or artist but was a businessman, an impresario in the arts. And so it goes.

In searching my personal files, the slightest degree of celebrity was *always* corroborated by angularity of an outer planet. There is something here that *is* speaking to us. The angularity dimension for prominence is closely followed by conspicuous conjunctions and then squares. The opposition seems the least frequent in occurrence.

For millennia, the outer three planets were *not* there in horoscopes. However, a glowing pantheon of the famous, those who punctuated history, do attest to the outer planets in their proper places, at the proper times. Imagine how astrologers felt when they were simply unable to explain from the measurements at hand that which was overwhelming! Misery and failure were easy perhaps: Saturn. But glory? Transcendence? Genius? Inspiration, vision, ecstasy? World perspectives, even in a smaller world; power; revolutionary change?

Fascinatingly, Alan Leo called Uranus "The Awakener." In our inspired perception over the last 200 years, we have given Uranus rulership over astrology. Are we indeed awakening to new visions and perspectives the next time we blink our eyes in the scheme of time?

Postscript

I want to welcome formally the awakeners in this book! Each of them eagerly tackled the assignments we created together: to bring the outer planets down to earth every way we could and to personalize them so that each of us and our clients might get in better touch with our portions of greatness. Thank you, writers, for your care and inspiration. Thank you readers, for being with us in the quest.

Noel Tyl
Editor

Jeff Jawer

Jeff Jawer holds a B.A. in Astrology from The University of Massachusetts and has been a professional astrologer since 1973. He is one of the pioneers in experiential astrology and is known for his work with astro-drama in the United States, Canada, Europe, and Brazil. Jeff holds professional certification from the City of Atlanta's Board of Astrology Examiners (for which he has served as chair) and the American Federation of Astrologers.

Jeff is one of the founders of AFAN and UAC and has been a leader in establishing astrologers' rights.

Jeff's articles appear in numerous publications as well as in Llewellyn's *Spiritual Metaphysical & New Trends in Astrology* and *Intimate Relationships*.

Among his travels, Jeff spent two years in France associated with Alexander Ruperti's Network for Humanistic Astrology. He met his wife Danick there, with whom he has conducted workshops in experiential astrology. Jeff and Danick and their two daughters reside in Atlanta, Georgia.

Prologue

The Discovery of the Outer Planets

Jeff Jawer

New discoveries enter consciousness at "ripe" moments. This is true for both individual unfoldment and for collective experience. Until the latter part of the 18th century, our solar system was bound by the ancient model of the seven: the Sun, the Moon, and the five planets. The inhabitants of earth viewed the sky as an unchanging family of these seven angels of light. The outermost of these was Saturn, whose pale color and stately march through the heavens symbolized the limits of human experience. It was Saturn that was blamed for loss of life, and it was to Saturn that we looked to measure the end of all things. While the telescope was invented in 1608, it took almost 200 years until the discover of Uranus smashed the barriers of space and mind. The moment was ripe.

The discovery of Uranus, appropriately enough, was an accident. Sir William Herschel of England did not use his telescope to record the positions of familiar bodies, but found pleasure in searching the sky for new and unknown objects. It was on the evening of March 13, 1781 that his attention was caught by the new planet. At first he was unaware that he had discovered the solar system's newest member. He did know, however, that this disk-like body was *not* a star.

It was not long before astronomers realized the magnitude of his discovery. Sir William chose to call the new planet Georgium Sidus after King George III, who granted him a stipend and honored him with a title for his work. Not unexpectedly, the name drew little favor from astronomers outside Britain. The German astronomer Johann Bode suggested the name Uranus after the sky god Urania.

This name was eventually accepted, although the very name Herschel after the discoverer, has been applied to the same planet.

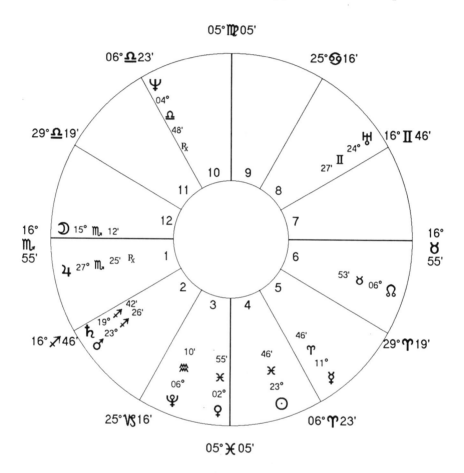

Chart 1
Discovery of Uranus
March 13, 1781, 11:00 p.m. GMT
London, England
0W10 51N30

Period of Revolution

Herschel's discovery did more than shatter our concept of the solar system. It heralded a period of revolution in politics and science that coincided with the birth of America. The esotericist expects the events of daily life to synchronize with the advances of science. In the discovery of Uranus, we have a perfect example of the convergence of many streams, all leading to the same end; invention, revolution, and transcendance. The year 1781 was the year of Cornwallis' surrender to the American forces and marked the publication of Emmanuel Kant's *Critique of Pure Reason,* a breakthrough in philosophy. Only two years earlier, the mechanization of spinning was completed with the invention of the spinning mule. 1782 brought James Watt's steam engine, 1785 the power-driven loom, 1793 the cotton gin, and in 1796 the invention of lithography. This remarkable burst of creative energy was matched on the political front as well, with the opening of the French Revolution in 1789, close on the heels of our American experiment in democracy. Mesmer brought hypnotism to light in 1778. The old barriers were down at last. Thomas Jefferson, an Aries, perhaps expressed it best when he wrote in 1787, "I hold it, that a little rebellion, now and then, is a good thing, and as necessary in the political world as storms in the physical."

The exact moment of Herschel's discovery is unknown. However, a horoscope drawn for the evening of March 13, 1781 works well to describe the birth of this momentous era in history (see chart 1). The chart is characterized by a mutable T-square among Uranus, a Mars-Saturn conjunction, and the Sun. The conjunction of Mars and Saturn is one of the most potent indicators of physical manifestation. Its placement in Sagittarius is particularly appropriate for the observation of distant objects through a telescope. The opposition to Uranus both describes what is manifesting, and as well, the concretization of the new age of invention and revolution. The Sun's position at the fulcrum serves to emphasize the significance of the event, although its position in Pisces might describe the uncertainty of the meaning of the new object at that moment. The orbit of Uranus was very difficult to plot, and disturbances to it (perturbations) led to the search for and eventually the discovery of Neptune.

A minor aspect that is often overlooked is the quintile angle of 72 degrees. Quintiles serve as important significators of talent or perception. In the Uranus discovery chart, Mercury is in a close quintile to Uranus. The creative genius of Herschel brings perception to a new discovery. The right of free speech might be seen here as well as in the trine from Jupiter to the Sun. This trine is also a clear indication of expansion, our awareness of a solar system expanded in size overnight.

The Moon's position in Scorpio is another factor that demands attention, *particularly since it was in that sign as well at the discovery of Neptune and Pluto.* The image of the researcher scraping away another level of life's mystery comes easily to mind. The Moon's discomfort in this sign might be due to the necessity of transforming habits when old patterns are broken. A contraparallel of Uranus and Pluto restates this theme of forced changes in consciousness brought by the event. The square from Pluto to the Moon's Nodes may also serve to remind us of the power of Uranus' discovery to undermine long-held connections among groups. All of this was yet to be embraced, discovered, by us—Neptune and Pluto still unknown in 1781.

Midpoint Pictures

The use of midpoint pictures adds depth to any chart reading. The chart for the discovery of Uranus shows Pluto conjunct the Sun-Saturn midpoint. We could call this "transformation of conscious limits yet to come." The Sun at the midpoint of Mars-Uranus is described as, "A sudden adjustment to new circumstances and conditions in life, injury, accident, operation, birth," in Reinhold Ebertin's *The Combination of Stellar Influences.* The Sun at the midpoint of Saturn-Uranus is described in the same book as, "Physical exposure to severe tests of strength, the power of resistance, rebellion, inflexibility. Separation." If the time used in our discovery chart is close to correct, we will also find that Sun-Uranus equals Moon-South Node. This is another powerful picture of deep changes in daily lifestyle, public interactions and consciousness.

The discovery charts of the outer planets should work like any other natal charts. Examination of the basic aspects and midpoints seems to bear this out.

The 25th Degree

The La Volasfera book of degree symbols describes the 25th degree of Gemini as, "An old book lying open upon a table, and beside it a burning lamp." The interpretation centers on the idea of a studious mind, mental powers. Kozminsky calls this degree, "A hand issuing from heavens holding a great scroll on which is a shining pentagram." We again have a symbol of literacy or intelligence. John Sandbach calls this degree, "the gardner of ideas." Jeryl Keane calls it studious, "...a person much given to serious study, usually of a scientific turn of mind." The Sabian Symbol for this degree is, "Frost-covered trees against winter skies." Rudhyar describes this as: "the revelation of archetypal form and essential rhythm of existence." Rhythm is often associated with Uranus. Certainly all these references to thought are appropriate to that which some consider the higher octave of Mercury discovered through Uranus.

The physical characteristics of Uranus also support the astrological interpretation. Uranus rotates on its side, making it the most eccentric of planets within its own realm. Its orbit, however, is relatively circular. Perhaps we have here an ideal expression of individualism. Its atmosphere is considered very clear due to methane gas. Sunlight penetrates deeply into it before being reflected.

Herschel is credited with discovering Uranus' moon Umbriel on April 17, 1801. The transiting Moon was in Gemini then, perhaps conjunct Uranus' discovery degree. Lassell's discovery of two more moons of Uranus on October 24, 1851 occurred when transiting Venus and Jupiter contacted the lunar nodes of the original discovery chart. Then, on March 10, 1977, rings were discovered around Uranus: the Sun at 20 degrees Pisces conjunct the Uranus discovery Sun; the Moon at 29 Scorpio joined the discovery Jupiter. The chart for the discovery of the rings shows a close parallel between Uranus and Mars. Perhaps the most interesting feature of that chart is the close conjunction of Uranus at 11 degrees 31 minutes Scorpio to the Moon-North Node midpoint at 11 degrees 52 minutes. Ebertin calls this combination, "Sudden experiences with others, suddenly entering into a union or alliance." The surprising discovery of rings around Uranus certainly fits this description well.

Chart Projections

If the discovery degree of Uranus holds special significance we should find it revealing itself through related event charts. From August 26–28, 1883 the island of Krakatoa in the Dutch Indies was an inferno of violence. Two-thirds of the island were destroyed in a great volcanic explosion, perhaps the largest the world has known, that left an estimated 36,000 dead and produced giant sea waves as far away as Cape Horn. *Transiting Uranus was at 22 degrees of Virgo, square its discovery point.* Transiting Mercury at 25 degrees Virgo was also squaring this point. A close square between transiting Sun and Pluto was also a factor in the event.

On July 23, 1967 racial violence exploded in Detroit, New York City, Rochester, New York, Birmingham, Alabama and New Britain, Connecticut. Uranus again was transiting square its discovery point from 22 degrees Virgo.

A total eclipse of the Sun on June 17, 1909 occurred at 26 degrees of Gemini. This eclipse was conjunct transiting Pluto at the time and conjuncted the discovery degree of Uranus. The year 1909 was the year that explorers first reached the North Pole.

On June 19, 1936, another total solar eclipse contacted the Uranus discovery point. The eclipse also squared transiting Saturn. 1936 was the year Germany occupied Italy and invaded Ethiopia; the year when the Spanish Civil War began. While these are not overwhelming evidence of the power of the discovery degree, there are the natal charts of individual events that correlate significantly.

The discovery degree of Uranus has been found to be primarily important in three categories of individuals. The first is with writers, particularly those who achieve wide recognition during their lifetimes. The second is with political reformers, and the third is with astrologers. Ralph Waldo Emerson was born with Mercury at 24 degrees Gemini. Charles Dickens and Arthur Conan Doyle both had Jupiter at 26 Gemini and Aldous Huxley had his Jupiter at 25 Gemini, the discovery degree of Uranus.

Franklin D. Roosevelt had his Mars at 27 Gemini, Eleanor Roosevelt had her Saturn at 24. Adlai Stevenson had his Neptune at 24. Marx and Engels were more properly radicals than liberals, although both groups might be characterized as Uranian. Marx's Neptune was at 25 Sagittarius opposing the discovery degree of Uranus, and his Pluto was square it from 26 Pisces. Engels had his Venus at 25 Libra, the midpoint between the discovery degrees of Uranus and Neptune.

The discovery degree is found in the charts of many famous astrologers. Rudhyar had Jupiter at 28 Gemini (and his Moon at 24 Aquarius, conjunct Neptune's discovery degree). Cyril Fagan had Mercury at 23 Gemini (tropical). Paul Clancy had Neptune and Mercury at 21 Gemini. Rupert Gleadow had Pluto at 24 Gemini and Alice Bailey had her Sun at 26 Gemini. Noel Tyl's nodal axis is 23 Gemini/Sagittarius 33, semisquare his Uranus and sextile his Moon. Careful observation of this degree in natal charts and in transits will prove valuable for future study.

Neptune

Inconsistencies of opinion, arising from changes
of circumstances, are often justifiable.
Daniel Webster, 1846

The discovery of Neptune in 1846 coincided with a time of great suffering and idealism. 1846 was the year of the Irish potato famine, the Mormons' arrival at the Great Salt Lake and the first use of ether for painless surgery. In 1847, Michigan was the first state to abolish capital punishment. Karl Marx's *Communist Manifesto*, a plea for the poor and hungry, was published in 1848. These were the years of increased concern for the downtrodden all over the world. The abolitionist John Brown and the publication of *Uncle Tom's Cabin* led to great social changes in the United States. Dickens wrote *David Copperfield* in 1849 to reveal the plight of England's poor. The poets Thoreau, Emerson, and Walt Whitman appeared on the scene. The California Gold Rush of 1849 fired men's imaginations, while the first commercial oil well brought us black gold in 1859, the same year Charles Darwin mixed us up with the monkeys with his theory of the evolution of man from lower forms of animals. The Theosophical Society and Christian Science were both founded in 1875 as an age of spiritualism grew in America and Europe. Abdul Baha, founder of the Bahai faith, was born in 1844. Annie Besant and C. W. Ledbeatter were born in 1847 and were to make their mark through the Theosophical Society. Even *Moby Dick*, Melville's classic sea story, waited for Neptune before appearing in 1851.

The first non-rigid airship appeared in 1852. The first color photo images were invented in 1848, and plastics first appeared in 1855 in the form of nitrocellulose. This was a period of time when spirits, ideals, dreams and fakery had a special place in our history. Dissatisfaction in the South led to secession, dissolving the bonds of union. They were eventually rebound, but not without considerable loss of life and limb. During this period we also saw the emergence of union in Italy and Austria-Hungary.

The discovery of Neptune was as full of confusion as the discovery of Uranus was full of surprise. Perturbations in the orbit of Uranus led astronomers to look for a planet beyond it that might account for its behavior. By hypothesizing a planet of certain mass and location beyond Uranus, they hoped to discover a new addition to the solar system. Englishman John Couch Adams and French astronomer Urbain Jean Leverrier both began calculations in the search for Neptune. Adams completed his work first and communicated his results to the Astronomer Royal and the director of the Cambridge Observatory. They were hesitant to follow up on the work of Adams and were beaten to the punch by J. G. Galle of the Berlin Observatory. Leverrier had sent his calculations to Galle, who discovered the new planet on *September 23, 1846.* James Challis of the Cambridge Observatory had located Neptune on August 4, 1846, but failed to recheck his observations, allowing history to pass him by.

The position at which Neptune was discovered was only one degree from the place predicted by Leverrier and only 2.2 degrees from the location predicted by Adams. It was quite lucky, however, as both men used the proportional distances between planets (known as Bode's Law) in their work. While this was accurate for the time of their research, a period 75 years before or after would have changed the picture sufficiently to make their calculations grossly inaccurate. The name Neptune was selected over the French idea of calling it "Leverrier." This, too, continued the practice of naming planets after the characters of western mythology.

Finger of God Pattern

Our chart for Neptune's discovery is calculated for 10 p.m. GMT, September 23, 1846 in Berlin, Germany (ee chart 2). This is a most remarkable horoscope in many ways. First, there is the conjunction of *Saturn* and Neptune! This conjunction clearly shows the manifestation of the new planet through the *reality* of Saturn. Note that Saturn also strongly aspected the newly discovered planet in the Uranus chart (page 14)! We also have the Moon *again* in the mystery sign Scorpio. Neptune is retrograde in the discovery chart, as will Pluto be in its discovery chart. It seems apropos that these two planets (Neptune and Pluto) should be found retrograde in their discovery charts since their levels of manifestation are almost always through unconscious rather than direct sense-experience. The remarkable conjunction of Saturn and Neptune forms a Yod pattern, or Finger of God, along with Pluto and Mars. Mars in Virgo as the focal point describes the process of mathematical calculation that led to deliberate discovery. Perhaps Jupiter in Gemini square Mercury in Virgo describes the two mathematicians whose calculations led to the same conclusion at about the same time. The Sun in

Libra might be another indicator of the sharing of credit that the scientific community conferred on Leverrier and Adams. The Moon is parallel in declination to Neptune in this chart. This would bring the public consciousness to this new planet, but might also describe the confusion about its proper discoverer.

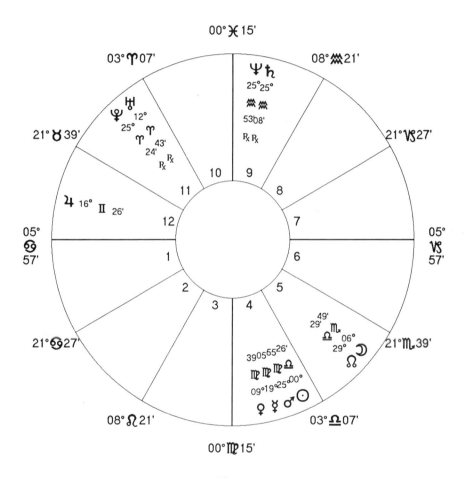

Chart 2
Discovery of Neptune
September 23, 1846, 10:00 p.m., GMT
Berlin, Germany
13E22 52N29

The midpoint picture Mars-Node equals Uranus is called "Active Cooperation" by Ebertin. Rather than the isolated good fortune that brought Uranus to the fore, we have a case of several scientists working together to bring Neptune to our attention. The midpoint of Uranus-Neptune is opposed by Mercury. Ebertin calls this, "A peculiar imagination, occupation with the metaphysical sciences and with supernatural problems, the investigation or exploration of the unconscious. A longing for far-distant places, plans without the possibility of realization, journeys." There is much in this description that fits our astrological concept of Neptune.

Neptune was found in the Libra decanate of Aquarius and in either the Sagittarian or Aquarian dwad (depending upon the system used). By counting the dwads beginning with the sign of Aquarius, we find Neptune in the Sagittarian dwad. In the light of Neptune's displacement of Jupiter as ruler of Pisces, we can expect an affinity for it in Sagittarius as well. Certainly the combinations of Libra (pairs), Sagittarius (search for knowledge), and Aquarius (scientific inquiry) are all applicable to the story of Neptune's discovery.

The La Volasfera picture of the 26th degree of Aquarius is particularly apt. It is, "A man walking blindfold towards the opening of a deep pit." The author goes on to explain that, "this indicates one whose thoughts and projects are liable to become chaotic and confused . . . it may be from ignorance or from want of alertness and responsiveness to his surroundings that he will come by hurt to himself, but save by the helping and directing hand of some wise friend or overarching love of Heaven, he cannot escape downfall and ruin." He calls it a degree of "Blinding."

Charubel says that there is *no* symbol for this degree, that it is a degree of mystery! Kozminsky says the degree, "denotes one of mystic and reformative learnings who may be impressed by the invisible forces for certain work on earth, but who may not be conscious of the part he is called upon to play . . . He should never permit himself to be hypnotized or entranced, nor yield his will to the power of another in the body or out of it. It is a symbol of Service."

Poets and Mystics

Jeryl Keane describes the degree as, "dramatic, not always emotionally stable, but certainly with a good deal of charm." The Sabian Symbol is, "a garageman testing a car's battery with a hydrometer." The degree symbols given here for Neptune seem to work extremely well in expressing the characteristics of the planet.

Neptune's discovery degree should have some impact on those born with planets in close aspect to it. The first category is the religious-spiritual group. Thomas More, a saint, was born with his Sun at 28 Aquarius. Meher Baba, a Pisces, silent much of his life, had Venus at 23 Aquarius. Evangelist Billy Graham shows Uranus at 24 Aquarius. Ayn Rand, somewhat anti-spiritual, shows Saturn at 22 Aquarius. The births of Abdul Baha, Annie Besant and C. W. Ledbeater were mentioned earlier with respect to the year of Neptune's discovery.

Two flyers, Howard Hughes and Charles Lindbergh, have Mars in close conjunction with the discovery degree at 27 and 26 degrees respectively. While many consider Uranus the planet of aviation, I have found Neptune to work well in this area. We are, I believe, describing two different phenomena. Uranus is certainly the technical achievement of aviation, while Neptune is the principle of aero-dynamics, floating through space.

Poets fare well with regard to the discovery degree of Neptune, as one would expect. Shelley had Pluto at 22 Aquarius and Keats had it at 26. Byron had his Venus at 25 Aquarius. Carl Sandburg had the Moon's North Node at 24. Jules Verne, author of fantasy, has his Mercury at 23 Aquarius. Manet, the father of Impressionist painting, had his Jupiter at 27 Aquarius. Most of the Impressionists, as a matter of fact, were born about the time of Neptune's discovery.

Two great men of history born on the same day had the Neptune discovery degree emphasized in their charts: Lincoln and Darwin both had the Sun at 23 degrees of Aquarius and Mars at 25 Libra, conjunct the Uranus-Neptune discovery midpoints! John Kennedy, another individual credited with feelings for the underprivileged, had his Uranus at 24 Aquarius.

As with Uranus, we would expect that the discovery point of Neptune should respond to transits. In 1642 in China, rebels destroyed a seawall that led to the deaths of approximately 300,000 people by drowning. Neptune was between 26 and 28 degrees Scorpio that year, square the discovery point. Perhaps the most interesting case occurred in May 1968, when the nuclear submarine "Scorpion" sank, killing 99 men. Neptune was at 25 degrees Scorpio, again squaring the discovery point. Neptune in the sign that was the same as the name of the submarine makes this a most interesting fact. The number 99 reduces to 9 numerologically (9 plus 9 equals 18, 1 plus 8 equals 9) is also considered a Neptunian number by some.

Pluto

Birth, and copulation, and death. That's all the
facts when you come to brass tacks.

T. S. Eliot, 1930

This quote from T. S. Eliot is about as concise a definition of Pluto as one could make. All the elements of Pluto are contained within those two short sentences. But, after all, isn't that what Pluto is about, getting down to root causes, elimination of excess, brass tacks? There is a wealth of quotations relevant to this outermost member of our solar system. Einstein wrote, "the most beautiful thing we can experience is the mysterious. It is the source of all true art and science." The year of this quote was 1930, the year of Pluto's discovery. In 1933 Franklin D. Roosevelt said, "The only thing we have to fear is fear itself." And in 1934, Benito Mussolini said, "We have buried the putrid corpse of liberty." These all express the symbolic power of this tiny planet at the edge of our solar system. From Pluto, the Sun is so distant it appears as only another star in the sky, yet to astrologers on earth Pluto has great significance.

The birth of Pluto in our consciousness in many ways has brought the god of the underworld to the fore. Though some are careful to separate Pluto from Plutus, god of great wealth, we cannot help but see a connection between the two. In 1929, the United States suffered the Great Depression's beginning, an event that would effect all the world in a few short years. 1929 was also the year of the St. Valentine's Day Massacre in Chicago, a high point (or low point if you like) for the American gangster (underworld character). The great dictatorships of the axis powers and the Soviet Union grew in the days of Pluto's infancy. Japan invaded Manchuria in 1931. The Nazis came to power in 1933. Hitler wrote *Mein Kampf* in the early 1920s, and was appointed chancellor of Germany in 1933. The years following brought us World War II, genocide, and atomic devastation.

1930 was the year of the first jet propulsion aircraft, following by only two years, the first differential analyzer or basic computer. In 1931, we developed the first cyclotron and produced deuterium (heavy hydrogen). In 1932, the positron, and eventually, in 1938, nuclear fission. FM radio made its way into the world in 1933, so things couldn't be all bad. But bad they were in many, many ways. The discovery of Pluto has opened up a level of technology unmatched in history. As our consciousness brought us to the edge of space, our machines have become powerful enough to destroy us.

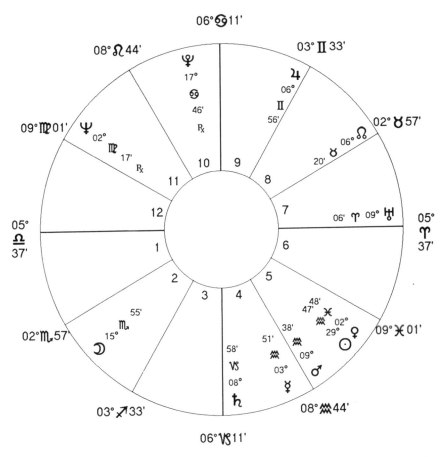

Chart 3
Discovery of Pluto
February 18, 1930, 9:00 p.m., MST
Flagstaff, Arizona
111W39 35N12

Dictators, Bombs, Repression

The search for Pluto was begun in 1905 by Percival Lowell and continued beyond his death at facilities he paid for. Pluto was found within six degrees of one of Lowell's predictions, but astronomers considered this a matter of luck as the required Pluto mass for his prediction was more than six times that of earth. Yet, Lowell did have his wishes fulfilled beyond the grave. His influence in the search for Pluto was so great that some consider the planet's name to be more than an accidental extension of his own initials, P. L. Actually, it was a young girl who named Pluto, some say after Mickey Mouse's dog. In any case, the mythology of the god of the underworld is an appropriate name for the astrological function of Pluto.

The actual discoverer of Pluto was Clyde Tombaugh, an Illinois farmboy turned astronomer. Tombaugh's parents hadn't enough money to send him to college, so he practiced telescopic observations on his own. He made drawings of his own observations of Mars and sent them to the Lowell Observatory in Flagstaff, Arizona. This so impressed the director that he offered young Tombaugh a job in photographic observing. His function was to scan the sky in an attempt to find Planet X, Lowell's name for the yet undiscovered Pluto. Tombaugh worked outdoors in an unheated dome, photographing that part of the sky where Lowell predicted the planet would be found. He would photograph an area one night, then photograph it again a night or two later. He would use an instrument called a blink microscope to compare the two plates for any motion that might show a planet. The plates showed an average of 160,000 stars each and the work was long and painstaking. Finally, on February 18, 1930, 25 years after Lowell began the search, Pluto was found (see chart 3).

Pluto was located at 17 degrees and 46 minutes of Cancer in the tropical zodiac. It was in wide opposition to Saturn, made closer by the contraparallel between them. The Moon is in Scorpio as it was in the two previous planets' discovery charts. *In all three cases, the common elements are hard aspects by Saturn, two oppositions and a conjunction, and the Moon in Scorpio.* All three cases were searches that resulted in new discoveries of planets. Saturn, the reality principle, and Scorpio, sign of deep investigation, work well to describe the nature of such events. Uranus was discovered by accident. Neptune was discovered based on calculations made independently by two men. Pluto was discovered by an obscure, self-made astronomer who didn't attend college until after his famous work. The search for Pluto was primarily financed by one man whose work was completed after his death.

The Pluto discovery chart shows a trine between Mars and Jupiter in air signs. This might refer to the expansive discovery made possible by high technology machinery. Pluto does symbolize atomic energy and the release of unlimited power, another expression of Mars-Jupiter. A square between Saturn and Uranus might indicate the many years' work involved in this scientific breakthrough, as well as symbolizing the necessity for our control of unexpected inventions that soon followed. On another level, it could indicate the repression of individual liberty symbolized by the great dictators of the discovery era. The midpoint of Sun-Saturn conjuncts Mercury showing the careful observations over a long period of time that led to discovery. Mars-Jupiter conjuncts Uranus, a symbol of expansive new discoveries or breakthroughs.

Pluto was discovered in the Scorpio decan of Cancer. This places it in its ruling sign just as Uranus was found in the Aquarius decan of Gemini.

The degree systems, however, do prove to be almost uncanny in some cases. La Volasfera calls the 18th degree of Cancer one of satiety. Charubel symbolizes this degree as, "A bull tossing a man with his horns." He says, "this denotes a willful person, one who will be always on the defensive, and too often on the aggressive. Personal property will have but little sacredness with him, his motto being, 'what I can get is my own'." Kozminsky sees this degree as, "An old man sitting alone in semi-darkness with an old book before him, from which emanate bright rays of light." He goes on to describe it as a dauntless search for truth and calls it a symbol of "essentials," another Pluto keyword. Sandbach refers to manipulation of others in his description of this area of the Zodiac. The Sabian Symbol is "A hen scratching the ground to find nourishment for her progeny." This might seem meaningless until we recall that the Pluto myth of taking Persephone below the earth for half the year was symbolic of the winter months when seeds rest beneath the ground.

Powerful Leaders

Pluto's discovery degree is prominent in the charts of powerful leaders, those with great wealth, powerful communicators, those involved with overt or repressed sexuality and some of those with mental powers that far exceed the ordinary. Julius Caesar and Henry VIII had the Sun conjunct Pluto's discovery point. Richard Nixon's Sun opposed it. Napoleon's Pluto opposed it from 16 Capricorn. Lenin's Uranus was at 18 Cancer, Mussolini's Jupiter at 19 and Hitler's North Node was at 16. Harry Truman's Mars was at 17 Cancer.

Among the very wealthy with contacts to the Pluto discovery degree, we find Andrew Carnegie, with his Jupiter at 15 Cancer. John D. Rockefeller. Aristotle Onassis had his Venus at 17 Capricorn in opposition to the discovery point. J. P. Morgan had his Pluto at 15 Aries and his Venus at 19 Aries both square the discovery point. William Randolph Hearst, the famous yellow journalist, had his Moon-Mercury midpoint at exactly 18 degrees Cancer, conjunct the Pluto point. In the realm of sexuality, we have Mae West with Venus at 15 Cancer, and Marilyn Monroe with the North Node at 18 Cancer. Sufferers of sexual repression include Alan Leo (a man with a celibate marriage) with Venus at 18 Cancer, Queen Victoria with Mars at 18 Aries in square, and J. Edgar Hoover with Venus at 19 Capricorn. (Notice that the planets contacting the discovery point are either Venus, Mars, or the Node in this category.)

Pluto is considered to be related to propaganda when in contact with Mercury or Jupiter. Powerful communicators with contacts to the discovery point were Daniel Webster with Mercury at 19 Capricorn, Richard Wagner with Saturn at 18 Capricorn and his Moon-Neptune midpoint at 15. George Bernard Shaw had his Mercury conjunct the discovery point at 18 Cancer.

Two other interesting cases are the famous seer Nostradamus with Mars at 18 Cancer and Saturn at 16 Cancer (and the Moon in Scorpio) and Buckminster Fuller with Jupiter at 18 and the Sun at 20 degrees Cancer. Many consider Fuller one of the towering geniuses of our age. While these degree contacts work well, it is the transits to this point that are most fascinating.

It seems no accident that Plutonium is a basic necessity for the production of nuclear bombs. When Pluto was discovered, its position was in the 18th degree of Cancer. The Atomic Age is said to have begun on July 16, 1945 at Alamogordo, New Mexico, when the first atomic blast took place at 5:30 a.m. The ascendant there was conjunct Saturn at 15 degrees Cancer. The Mercury-Uranus midpoint was 17 Cancer 29. Uranus-Neptune conjuncted Pluto, Sun-Node conjuncted Saturn, Venus-Pluto conjuncted the Sun, all within orbs of one degree. The first atomic bomb dropped on Hiroshima, Japan was on August 6, 1945. Transiting Saturn was at 18 degrees Cancer conjunct Pluto's discovery point. On October 31, 1952, the United States tested the first hydrogen bomb. Transiting Uranus (as in uranium) was at 18 degrees Cancer.

At the present time, Pluto has come within the orbit of Neptune. This rare event might indicate that power or force will break through Neptune's veil of piety. Religious violence has already manifest itself most unpleasantly in Guyana and Iran. This might continue to be an issue until Pluto again moves outside Neptune in 1998. In a more positive vein, we might hope that concentrated efforts will enable us to transcend the limits of our imagination in the years to come.

Throughout this prologue, the basic point has been to remember that the moment of any beginning is an appropriate one. This is true for individuals, as well as planets, plants, or puppy dogs. Too many who study astrology fail to remember that each life has its purpose and its time. Our earthly perspective often makes history look like a fearful thing, but this is not so. Each moment is right, each birth the precisely correct, fully ripe time for emergence. Our understanding of these forces can help us eliminate prejudices and doubts when bringing our astrological skills into the service (not evaluation) of others. The following is from the Taoist Book of Days:

> *Birth is not a beginning. When things are born, it is always the result culminating from good conduct and contentment that establishes calm wherein things act together in harmony. This evolvement is positive: creative forces unite unobstructed, producing a new time of flowering, a time of meaningful manifestation. All beginnings are a result of harmony, for all new things emerge when the necessary creative forces unite without obstruction.*

Joanne Wickenburg

Joanne Wickenburg is a practicing professional astrologer, serving a large clientele in the greater Seattle area. She has lectured extensively throughout the United States and Canada, and markets an internationally recognized correspondence course in astrology. Joanne has been a faculty member at many conferences, including AFA, UAC and NORWAC, and is past President of the Washington State Astrological Association, where she was instrumental in creating a certification program for astrologers. She was presented the Most Inspirational Astrologer award in 1982. Joanne is also a certified neuro-linguistic practitioner.

She is the author of many popular books on astrology, including *A Journey Through the Birth Chart, In Search of a Fulfilling Career,* and *Intercepted Signs—Environment Vs. Destiny.* She is the co-author of *The Spiral of Life, The Digested Astrology,* and *When Your Sun Returns.*

Bringing the Outer Planets Down to Earth

Joanne Wickenburg

Have you ever done something that you were taught was impossible? Perhaps you drove your car for a distance of ten or twenty miles and, when you arrived at your destination, you didn't remember the trip... you realized, after the fact, that you had been driving on "automatic pilot." How much time had elapsed? At what speed had you been driving? How could you have safely driven the car and yet been unconscious of the process?

Or maybe, on another occasion, you responded to an unexpected situation in a manner that was totally uncharacteristic of your usual behavior. You might have opened your mouth and heard something come out that was a complete surprise. At some time in your life, have circumstances required you to do something you had never done before? Something you were taught, or had always told yourself, was an impossible feat? Or maybe you witnessed an event that you later discovered never really happened. You might have vividly remembered a conversation that never really occurred.

Have you ever committed to a relationship with someone who turned out to be very different from what you originally believed? How could you have been so blind not to see what now appears so obvious? Have you ever fooled yourself in other ways and wondered later how you could have been so naive?

These kinds of experiences can only happen when you are functioning *outside* consciousness. All of these experiences are normal *modus operandi* for Uranus, Neptune, and Pluto.

Uranus, Neptune, and Pluto represent unconscious "parts" of you that are constantly attempting to show you that there is more to

31

life than what text books lead you to believe; you can do more with your life than what you have been taught by the familial and social structures that surround and shape your everyday life. Sometimes, in the process of making their energies known to you, the outer planets create disruptions, uncertainties, or fears. At other times, these same planetary energies create excitement, exhilaration, vision, inspiration, profound understanding and liberation from the limitations of the past.

The outer planets represent "parts" of you that want you to be all that you can be, rather than being content with simply who you are. They represent "parts" of you that want you to explore what's unknown, look beyond the immediate for answers, experiment with life, and constantly grow as a result of your risk-taking adventures. These adventures can be physical, mental, emotional, or spiritual, but they are adventures never-the-less, and they always lead you to a surprise destination.

Each one of us is made up of many different "parts:"

Moon: the part of you that wants safety and security.
Mercury: the part of you that wants to learn.
Venus: the part of you that wants to love and to be loved.
Sun: the part of you that wants to shine and be confident.
Mars: the part of you that wants to be independent and assertive.
Jupiter: the part of you that wants social interaction and opportunity to expand in the outer world.
Saturn: the part of you that wants stability, recognition, rules and, yes, even limits.

While these "parts," represented by the personal and social planets, find avenues to get what they want within society's existing structures, the "parts" of you represented by Uranus, Neptune, and Pluto are much more complex. They represent urges that encourage you to move beyond reality as it is defined at any given stage of your life. The outer planets challenge you to explore the unknown.

URANUS

Uranus represents a "part" of you that wants you to take risks. It wants you to explore and experiment with life. It represents the part of you that wants you to be more than what your limited experience has proven possible. Uranus is the liberator, the part of you that wants to free you from overly structured boundaries that prohibit access to the unknown. Uranus is the rebel. It thrives on excitement and is repelled by rules, regulations, or structured organization. It represents a living force inside of you that sometimes must go to extremes to make its needs known to your conscious ego.

Like any family unit, the planets, representing your internal cast of characters, must learn to function with mutual respect and recognition of each others' importance. When one "part" of you attempts to dominate or control other members of your "family," no matter how good its intentions might be, internal strife and imbalance are experienced. This internal strife is projected onto and into your external activities.

For example, if the "part" of you that wants security and safety (Moon) attempts to block the natural expression of your inner rebel (Uranus), a personal crisis is experienced. Two individual "parts" of you are attempting to function at cross-purposes. Uranus, like an out-of-control adolescent, will retaliate by creating frequent emotional upheavals or inappropriate behavioral outbursts until you recognize the importance of its role, which is to stimulate change, progress and evolution. Until the part of you that wants guaranteed safety (Moon) realizes that stagnation, not security, is what results from lack of fluidity and movement, Uranus will create crisis after crisis in its attempt to prod you forward.

In the example just given, it is of equal importance for Uranus, as one member of your inner "family," to recognize, respect, and appreciate the needs of the Moon. When functioning creatively, the part of you that wants protection and security (Moon) is familiar with the part that wants change and progress (Uranus). When these two functions work together, as a team, you know that it's possible to explore and experiment with life creatively and still feel safe and protected. When this outcome is attained, you can be assured that you have integrated these two planetary forces in your life.

Uranus thrives on chaos. When your life feels completely out of control, as if you are riding on the most exciting, but frightening, roller coaster ride, the "part" of you that is Uranus is ecstatic. Uranus thrives on excitement and risk. Its purpose is to help you evolve, to discover dimensions of life that go beyond the limits of social definition or permission. It may choose, or find it necessary, to create this outcome by provoking crisis. The more unbending, rigid, or fearful you are, the louder Uranus must holler to make its needs heard, the more dramatic its actions must be. Sometimes, like an adolescent rebelliously trying to break free from family restraints to discover his or her true identity, Uranus seems to go too far in its attempt to find release. If you see this beginning to occur in your life, remind yourself that a "part" of you, named Uranus, wants and deserves to be heard, wants and deserves a chance to have center stage, wants and deserves a chance to contribute to your personal evolution.

It is important to recognize and appreciate the reasons that stand behind the disruptions Uranus is so frequently blamed for creating. The *intent* of the action, rather than the action itself, is this planet's only concern. Uranus is not concerned with what it considers trivia: things like possessions, social protocol, security or obsolete beliefs. It simply but dramatically wants you to *change, to grow, to explore,* and *to experiment.* When it deems that the time has come for change, and you consciously refuse to flow with it, Uranus will find whatever way it can to do its job. If it has to create upheaval, then so be it.

It has been said that the outer planets are "bigger than you are." They deal with energies and issues that are greater than personality, even though they manifest through it. Uranus, for example, *will* promote change, whether you consciously want change or not. It *will* keep your life topsy-turvy until you finally acknowledge and own the important role it plays in your life.

Uranus is called evolution, progress, change. Fighting progress is seldom a productive decision. Uranus encourages eccentricity, eclecticism, and detachment. It challenges you to let go of the past. It invites and welcomes surprise, excitement, and originality. It rules the unexpected because it is often the surprising, unexpected events that make you aware of something about yourself that you never knew before, and probably never would have discovered, had it not been for Uranus' surprise intervention. Sometimes its surprises are frightening. Other times they are stimulating, provocative, and exciting. How you respond to the changes it encourages can only be defined by how you, and all of your complex "parts" (planets), view progress.

When Uranus is "playing" with your life, it is important that you consciously touch base with all other members of your "family." For example, if you do not consciously access the Moon (your urge to protect and be protected), you could attract stressful and un-settling situations that are unduly dangerous to your emotional well-being. Accessing Mercury, on the other hand, encourages you to ask: are my rebellious urges intellectually sound?

Venus/Uranus issues revolve around relationships and per-sonal values. If Uranus interacts with Venus in your chart, you need exciting, stimulating relationships. Uranus constantly challenges the part of you that wants to please and be pleased, love and be loved. For Uranus to be satisfied in any Venus-ruled affair, it needs to see the relationship moving, progressing, changing.

At the same time, it is important that you don't get so involved in creating constant change in relationships that you fail to acknowl-edge their value (Venus). If Uranus dominates, valued and valuable relationships are often lost, and the part of you that wants love (Ve-nus) feels cheated. Relationships are exciting, but they are usually unstable and not satisfying. On the other hand, when these energies work in harmony, and the needs of both planets are met, relation-ships are exhilarating, vital, exciting, stimulating, and progressive.

This same principle is applicable when assessing any and all aspects in your natal chart. Aspects simply indicate *the degree of ease or discomfort experienced between any two "parts" of yourself.* In all cases, the slower, or more distant, planet represents a part of you that is attempting to shape the expression of the faster. It is attempt-ing to work *through* the function of the faster planet in order to make its needs known.

For example, consider a square between Uranus and Mercury. Uranus wants Mercury to think in progressive, possibly unconven-tional ways. Uranus challenges the Mercury-mind to take risks, dare to explore mental concepts that go beyond those you already understand. Break out of a traditional or conventional mind-set and explore the unexplainable, explore the unknown. Because the square suggests that this challenge is not easily met, one of two things could result. If Mercury shuts out Uranus, and refuses to in-vestigate progressive ideas, Uranus will rebelliously retaliate by creating mental "short circuits," unrest, and disturbance. This can happen in any number of ways. At the other extreme, if Uranus dominates and doesn't respect Mercury's role, the mind will func-tion erratically and with extreme eccentricity. The way you express your Uranian energy simply won't make any sense to others.

At a positive level, this combination contributes to genius. Regardless of whether the aspect is easy or stressful, cooperation between the "thinker" (Mercury) and the "rebel" (Uranus) is the ultimate goal. Easy aspects, such as sextiles and trines, suggest that an amiable relationship was established at birth between these two inner "parts" of you. For example, a sextile suggests that constructive tools are available to assist the two energies in forming a productive relationship. Challenging, provocative aspects, such as the conjunction, square, quincunx, or opposition, require effort to integrate the energies. But regardless of the aspect, Uranus/Mercury contacts always imply a potential for ingenuity and exceptional originality.

Whenever Uranus overwhelms or ignores the needs of your other "inner people," instability and disintegration occur. For example, consider what might happen the first time you meet an opportunity to go skydiving...something you've always wanted to do. A part of you (Uranus) is excited. You can almost hear its silent voice saying, "Go for it! Its what you want! It will be exciting! Liberating! It will change your life forever! Jump!"

At the same time, another part of you, described by the Moon, is afraid. It knows that sky diving involves some element of risk. It recognizes that you have no past experience to assure you that you'll come out of this safely.

If you fail to skydive, even after you learn how to use the equipment and carefully observe the landscape to see if obstacles block your path, you are allowing the Moon to dominate Uranus. These two "parts" of you are not operating cooperatively. In this case, Uranus is left unfulfilled, possibly seeking revenge! Uranus wants to add a new dimension to your life, and you are denying it freedom.

On the other hand, if you go ahead and jump *without* recognizing and respecting the Moon's wish to protect you, you put your life in grave danger. Leaping before looking has potentially devastating results. Remember, Uranus does not have the strong survival instincts provided by the Moon. Uranus has no logic (Mercury). Uranus knows no rules (Saturn).

Whenever assessing how planets interact, realize that *the slower, more distant planet carries the greater shaping power.* It is attempting to shape and direct the functions of all faster planets. In the case of Uranus/Moon, Uranus challenges the Moon to redefine its old ideas about safety. If the Moon fails to do so, Uranus reacts by creating instability, and the Moon "part" of you experiences emotional imbalance and insecurity.

This same principle applies when evaluating how Uranus interacts with all personal and social planets. Its role is to create change in both your personal life and in how you function as a social participant. It wants you to be more tomorrow that you are today. It wants to liberate you from boundaries that limit future possibilities. The "parts" of you defined by planets in easy aspect with Uranus welcome its liberating promises. Planets in challenging aspect represent "parts" of you that are reluctant to change, or lack experience in doing so gracefully.

One of the most exciting, if not potentially dangerous, combinations of planetary energies is seen in Mars/Uranus interplay. Mars represents the "part" of you that wants you to be assertive, action-oriented and independent. It can easily become overwhelmed by the Uranus challenge. Uranus wants you to take risks every time you go after what you want (Mars). It challenges you not only to pioneer new trails in life (Mars), but to use untried, unconventional techniques in doing so. While this particular combination can be extremely exciting, it can also be very unstable and volatile. Anger often erupts unexpectedly, actions can be initiated erratically in Uranus' attempt to show you that you can do more than what you thought possible.

If Mars, in its attempt to maintain independence by doing things its own way, refuses to change its mode of expression, Uranus will instigate crises to show you that things can be done differently in the future than they have been done in the past. This aspect is truly revolutionary. Because of its potential volatility, if you have these planets in stressful aspect in your chart, you have a dynamic responsibility to understand and direct the energies.

Jupiter and Saturn are considered the "social" planets. They represent the "parts" of you that want you to function in society. Jupiter wants you to expand, to grow, to take advantage of all of society's facilities. It urges you to go outside your own limited environment to expand your understanding of life. Saturn urges you to be responsible once functioning out in the world, to learn to respect social boundaries, and to abide by the laws it has designed to keep life orderly.

When Uranus is in aspect to social planets, it challenges you to break out of not only personal attitudes, desires, and beliefs, but to play a part in changing outdated social attitudes and systems. You have a unique ability to use your rebellious, individualistic talents to make changes in the world around you. These might be political (Saturn) or philosophical (Jupiter). If Uranus' urges are not utilized in a positive way, they manifest in socially irresponsible behaviors that label you as a "rebel without a cause."

The House containing Uranus describes where you will go through major changes, possibly chaotic instability. It describes an area of life where you need to recognize and appreciate your inner rebel, your unconscious desire to break free from socially conditioned beliefs, to detach from any attachments or personal possessiveness you might have toward that field of life experience. Dare to explore and experiment when you meet situations and challenges in the area of life described by Uranus' House. This House shows where you need to be "different," where you are challenged to defy systems and preprogrammed methods for finding personal happiness. Here, you need to be experimental, detached and exhilarated by visions of future possibilities.

Astrologers often blame Uranus for creating events of upheaval. Perhaps it's time to consider it from a different perspective. Does Uranus, the planet, bring crisis to you? Or does it represent a part of you that helps you live through it? Major changes or crises occurring in Uranus' House seem, and sometimes are, out of your conscious control. Circumstances, even tragedies, spur your inner Uranus to emerge to help you solve problems and face challenges in a way you never knew you could, and probably never would have, had a crisis not occurred. Uranus helps you to break free from attachments, or a limited mind-set, and discover new dimensions of yourself.

As an example, consider the life of Helen Keller, who had Uranus in the third house of her chart. Her inability to communicate, to hear or to speak, was her greatest tragedy. The very limitation caused a need to call on her Uranian potential. By rebelling against her limitations, she unleashed her own genius and freed herself from bondage to her handicap.

The more strongly you hold on to old beliefs and security patterns in the area of life described by Uranus' House, the more likely you will be to attract instability and crisis. Uranus' message is: *dare to be different. Dare not conform.*

With these concepts in mind, consider how this exceptional planet might operate in the various Houses of the horoscope. As space does not permit an extensive evaluation of Uranus through each of the twelve Houses, I have condensed the following definitions to their core significance.

1st House: You need to approach life with a belief that each step you take is an adventure. Dare to show others, through personality, mannerisms, appearance, and dress, your originality and eccentricities. Direct your own chaos, or be controlled by it.

2nd House: You need to find progressive, even unconventional means of survival. Explore unique methods for financial and personal maintenance. Dare to question and rebel against traditional values that you feel are limiting. Financial stability may be erratic. Take advantage of it rather than allowing yourself to become a victim of it.

3rd House: You need to be an independent, progressive thinker. Gather information from unconventional channels. Dare to express your innovative, if somewhat eccentric, views to those in your environment in a unique and exciting way. Dare to challenge existing educational and community facilities and policies. Welcome the collapse of outdated ideas rather than becoming a victim of them.

4th House: You need to define security in a whole new way. Rather than holding on to the past, to family or tradition, realize that, for you, security can only be acquired by detaching from the very things that most people rely on for emotional grounding. Discover who you are apart from what family and heritage taught you to be.

5th House: You need to express your originality and your eccentricities through creativity. Dare to explore unique modes and techniques of creative expression. You probably have unusual talents; cultivate them. The part of you that enjoys taking risks will be evident not only in your romantic attractions, but when you participate in all activities that encourage drama in self expression.

6th House: You need a working routine that involves an element of risk; originality and experimentation should be encouraged. All daily routines, including those involving health maintenance, need to be designed out of unconventional strategies.

Instead of fighting change in the work place, be an agent for change within it.

7th House: Relationships challenge you to look at life from a unique perspective. You attract unique, unusual people because a part of you wants others to demonstrate the advantages of detachment and change. Through personal interaction with others, you are awakened to a new way of perceiving life and your role within it. Welcome surprises and changes in relationships rather than becoming a victim of them.

8th House: You need to take risks that provoke changes, not only in your own perspective of life, but in the experiences you share with others. Life experiences are "recycled" here. You need to design creative, unique, if not unconventional, ways to create changes that contribute to shared enterprises.

9th House: The religious structures within your society are not sufficient to give your life meaning. You will be challenged to develop a unique, progressive, unorthodox philosophy. You need to detach mentally from your particular community and its mind-set in order to understand better the ideas, cultures, races, and philosophies that are "foreign" or alien from your norm.

10th House: You need to be recognized for your originality and unconventional approach to the world. In career, you need to be on the cutting edge. Professional fulfillment comes once you trust your professional instincts enough to experiment and explore new possibilities regarding success.

11th House: You need to surround yourself with innovative, progressive, exhilarating people who encourage you to take risks and to contribute your unique ideas toward humanitarian movements. Don't be afraid to rebel against limitations in order to pursue future goals.

12th House: You have a rich past to call on that helps you deal with changes. "Skeletons in the closet" often come out in unexpected ways that make you look at life from a different perspective. Crisis and personal upheavals can provide unique opportunities to break out of old cycles that have impeded progress. Find unique methods of helping others who have experienced similar crises as those you have known.

NEPTUNE

Illusive, evasive, mystical, and idealistic, Neptune represents a "part" of you that can never be defined in concrete terms. It represents all that is, and yet is not. It is the greatest illusionist known. It represents all things unworldly, things having no form, ideas that cannot be substantiated, beliefs that are truth but cannot be proven, the things that we fear but know not why.

Neptune represents a part of you that wants you to believe in an intangible world, a part of you that is not concerned with form, structure, and experience as you consciously know them. It represents a part of you that wants you to dream, to fantasize, to experience life with no limits, life with no form, life with no responsibilities, no expectations, no physical boundaries to limit your imagination. Neptune is the "ethereal" you. It wants you to experience life without structure. It represents your dreams, your fantasies, your doubts, your fears. It is your faith, your idealism, your desire for a perfect world, your urge to escape from its existing imperfections.

When you see your world as imperfect, the Neptune "part" of you wants to reject it, to escape from imperfections, to imagine a better place, a better world, a better life. Neptune rules escapism, addictions, fears, phobias. All of these states of consciousness are unreal, imagined; they have no form, yet they are powerful forces that could dominate your life—but when fear is conquered, it no longer exists. When addictions are mastered, they no longer have power. They never had form in the first place. They were simply but profoundly, merely but powerfully, only states of mind.

Neptune rules confusion, the misty atmosphere, the foggy mind. Once the confusion of your mind or the fog that clouds your vision is lifted, Neptune's influence will have passed, having left no physical remnants behind to prove that it ever existed. By the time you understand Neptune's purpose, it is no longer a Neptunian issue.

The part of you named "Neptune" knows that there are some things that cannot be explained in logical terms; some things must simply be accepted as truth or untruth. This is seldom a comfortable state because it goes against all reason. The educational system, for example, probably taught you to use logic, to find evidence to validate your beliefs. Neptune denies evidence. Neptune defies logic.

Neptune wants to take you into a world that has not yet been charted, there are no maps available to help you navigate or find your way. It represents a part of you that wants you to know what it feels like not knowing where you are. Neptune wants you to trust it, to have total faith that there is a "part" of you, named Neptune, that will guide you into a world you never knew existed. It wants you to see colors more radiant than any of the colors of Earth's rainbows. It wants you to hear music that is so beautiful it could never be reproduced. It wants you to see beauty that is more exquisite than any human could define.

Some of us attempt to reach this state, the "bliss," relying on something outside of self, outside of our own inner Neptune. We may look to another person to fulfill our fantasies; we may use drugs or alcohol to reach this altered state; we may run away from life and its realities in our pursuit of happiness. We will ultimately run into Neptune's smoke-screen. The images we see will not be true beauty; they will only be deceptive and flawed reproductions. The music we hear is not perfectly pitched; instead, it hurts our ears. The people we select to fulfill our fantasies will disillusion us. We will live in Neptune's unreal world, but it will be a convoluted world, with distorted images and false idols. And we will probably blame it all unfairly on Neptune, whose only intent was to show us a world of beauty, love and perfection.

The more the conscious ego attempts to control and direct Neptune's energy, the more distorted vision becomes. The Neptune "part" of us knows that inspiration cannot be experienced while we are overly focused in a singular direction. It clouds our vision in order to distract us from the "real" world. If, out of fear, you get lost in the fog, afraid to move through it because there is no guarantee of what lies beyond, you will soon find yourself immobilized and blinded by your own fear. Neptune, like all members of your "inner family," is persistent. It will continue to cloud issues, hoping that you will respect its purpose and trust its judgment, believe in its integrity. Like any family member, if you choose to ignore its importance, Neptune eventually begins to act up. It will try, in whatever way it can, using whatever means it has available, to gain your attention. Neptune's attention-getting device is confusion. It makes it impossible to separate inspiration from illusion, vision from unrealistic fantasy, truth from untruths, denial from release.

Someone once said that Neptune represents the "umbilical cord that connects man to his creator," suggesting that through meditation and other forms of ego-dissociation, we are fed spiritual food that sustains our physical lives. Others have called Neptune delusion, fear, escapism, and disintegration. How could both definitions have merit?

Without accepting the spiritual food that Neptune provides, your "ethereal self" experiences malnutrition. Fear, escapism, disillusionment, and so forth are symptoms of *spiritual malnutrition*. They, like fear, are the effect, not the cause, the result, not the intent.

It is important to keep these concepts in mind whenever evaluating how Neptune functions in the birth chart, how it makes itself known in everyday life experiences.

Earlier, I made reference to driving a vehicle on "automatic pilot," something almost every driver has experienced at some point in life. Where were you when you were driving? What was going on in your mind? Somehow you disconnected with the "real" world, yet you were still functioning effectively within it. You may not consciously remember where you were, but a part of you called Neptune did know. Were you daydreaming? Astro-traveling? Unconsciously meditating? Whatever you were doing, you probably reentered consciousness feeling different in some way. Obviously there was unconscious activity at the time of your lapse of consciousness. If you remembered exactly what it was, would you attempt to judge it? By doing so, you would lose the real essence of the experience.

These moments of "tuning out" are important. Neptune deserves this kind of time in your life. If you don't consciously choose to respect your inner need to dream, to fantasize, to welcome inspiration, Neptune will find a way to fill its needs in whatever way it can. It will cloud your vision at inappropriate times; it will cloud your judgment when good judgment is essential; it will do what it must do to enlighten you to the fact that it exists and wants to be a recognized, respected part of who you are.

There is a time and place for everything. If, for example, you "tuned out" while driving, but you had no past driving experience to call on to guarantee safety, disaster would surely result. As an experienced driver, you could afford to ask Neptune aboard for the ride only if the part of you that has safety concerns (Moon) is in the front seat, too.

Have you ever done something without full control of all your "faculties?" What is a faculty, anyway? Is it not a group of people working together for a common cause? Conventions have faculties, and so do you. Your inner "faculty" consists of all your inner parts, the planets. If you drive under the influence of Neptune, without including the rest of the team (planets), the journey is sure to be a dangerous one. One "member" of your faculty may have the "chair" for its moment in time, but it needs to respect and include all other participants for an effective group outcome to be reached. In other words, Neptune deserves its time in the spotlight. You need what it has to offer—but discretion is equally important. It would not be appropriate for Neptune to take your mathematics test, nor would it be appropriate for Mars to meditate. Mars' role in the "faculty" profile is to motivate and act. Neptune inspires that motivation.

Webster defines the word "inspiration" as: *motivation by divine influence.* One of Neptune's major intents is to dissolve overly rigid structures that inhibit or restrict inspiration. It must dissolve the boundaries between the conscious and unconscious mind in order to receive inspiration. Neptune also dissolves the social, political, religious, and personal behavioral boundaries that prohibit personal or collective growth when it deems it to be is time for a new ideal to come to life.

Whole generations of people are born with Neptune in the same sign, showing the kinds of beliefs that need to be dissolved so a new order can come into being. For example, the Neptune in Libra generation collectively dissolved societal beliefs about relationships and what marriage and commitment were all about. This generation challenged old ideas about equality. Racial and sexual stereotypes began to change dramatically, as did the significance and importance previously placed on the institution of marriage. The Neptune in Scorpio generation collectively dissolved old beliefs about sexuality and even death. Neptune in Sagittarius will be urging society to dissolve overly rigid religious beliefs. It has already started: many traditional religions have made significant changes; religious cults have been prominent in the news. Now Neptune in Capricorn is having a heyday dissolving obsolete political systems that no longer fill the needs of the people. It can be said with great predictability that by the time Neptune leaves a sign, society will have formed a totally different belief about the issues that sign represents. In some way, you will play an important part in this process. Many of your old beliefs will change because of what's happening in the world.

The same principle can be applied to Neptune's role in the natal chart. The House containing this powerful planet shows where you will go through "dissolving" experiences. It describes an area of life where you need to walk into the fog, face the unknown and develop faith in your inner commitments. Its House describes an area of life where you may feel lost in a cloud of confusion. It's hard to focus here. It's difficult to define what you want, and once you do define it, you realize that it is not real. What you want has no physical form, no actual place in reality. Here, you need to look beyond reality to be "motivated by divine influence." Be open to inspiration, not illusion; develop a rich fantasy life, but don't project it onto the physical objects or people ruled by that house. Know that you need an element of the "unreal" to be happy here, but don't try to make what's real not; allow yourself time to daydream, to ponder. Look for what's beautiful, but don't try to own it; create your own fantasy, but know what it is. Learn to detach, to let go, to allow barriers to disintegrate and dissolve in order to experience true freedom. Don't use substances, people, or beliefs associated with Neptune's House for escape, but instead become free from dependence. When you feel there is no substance to rely on, realize that substance can weigh you down. If you feel that nothing is real here, examine what real really is. Is real what you really want?

Inspiration can be like a doubled-edged sword. It's a wonderful state to be in, but *once inspiration has turned into reality, inspiration no longer exists,* Neptune is no longer involved. One of the biggest dilemmas people face when Neptune plays with their lives is finding *new* inspiration once a dream has come true. Dreams, because they include mystery, intrigue, romance, and illusion, are often more satisfying than true life. Once fantasies have come true, they no longer exist, and Neptune again feels left out. Its only recourse for survival is to create another illusion or dream, to find a new inspiration.

The House containing Neptune shows where these conflicts emerge in your life, where a part of you wants to create, to dream, to experience the unreal. In the process of trying to create an ideal reality, based on your vision of what could be, you can easily get lost in the dream and lose your *real* place in life. You can easily fall prey to deception, because you so want to believe in what doesn't exist. You can devise tricks that give you a temporary sense of "ideal dissociation," but be sure that they won't work for you very long.

There may always be a sense of lack in the area of your life ruled by Neptune, a dream that may never come true. The truth of the matter is, when fantasy is realized, its very "realness" is not as exquisite as your vision perceived it to be.

In Neptune's house, you need to trust in the belief that there will be another dream, another fantasy, a new inspiration emerging to replace what has been lost. "Believe" is a keyword for Neptune. You need a dream, an ideal, something impossible to aspire to, or you won't be satisfied here. Don't expect the real world to act out your fantasy for you. In the real world, there is no perfection.

Artists and novelists attest to the fact that, once their inner visions have become real, they experience a great sense of loss. Only until they are actively pursuing another dream do they feel they are in their true element. The process of creating is more important, more inspiring, more fulfilling than the result can possibly be. If you approach your Neptunian experiences with this principle in mind, you too will find your bliss. The Neptune "part" of you will be not only satisfied, but it will become one of the most treasured members of your "faculty."

The greatest problem associated with Neptune is that it is easy to confuse its message. You can fool yourself by convincing yourself that the real is unreal, the reality is the fantasy. You put yourself in positions of making unrealistic value judgments. You make yourself believe things like, "this person is my dream come true," or, "this money will allow me to live out my fantasies." These beliefs are convoluted and suggest that you've not heard Neptune clearly. Substance is not fantasy, but fantasy can come true.

Planets in aspect with Neptune describe how other participants in your "family" interact with Neptune's energy, how your unconscious energy and potential (Neptune) express themselves through your conscious personality (Moon through Saturn). Aspects to Neptune show how you live out your fantasies, ideals and beliefs. Do they manifest through creativity or fear? For example:

Neptune/Moon: Are you secure in your beliefs? Are you able to dissociate and still remain safe?

Neptune/Mercury: How do you communicate your ideals and your dreams? Have you allowed your conscious mind to express them, or to distort them into something they're not?

Neptune/Venus: How do you live your ideals out in relationships? Are you trying to make others your fantasy?

Neptune/Sun: How do you express your ideals through ego? Is your consciousness fooling itself?

Neptune/Mars: How do you act your ideals out through assertive behavior? Are your desires based on honesty or a lie?

Neptune/Jupiter: How do you use the opportunities society offers to make your dreams realities? Are you expecting the world to make your dreams come true?

Neptune/Saturn: Are you looking beyond social structures and systems to find what you really want? Or are you blaming the system for your unfulfilled fantasies?

Are you living out the *true essence* of Neptune? Or have you allowed your conscious ego and personality to attempt to direct it and distort it instead? The nature of its aspects shows how Neptune expresses itself through your various personality "parts." Individual aspects encourage you to ask the following questions:

Conjunction: Are your ideals instinctively projected through this planet's function?

Opposition: How are your beliefs and fantasies reflected back to you through others' responses, or have you identified with your fantasies instead?

Square: Do you lack natural skills, so you must learn through trial and error?

Sextile: Are your ideals expressed through productive enterprise with style?

Quincunx: Do you discover ideals through distractions?

Neptune's aspects simply define the relationship between the inner and outer you, your inspiration and its outer actualization.

Because Neptune knows no boundaries, its significance is especially difficult to grasp, as is a true understanding of the vast possibilities it offers. When you stop viewing Neptune as a thing out in space whose energy is invading your life and accept it as representing a part of the total you, you will be empowered and awed by your own creative vision, your ability to experience a unique kind of "weightlessness" that enables you to transcend all physical boundaries and experience bliss.

PLUTO

Pluto symbolizes the most powerful and compulsive energy known to mankind. Pluto represents a "part" of you that you may not want to know. It is a part of you that requires true insight before it can be used in a positive way. It represents a part of you that wants you to know both the glory and the dangers of power.

Have you ever known compulsion? Have you ever "lost yourself" to some compelling urge that you could not control? A part of you named Pluto loves the intensity of such sensation. It thrives on obsession, the state of feeling driven by a power greater than your conscious ego can control. Pluto wants you to do something with your life that requires risk (Uranus), faith (Neptune), and one more important ingredient: a desire so deep, powerful, and compelling that you have no choice but to go with it at any cost.

Like all planets, Pluto's energy can manifest through positive or negative experience. Unlike other planets, when Pluto is functioning in your life, there is no escape. You can shut off your mind temporarily (Mercury); you can turn off your emotions (Moon). But when Pluto emerges into consciousness, you can't help but play by its rules.

Pluto can bring out the best and the worst of who you are. At a positive level, it creates a compelling urge to do something with your life that "makes a difference," to participate in some significant collective movement to change the world. Pluto's compelling power can also bring out the most destructive, abusive, dark side of your soul. When the latter is the case, you become obsessed, even temporarily possessed, by a compelling drive to live out the dark side of reality, the worst of the social condition.

Through Pluto's compulsions, you demonstrate the best and the worst of human potential. This planet has been blamed for creating not only compulsive addictions, but atomic and nuclear weapons, social monsters such as Adolf Hitler and Charles Manson. Through these men's lives, and what they collectively represented, the world was shown terror in its rawest and cruelest form.

It is important to realize that Pluto did not create these atrocities. They are only the result of the misuse of its power. Pluto is the part of you that wants you to tap into, and use, your *own* power. But when left undirected it can be misused, leading to abuse aimed at yourself or onto others.

On the other hand, when you make a conscious commitment to direct your power to create positive change, Pluto provides the compelling energy needed to trans,form not only your personal life, but to participate in the transformation of the lives of others.

Rudhyar once said that Pluto represents "the part of God that became trapped in his own creation." It represents the power to create and the power to destroy. It is a power greater than personal, a power absorbed from the collective, a power that can be used to either contribute to collective change or to contribute to its destruction.

Unlike in any other time in history, people must now begin to recognize not only the responsibility they have regarding personal survival but how their actions affect our planet as a whole. Pluto's House position describes where you need to confront the reality that you are only one cell in the body of mankind. No matter how small your role is, if your "cell" is diseased, you are contributing to the planet's decay.

When involved in the area of life covered by Pluto's House, it is wise to ask yourself the following questions: how does my life reflect the conditions of society? Am I losing myself to "worldly" things, or am I offering the world my power? Am I contributing to social evolution, or am I contributing to its destruction?

Pluto represents ultimate power: power to create and power to destroy, the power of evolution and the power of regression. At some time in your life you will live out its power regardless of your level of consciousness. In some way, even though you may not consciously know it, you will be "used" as an example, demonstrating society's potential or its greatest mistakes.

What you attract, and what you create, is a reflection of not just your ego, but the consciousness of the collective. Therefore, when meeting the experiences ruled by Pluto's House, you need to ask: How does what I'm doing here make a difference in the world?

Just as Pluto is the farthest out planet in our solar system, it is the most distant or "far out" part of yourself. It can be considered the "final chapter" of your life, representing the greatest goal you are capable of attaining. Pluto's House shows where your life will falter or fail based on what happens to you, and how you respond when it happens. It shows where compelling urges that often make no conscious sense do shape the destiny of your life.

Pluto represents the "part" of you that creates intense, power-ful experiences that compel you to do something. It wants you to experience rebirth. Its House shows where old, socially conditioned beliefs must go through a "death" experience before you can actu-ally "live." Pluto wants you to do something with your life that con-tributes to the lives of others. It represents the "ultimate invoice" that itemizes the costs you must pay to own life.

At one time in history, a person exhibiting power beyond what family status and social caste afforded was considered "possessed." We now know that everyone, no matter what lifestyle they came from, can become much greater and more powerful than society's standards require or allow. Uranus, the first of the outer planets, provides the urge to rebel against personally or socially induced boundaries or restrictions. Neptune's role provides a dream of a bet-ter place. *Pluto is the reason that Uranus and Neptune exist.*

If the other members of your "inner family" are not well devel-oped, Pluto's power, when tapped, cannot function at its maximum potential. Often the results lead to major power struggles, issues around dominance, abuse, or compulsive behaviors that over-whelm you. This is particularly the case when people attempt to own Pluto's power, to identify it as part of their egos.

One thing is certain when considering Pluto's role in your life: you *will* be changed. The Pluto "part" of you will not forever remain content to leave things as they are. It wants you to recycle your life, your goals, your sense of who you are. It wants you to recognize your larger role in life, your need to contribute to others. Pluto allows you, encourages you, compels you to live out something greater than ego. If you fail to acknowledge that you are one "part" in a larger world and must, like your own inner "parts," function with others as a team, the world will likely rebel against you, just as your "inner family" quarrels when its members don't function in harmony.

It is always important to remember that Pluto is "greater than self." The changes it promotes in your life always reflect changes that society is also experiencing in its process of growth. The sign Pluto occupied at the time of your birth will be shared by your entire generation. It describes the kinds of changes society, as a collective unit, needs to address throughout the course of your generation's influence:

Pluto In Gemini: The world was introduced to mass communication that changed the world.

Pluto In Cancer: Major changes occurred in the structures of the "family." Security was redefined due to global changes taking place.

Pluto In Leo: Dramatic liberation regarding self expression. The "me" generation was born.

Pluto In Virgo: Major technological developments ultimately changed the course of history.

Pluto In Libra: Equal Rights became an issue, women's liberation began. Major changes occurred in society's beliefs about relationships.

Pluto In Scorpio: Major changes in society's understanding of sexuality. Society confronts its own power not only to evolve at a rapid pace, but its potential to destroy itself.

In some way, you will live out the prophesies of Pluto's sign placement through the experiences described by its House. You will play some part, big or small, in shaping humanity's consciousness. You will live out not only the promises, but the diseases that evolution involves. At times you may feel you are being used as a "vehicle" to activate or mobilize some greater-than-personal purpose.

Pluto wants you to be something more than ordinary. Because of this, you may at times experience an innate, almost perverted desire to destroy the stereotypes that society has projected on you. A part of you named "Pluto" wants you to feel compelled to make profound changes in your life. It wants you to know obsession. It wants you to be something more than you are. It wants to use you as a vehicle for change. It wants to use you as an example for others to gauge how far they have come.

Have you found and directed your power? Have you used it to recycle your life? Or have you dissociated from it and, by doing so, inadvertently given it to someone else who now uses it to control?

1st House: You project your power and intensity into all that you do. Pluto here wants you to discover yourself, turn yourself inside out until you know a new you. Then, present your power to the world as different from what is expected of you. Know and embrace the very depths of who you are. When meeting new experiences, question and sometimes reject what you see. Dare to look beneath the surface and never accept what's superficial. *Develop power through personality.*

2nd House: You need to develop a powerful reservoir of personal strength. You need to cultivate resourceful survival skills and then share these skills with others. Know how to stand alone and question values that others blindly accept. Know that you can survive independently by developing a strong belief in your own integrity. Your ability to access power is the greatest asset you possess. Use it wisely. *The power of survival.*

3rd House: Always look beyond the obvious to find answers to your questions. You need to learn how to access information from your environment, transform that information, and then give it back to the environment as something new and more meaningful. Discover the depths of the human mind, and the power of communication. In some way your thoughts and how they emerge in words make an impact on your world. What you do with your mind reflects the mental state of the environment around you. *The power of communication.*

4th House: Throughout your life, you will be challenged to tear down old emotional structures and build new ones that not only support your emotional needs but contribute to others' emotional stability. Conditions in your early home life in some way reflected the condition of the world. Once you have developed a profound understanding of the importance of family and security, you need to take part in changing society's obsolete beliefs. *The power of emotion.*

5th House: From deep inside, you feel a compelling need to express power through creativity. You need to use your creative skills to stimulate social change and transformation. You may feel compelled to take significant risks in love that lead to a complete change in your belief regarding what love is. "All the way, or nothing at all" is a mantra you know well. You want to experience the depths in all things designed to give pleasure. *The power to create.*

6th House: When confronting dilemmas, you need to go "all the way." Know your own mistakes by living them to the fullest. Then use your resulting understanding to help others through similar crisis. All work considered routine by most can become extreme obsessions to you. You feel useful only when afforded an opportunity to dig deeply to find answers. The workplace must provide a vehicle to bring about change and an opportunity to see something new result from it. *The power of routine.*

7th House: You discover your power to create profound change as a result of relating with others. Be prepared not only to make a powerful impact on others, but to be powerfully changed by the roles they play in your life. Through intense power-exchange, you discover the depths of your being. At one level, you could attract abusive relationships that force your power to emerge. At another level, the profound changes you experience have a powerful influence on others. Be willing to witness your own power reflected in their responses. *The power of relating.*

8th House: You are acutely aware of what needs to be sacrificed or eliminated in order to maintain meaningful relationships. Pluto here is one signature of a psychologist, infusing an urge to get to the very core of human experience and to regenerate life in the process. You need to develop an acute understanding of what's inside others' psyches, what makes people tick. Use this knowledge to help create positive change. Merge your powers with those of others in order to create transformation. *The power of union.*

9th House: A "part" of you wants to know what works for people, what enables them to expand beyond limited ideas of what's possible. It wants you to search the world, mentally, philosophically, or experientially, to discover what can make your world a better place. Pluto wants you to destroy prejudices that separate groups of people, rather than being controlled by them. It wants you to dig under the surface of societal beliefs until you find a "core" that unites all of mankind. You must confront prejudices (your own and others') in order to destroy them. Find beauty in what's different rather than living in fear of what you don't understand. *The power of philosophy.*

10th House: Your destiny is to make an impact on the world. Welcome collective power and allow it to live through you. Express it through profession, through the social role you play. This position practically guarantees power; use and direct it wisely. You will be a vehicle of change and will be recognized for the powerful role you play in the world. Whether that role is regenerative or destructive is a choice you will have to make. *The power of position.*

11th House: You will attract powerful friends and associates that show you what needs to be changed in the world. Your own power will surface because of their influence on your life. Life will challenge you to promote progressive changes, to live out an ideal of a new world, a new order. Fight for change, be obsessed with the desire to create it. You are a spokesperson. You can manipulate people because you have "group power." Use this power wisely. *Group power.*

12th House: You have a powerful past to call on to create major changes behind the scenes. You need to use it to help society correct past mistakes and failures, to transform them into successes. Personal problems can be transformed into social contributions, but some personal sacrifices may be required. Get to know the power that comes from isolation, time spent alone, meditation. Something is being lived out through you that may not be obvious, but it is making a powerful statement to the world. *The power of isolation.*

Aspects between Pluto and the personal planets describe how Pluto lives through personality. The planets involved describe "parts" of you that will be "possessed" by Pluto's intensity and desire to create change. The nature of the aspect describes the ease or difficulty you experience when living out Pluto's mission. Are you sufficiently secure within yourself to allow Pluto to use your personality as a vehicle of change? The outer planets function beyond consciousness. You can choose to direct them consciously, but you can't stop them from pursuing their "causes."

What you live out through the experiences of Pluto's House will in some way make an impact on your world. You may not be aware of the power of your actions, but it is there and others see it. You may, instead of consciously using the power this planet provides, attract it from outside sources. This can be dangerous because it infers that you're out of control, that you have given your power away. We see this in gang members who give their power to the leader. We see it in abusive relationships, where one partner allows the other to dominate and control. We see it all around us, but it is often masked, making it difficult to define. We saw Pluto at work in Jonestown, where an entire community was destroyed because each individual gave their power to one person who couldn't possibly handle it all.

Pluto shows where you are living out deep-seated sociological issues that need to be transformed or recycled. It describes where you are challenged to investigate, to look beyond and beneath the obvious, to probe the very core of the meaning of experience. If you dig deeply enough, you will ultimately find a link that connects your personal experience to what's going on in society. Here, you can contribute to a better world, or you can be part of its current problems.

The outer planets are "parts" of you that collectively want you to be more than you *have* to be. They want you to be more than your consciousness believes is possible. The outer planets challenge you, provoke you, test you. They represent "parts" of you that invite progress, excitement, and change. If you knew the outcomes of their intents, their powers would be dissipated, and you would miss the adventure of life.

The Outer Planets and the Inner Spirit

Jeff Jawer

Beyond the gates of Saturn lie liberation and madness, inspiration and folly, illumination and death. Each step beyond the known is fraught with danger and opportunity, simultaneously a journey away from and toward the self. This is the story of the outer planets, Uranus, Neptune and Pluto, each of which takes us to higher levels of consciousness and new possibilities of experience. The price, however, is steep: loss of control and loss of orientation in unfamiliar worlds of mist and turbulence. Just as the discoveries of the outer planets corresponded with great social changes, they touch us individually to leave us unlike what we were before. They are bridges, each one, to another world, one in which the highest aspirations of the personal connect with our collective urge to evolve and grow.

The word "spirit" comes from the Latin "spiritus" or breath. It is breath which gives us life and connects us to the atmosphere in which we live. It is also that which separates us, which reminds us with each exhalation that we are unique, just as each inhalation reconnects us with the whole. The paradox of existence can be summed up in breath, the constant coming and going, connecting and disconnecting, the eternal dance of the individual and the whole.

For thousands of years, the planet Saturn has stood guard as the cold, pale sentry against the worlds beyond our Sun. These two poles of the solar system, the Sun and Saturn, marked the beginning and the end of our earthly experiences. The Sun pulled us toward the center, literally keeping the solar system together, while Saturn, the great Timekeeper, set the outer limits of experience. One brilliant and blinding, the other cool and distant, held together the

57

world as we knew it. Certainly, there were individuals who surpassed these limits and moments in lives which went beyond the known and touched the worlds of Uranus, Neptune and Pluto. But these were forbidden places, outside the domain of Church and Crown, which were entered secretly, if at all.

Before the discovery of Uranus in 1781, Saturn's laws bound us to the land. Travel was rare, shifts in social status uncommon, people and animals tilled the soil as they had done for thousands of years. This was the period before industrialization, when the crafting of objects by hand required considerable time and patience. The two centuries that have followed have been marked by a dramatic increase in the use of machines to produce goods, assist agriculture, and facilitate travel. The world has broken loose from its moorings. and the old order has given way. The new political freedoms symbolized by the American and French Revolutions accelerated the demise of Saturn's authority. We were free; free from kings, free from the plow, free from eons of human history.

With freedom, though, comes alienation. When the old order no longer applies, *we no longer know where we stand*. Uranus symbolizes this combination of freedom and alienation in all of us. Collectively it has accelerated economic and social movement enabling workers to become owners, subjects to become rulers. Personally, it enables us to be individuals, to invent new ways to be and to express ourselves more freely. But the pain of Uranus is that we can no longer rely on the past as a guide to future actions. We are like strangers in a strange land, people in a new place unfamiliar with the rules and customs. Naturally this makes us nervous, uncertain, out of synch. This is the role of Uranus, to break us out of the old rhythms of Saturn, creating a new syncopation which is both stimulating and jarring. Uranians are weird, nervous, exciting, inventive visitors from other worlds here to shock and surprise us, to awaken us, sometimes violently, in our desire to remain asleep.

We are all Uranians somewhere. Even the most solid and conservative person has idiosyncrasies. Each one of us has unique ways of seeing, eating, walking, dressing, kissing, and so forth. To be human *is* to be Uranian. It is to stand up against the force of gravity, the weight of Saturn, and to create anew the experience of life in which the individual counts. The position of Uranus in the natal chart will describe where and how you blaze a new trail. The House shows the environment in which the old rules do not apply, in which new rules must be invented. The sign shows us how this is to be done; in Cancer through emotional instincts, in Leo through playful creation, in Virgo with consideration of utility. Each of us is challenged to be weird and different somewhere in life, and the natal chart shows us where and how.

Naturally, we are not all Uranian to the same degree. Those charts marked by significant aspects from Uranus to the Sun, Moon or Ascendant, for example, show individual lives which will emphasize the issues of inventiveness, originality, and difference. Charts heavy in Aries, Sagittarius, or Aquarius may indicate individuals more open to the experimentation of Uranus. Taurus, Cancer, or Capricorn, on the other hand, can show greater resistance to the new and strange.

Regardless of our chart , each of us does have *resistance* to Uranus. It is only natural that we remain attached to the timeless rhythms of Saturn, to the biological needs for order and consistency, as well as to the psychological needs for control and safety. All human beings need order to survive, yet all humans, and humanity itself, need Uranus to bring them into the future. Human beings are not simply a self-replicating species. We are different from other species in our capacity to create variety and change. This is our Uranian function as the "weird" animal, the one different from all the rest.

Integration of Uranus

Personal success in integrating Uranus stems largely from our relationship with Saturn. If Saturn is strong, if our sense of reality and purpose is clear and solid, we will have the stable base necessary from which to launch our Uranian rocket of discovery. The more we have accepted the realities of Saturn, its responsibilities and limitations, the better prepared we will be to go beyond and discover the next level of existence.

It is paradoxical that a healthy Saturn makes for a healthy Uranus, but it's true. For example, a Uranian is likely to feel different from others. Being different can be a gift or a curse. If this person has a solid sense of self-respect, a clear awareness of himself and a healthy ego, being different can be fun and exciting. If, however, Saturn is underdeveloped, if self-confidence is weak, reality poorly defined, ego boundaries absent, then Uranus is going to be threatening. Being different for this person can mean alienation and separation, not individuation and genius. Someone with original ideas but no skills to express them will be frustrated. Someone with Saturn's mastery of techniques, though, can anchor inventiveness in form and use originality in ways which are healthy and connective. Without Saturn is painful, like taking a jolt of electricity without proper grounding.

The same is true on a collective level. Societies that are shocked by Uranian events such as revolutions, natural disasters, or rapid technological change, need solid structures to absorb these jolts to the system. Maturity and patience can allow the new and unknown to integrate with that which is already in place, allowing Uranian differences to flourish.

A healthy Saturn is *not* a rigid one. When shocks hit a person or a society, it is necessary to be flexible, to be able to adapt and accept a variety of approaches for dealing with sudden changes. Uranus imposed on a rigid Saturn will almost always bring pain and suffering. The new Uranian forms demand that the old system change. If Saturn is not present, burn-out will occur (no grounding); if Saturn is overly present, breakdown will occur.

We can see this in another way by looking at the skeletal system in the body as a model for Saturn. We need bones to have form; without them we could not evolve beyond the level of jellyfish. However, if the skeletal system is too rigid,the muscles can not move freely, and we cannot act. If we become too calcified, we become arthritic, unable to move without pain. Saturn requires lubrication to balance its form-holding function with fluidity (of spirit, of belief, of body) so that we do not become crystalline.

Uranus, being different, is a challenge to our identity. The Sun, symbol of identity, is transformed by Uranus. The ego as king is overthrown by the rebellion of Uranus. The "I" is no longer the primary point of reference. The Sun must now see itself as a star, one of many in the larger galaxy, not the center of the universe itself. No longer contained by Saturn we have become beings with two poles, one the Sun and the other the galaxy. On a personal level this refers to the function of Uranus as a planet that brings us in contact with issues outside the self, the strictly personal world of my will, my body. We are no longer Suns, each one the center of the universe, but stars among the many in the constellations above.

Uranus then is a bridge *from the personal to something more than personal*. It is not strictly collective—Uranian experiences feel extremely personal at times—but they are individual in a new way. They are individual but connected with ideals, ideas, principles, and experiences that impact the human race collectively. (See Dane Rudhyar's *The Galactic Dimension of Astrology*, Aurora Press, for the origins of these ideas.)

The connection of the personal with the collective is an essential idea for working productively with the outer planets. The madness of the outer planets is about stepping *outside the ego*, the known world of the old self, and participating in a broader stream of consciousness in which the personal self reunites with the larger spirit of humanity. The outer planets mark those places where personal breath connects with collective breath, where the lungs of each individual fill the air sacs of the human race and nurture the life force of the species as well as of the individual.

This means that we cannot integrate the outer planets on a *strictly* personal level. The insanity of the outer planets is that the personal ego is too small to contain their revolutionary forces! The individual must connect identity with all of humanity in order to place the outer planets in perspective, *to make them livable*. None of us would go through the considerable effort to integrate Uranus, Neptune, or Pluto if we did not have the presence of all of humanity in which to connect it. Therefore, in addition to grounding Uranus in Saturn, in addition to the personal discoveries of working with the outer planets in our personal lives, there is the possibility, even the need, to understand that your personal experience of Uranus, your feelings of weirdness and nervousness, are not just for you but for all of us. Your willingness to take risks, to go beyond the old rules and invent new forms of being and expression is not for you alone. Thus, all outer planet influences remind us that we are more than Suns, more than independent egos. We are stars in a vast interwoven galaxy.

Uranus functions primarily on a mental level. It is the nervous system that is most likely to be challenged and changed by Uranian influences. We could say that wherever Uranus touches us there is new information coming in. If our nervous system is strong enough and flexible enough, we can assimilate the information. If we can accept new signals or new feelings that sound like gibberish, we can profit from Uranus. Our task is to accept the unknown, to allow ourselves the excitation of the nervous system without shutting down while we reprogram ourselves to use this new information. If we shut down in the face of Uranus, that is, if we deny or project its influences, whether in the natal chart, by transit, progression, solar arc, etc., it will have its way in the crudest of forms: accidents, shocks, unexpected events and so forth. We must remember that events are the densest form of energy, and that energy will explode if we deny it access on the psychic (astral) and emotional (psychological) levels.

Since Uranus is so revolutionary, we are obliged to take a leap of faith; we need to go beyond the old without experience and with no guarantees of success. If we accept this uncertainty, we give Uranus space to act freely, without resistance but with the support of what we *do* know and have accomplished through Saturn. If, for example, Uranus is in your 6th House, the event level suggests surprises at work, sudden changes of jobs, rebellious employees or being a rebellious employee. The psychological level suggests that you need freedom at work, the need to define your own tasks and a changing work environment. Physically this can correspond to a highly sensitive nervous system with sudden changes or unusual patterns in health.

On its highest level, Uranus in the 6th indicates breakthroughs in daily function or routine, that you are here to invent new ways in which to fulfill the tasks of work and body. If you are open to this, you can create working situations that are revolutions in your chosen field or fields. You can break the old limits of the body enabling new understanding to emerge. Perhaps, as well, old ideas about work and service, maybe as ways in which we are enslaved, can be changed so that these become areas of excitement and discovery.

Uranus works in fits and starts, not in a simple straight line progression like Saturn. Therefore be prepared for volatility in 6th House matters with Uranus there. This applies to whatever position Uranus holds in your birth chart (as well as by transit). You can lose a job one day without warning and gain an exceptional position another day in an equally unexpected manner. You may even create a job that never existed before. Work and health may not be places of certainty, but they become laboratories in our experience of life.

Embracing Neptune

Uranus (Ouranos) was a sky god; energy that comes from above and works primarily on the mental level through the nervous system. Neptune was the god of the sea. That energy works more through feelings, water, the lymphatic system. To a certain degree, we can say that the function of Neptune is to *reconnect* what has been broken apart by Uranus. But, since Uranus has taken us beyond the limits of Saturn, that place of reconnection is not in the self or within the ego, but with the cosmos. Uranus points us toward the great beyond, it shows us how to be more than of this earth, this limited material plane. Neptune does more than show us, it gives us *the emotional experience of connection with the universal*.

With Neptune, all boundaries and barriers are erased. The battle between I and Thou is resolved in the universal Us. That is why Neptune is associated with compassion, the ability to feel beyond ourselves and be in touch with the suffering of others. As pointed out in the Prologue, "The Discovery of the Outer Planets," Neptune corresponds to a time of idealism and spirituality in the mid-19th century. The goal of Neptune is not to individuate or to invent, but *to belong* in the largest possible sense.

On another level, Neptune is a response to the Moon and Venus, two feminine planets that are associated with emotional ties. Although different from one another, both the Moon and Venus have to do with emotional identification, whether with family, lovers or friends. (Please see my article "Paradoxes of Intimacy" in *Intimate Relationships*, Llewellyn's New World Astrology Series, for more on this.)

The key here is that *both* planets deal with emotions. Their points of reference come from our own direct experiences and reflect the values of our family and culture. As an outer planet, Neptune takes us beyond these value systems. Neptune allows us to belong to groups outside the family, the old tribes of blood and kinship. The family of Neptune is that of all living things. It is not even exclusively human. While Uranus may represent the possibility of meeting (or being) an extra-terrestrial (someone from outside our system), Neptune represents the possibility of loving that strange being.

Uranus has little or nothing to do with love. Much of the idealism that is associated with Uranus comes from the sign Aquarius. Uranus is a revolutionary, but it functions *outside* feelings per se. With Neptune, we become aware of the emotional consequences of Uranus, of the voyage outside the old world. The gift of Neptune is communion, the highest level of merger, beyond that of sex or intimacy in the usual sense. This is why there is such a strong spiritual flavor to Neptune, i.e., the desire to reunite with spirit.

This seems to be a logical step after the separative and often alienating experience of Uranus. Adolescents who frequently express Uranus in their rebellion against family recreate the sense of family with their friends. This fulfills their need to belong even as they identify themselves as rebels. The communion they seek can be Neptunian in all possible senses. They share dreams and fantasies, ideals and illusions, means of escape (music, alcohol, drugs) all in the name of friendship. These budding individualists seem all too willing to conform to the new norms defined by their new tribe. Their appearance, language, tastes in music and clothes, and professed values have a surprising uniformity for those who are rebels. This Neptunian loss of individuality is a natural progression after Uranus' often brutal separation from the old order.

If communion is the high side of Neptune, lack of discrimination would be the down side. The inability to distinguish the relative values of people and things is one of Neptune's specialities. Spiritually inclined individuals who want to love everyone can spend energy giving to those who are unable or unwilling to receive. Thus Neptune becomes a martyr, a victim of its own lack of discrimination.

If there are no boundaries or rules, then there is danger of becoming lost. Neptune can do this in myriad ways: through romanticism, spirituality, alcohol, drugs, idealism, the "truth," carelessness, and lack of self-respect, just to begin the list. The sword of Neptune doesn't look very sharp, but it clearly cuts two ways, it connects *everything;* individuality and choice are lost. Thus with Neptune, there is a loss of one's emotional center, the ability to feel what belongs to oneself and what does not. While this can dissolve barriers and allow inspiration to occur, we can understand why so many creative people are lost in Neptune: it is because this place of connection is so vulnerable and unprotected that one easily loses one's way, loses oneself.

There is inherent in Neptune the possibility for forgiveness as this planet, more than any other, may help us wash away the sins (errors and pains) of the past. When experienced consciously, the forgiving of Neptune comes after we feel and understand on a personal level what has transpired. We are then ready to move on to the higher state of forgiveness. In this way a process of personal connection and releasing is completed.

However, when we jump to Neptune without having first encountered the Moon, the personal aspect of emotions, we cleanse nothing. We push things under the rug of illusion. This side of Neptune is self-deception. There is no redemption when the journey has not been made. We do not complete something by skipping steps along the way. When idealism or spirituality is used to escape the personal, we move farther and farther away from our emotional center and we are less anchored in reality.

If Neptune's forgiving and forgetting negate the personal, we do not advance, we do not purify the past (or release old wounds). We paint over the rusty old spots without scraping off the rust. We may look smooth and shiny on the outside, but the wound remains on the inside. Without the substance of the Moon's personal experiences, Neptune brings only illusion, not fulfillment.

The material or event-level experiences of Neptune are negatively connected with weakness, a lack of muscle or emotional tone. This leads to a failure of will, a passivity, even victim consciousness. Superficially, entering the monastery or the ashram might look like a spiritual step up. But for those who are retreating from a world in which they cannot cope, it is a step out, out of themselves and into a parasitic state of being. When spiritual retreat comes from strength, a strong position as an individual, saints are born.

Neptune in the horoscope shows us where we may be weak, in retreat, idealistic or unable to hold our ground, to maintain our integrity. The ocean is too great a force for any of us to resist. The desire to merge beyond the level of accountability (personal responsibility) is strong in all human beings. Neptune's House placement may show us where this is likely to occur. This can mean that we are unable to meet issues here in a personal way. This can mean avoidance, but it can also mean that this is an area where communion and higher dimensions of feelings are possible.

A negative expression might be the creation of an illusion or fantasy. If Neptune is in the 10th House, an individual might not feel able to be assertive professionally or to accept recognition of success. Weakness in this area can be connected to an *idealized* notion of what one's career should be, perhaps a vision so perfect that it cannot possibly be lived out.

Idealization is a Neptunian way to *avoid reality*. The unhealthy 10th House Neptune can feel unreal in the world of professional responsibility. Being a fraud or feeling like one is possible here. On the other hand, a healthy Neptune, one that operates in harmony with other elements of the chart, can function quite differently in our example. This would indicate the possibility of having a career in which idealism manifests concretely, in which inspiration and imagination function for the good of the individual and society.

This link between the individual and the collective is shown in two ways. First, the 10th House is the place in which our individual energies are most strongly connected to collective responsibilities. Second, as an outer planet, Neptune is most likely to fulfill itself by linkage with something greater than the individual. How to balance individual and collective needs remains the challenge.

If we stay on the individual level with Neptune, we are often deceived, disillusioned and marooned on an island of doubt and self-pity. If we sacrifice the person with Neptune, we also lose ourselves, this time in a world made by others, be they gurus, stock manipulators or the needy. Our interest in our own welfare is a vital guide as to where we can go. In this sense, an image of inner light and compassion for self, balanced by compassion for all, may provide us with the bearings we need. Our hunger for communion, to belong, when met through the personal symbolism of the Moon, permits us to move to the higher levels of community without loss of self.

If the lesson of Neptune is "let go and let God," we mustn't forget that "God helps those who help themselves." The spiritual rewards of forgiveness, compassion, and communion are those of Neptune. This planet can show us the way to a higher aspect of self, one that is not just mentally connected but emotionally connected to sources of light and energy outside the self. The forgiveness that is most important is the forgiveness of self. We can not truly forgive others if we can not forgive ourselves. It is Neptune that can lead us to be more of ourselves, ideally without loss or sacrifice of the essential self.

Knowing Pluto and the New Way

With Uranus operating on the mental level and Neptune on the emotional level, we are left with the challenge of finding the appropriate description of Pluto's field of action. Pluto was, of course, the Lord of the Underworld, master of Hades, a keeper of secrets and guardian of the unseen and forbidden realms. Such an inner turn seems out of line with the evolutionary thrust of Uranus and Neptune. How can this planet of darkness bring us to higher understanding? How can a god connected to the earth be a means of going beyond the earth? These are not easy questions, but possible answers have to do with the essential meaning of Pluto.

Pluto is not about matter, *it is about knowledge*. This in not knowledge that comes from studying; rather, it is the knowledge of what lies within. Pluto holds the key to the code of energy and matter. Its relationship to nuclear energy mentioned in the "Discovery" prologue shows us that Pluto's power is not in its substance (it is a very small planet), but in its capacity to release vast amounts of energy. $E=MC^2$ is Pluto talking. It is about breaking loose energy that is encoded in matter. By breaking the ordinary atomic structure enormous amounts of energy become available for both constructive and destructive purposes. On the personal levels, Pluto can break loose our life structure, releasing tremendous energies that can be either destructive or constructive.

Pluto touches us at the fundamental level of energy consciousness. Our very survival, even the survival of humanity, comes into play. We are no longer dealing with Neptune's idealism. Pluto has absolutely nothing to do with idealism. Its purpose for being is survival. When we contact Pluto's energies, the very question of existence comes into play. This is why most of us don't want to have anything to do with Pluto! Yet sometimes we have to lose that which we think we need in order to discover what we *truly* need. This purifying and purging aspect of Pluto can be frightening indeed.

Very often the House position of Pluto in the natal chart will be an area of life in which we are uncomfortable. We may feel out of control, controlled by others, and react by becoming totally controlling ourselves. This is not something that is easy to understand. We are beyond reason and are in the realm of the most primal forces of nature. Here at the outer limit of the solar system, we find the means to propel ourselves further toward the galaxy, the unknown, *or we self-destruct*. Naturally, few of us feel that we can work with Pluto; we feel rather that Pluto works on us, most often in the forms of undermining and manipulation. But it is through this cutting loose of old, unneeded ideas, feelings, relationships, etc. that Pluto helps us clear the way for new growth.

Plutonion dimensions force us beyond the logical and often put us in contact with our most fundamental fears. Fairness has nothing to do with the situation, at least on an intellectual level. Pluto's work is on the lower chakra, the most primal point in the body. In this way, Pluto can help us get past rationalization and face the core of an issue. The "healing crisis," for example, is a Plutonian event, a time when conditions, be they emotional or material, worsen, usually to the point where we can imagine only the worst possible outcome. It is at this time, when the deepest elements of feelings come to is the surface, that we are closest to completing our "unfinished business." This is also why this outermost planet of the solar system often brings up issues or people from the past: it is the purging process, the preparation for a new stage in our lives that requires us to look at all of that we have tried to bury in the closet of our unconscious.

On the level of pure energy, Pluto *is* completely fair. We are reminded of the price that must be paid to renew life, to surpass the static and familiar patterns of the past. One more look at our greatest fears may be the final step of healing that allows us to finally let go and go on.

If we think of life as a building, Uranus is the wrecking ball that brings the old walls crashing to earth. Neptune represents the erosive forces that seem to erase all recognizable images of the old structure. And it is Pluto that goes further: Pluto digs below the surface, unearthing the original foundation, the core intention, so that all vestiges of the past are released. In the process, whatever is essential to the future will be rediscovered and offered to us, in a totally new form. This renewal of the essential is central to understanding Pluto and its relationship to death. The death dimension of Pluto is that which strips away all that is not needed, but the core always remains. To allow the death or the release process to occur is the best way to work with Pluto. It requires understanding, though, that whatever is lost on the surface, or in form, *is retained in essence.*

On the material level, Pluto can then be seen in all the devastating and overpowering forces of life. Only that which comes from the very core of life, the code of life, the DNA, can provide us with what is needed to truly transform ourselves. Plutonian events ask us if we *really* want to rebuild as before. They show us the price of our desire to retain the past, which must then be considered in undertaking any new action.

On a psychological level, Pluto can correspond to our inner demons, our nightmares, the most hellish visions that we can imagine. But, the Lord of the Underworld is also the God of Wealth. This means that in our darkest fears, in our unconscious shadow material lie the very keys to our own transformation and a wealth of new experiences, power, and fulfillment. A paradox of Pluto is that it has to do with both holding on, in the forms of desire and obsession, and the need to release. Both desire and letting go of desire are worthy means for achieving our ends. The trick is in understanding which is appropriate at which time. Fortunately, the necessity to deal with essentials often brings us toward the awareness of what is needed in any situation.

The fundamental point of Pluto is that *nothing essential dies.* Old forms may give way painfully, but the most vital elements of existence will continue. This means that working with Pluto is all the easier when we are willing to see what parts of our hopes and aspirations, ideas and perceptions, have become outmoded and are no longer useful. I like my friend Angel Thompson's idea that Pluto is about "addition by subtraction." This asks us how we can grow by letting go of something we no longer need. The passage of Pluto in our lives is one which always changes us. If we are not able to accept this externally, it will work inwardly on the very cells of our bodies, on the very core of our soul.

As with Uranus and Neptune, Pluto represents a bridge to a reality beyond that of ordinary existence. When Pluto calls, we become agents of change for the planet earth. Wherever Pluto is in our natal chart can show us where we have fear, fear of death or the inappropriate use of power. But, this House is also the area where we can transform ourselves and impact others in meaningful ways.

I believe that one of the fears in working with Pluto is tied to *the power that can be released.* You can check out your relationship with this aspect of Pluto by asking yourself what the word "power" means to you. If your images of power are negative, then it will be all the more difficult to work with Pluto. If, however, you understand the neutrality of power, then Pluto can be your ally. What you *do* with power is important; power itself is neither positive or negative.

Aspects of the Three

The influences of Uranus, Neptune, and Pluto in a natal chart are most evident when they are in aspect with other planets. Soft aspects, the trine and sextile, indicate an ease in integrating energies.

Therefore, someone with Uranus trine the Sun moves easily between the self-consciousness of the Sun and the revolutionary impulses of Uranus. The old will, Sun, and the new will, Uranus, work harmoniously with one another. Neptune in harmonious aspect with any planet suggests that idealism, imagination and compassion work in just proportion with the other planet. Thus, someone with Mercury trine Neptune is able to integrate logical perception and imagination rather easily. When Pluto is in trine or sextile to another planet, the energy of the planet is readily renewable. Pluto in this form gives the capacity to recover and survive. For example, someone with Pluto in trine to the Moon is able to experience very powerful emotional situations with the ability to easily find the essential points and reinstate emotional balance.

Hard aspects, primarily the conjunction, square, and opposition, but also the lesser hard aspects such as the quincunx, semi and sesqui-squares, are signs of challenge between any pair of planets. These mark the most radical points of shift in one's life, the points of difficulty, but also the opportunities to make significant breakthroughs. When the outer planets form these aspects with other planets or significant points such as the meridian (MC/IC), horizon (ASC/DSC) or Lunar Nodes, we have clear signals of *transformational challenges*.

In every case, it is vital to remember that we are dealing with forces that can not be overpowered by the will of the Sun nor contained by the rules of Saturn. Our conscious participation in the mutations brought by the hard aspects of the outer planets not only eases our burden but contributes to the whole of humanity. In the following section on the outer planets in relation to the other planets, I will focus on the hard or challenging aspects. If you have trines or sextiles, you are not likely to need much advice or explanation. Simply keep in mind that you are instinctively able to blend the meanings/energies of the two planets involved.

The outer planets in aspect to the Sun are of great importance. The Sun is essentially self-centered. The outer planets then provide direct challenges to this sense of self or core "I." In most cases, the Sun is going to reflect one's relationship with his/her father. Hard aspects may show elements of challenge with the father which may later be projected onto other authority figures. This means, too, that one's own authority or capacity to project oneself into the world will be diverted by these outer planet energies. Generally speaking, these outer planet aspects to the Sun demand that the ego go beyond itself, that it include ideas, images, feelings, or experiences that are outside the ordinary. This also means that the ego can be I inked with more collective forces and that the express ion of the self can have an impact in changing those around us and society in general.

⊙ When Pluto is with the Sun, we are dealing with the contrasts of dark and light or death and life. While the Sun wants to shine and assert itself openly, Pluto acts indirectly, covertly, and often in destructive ways. Thus Pluto, in hard aspect to the Sun, can mean destruction of self. Of course, this may be subtle as in the case of someone who undermines his own career or personal life. There can be ambivalence or mixed feelings about succeeding and about creating. While Pluto can bring a certain obsessiveness to the ego here, its expression is rarely going to be overt or direct.

When considering Pluto, we must always think about power, Pluto's power to know the ways of life and death. Pluto-Sun can indicate power struggles with father or with authorities, even a struggle with one's own use of power. These aspects can indicate a profound distrust of self that may come from a distrust of father, father's own distrust of himself and his lack of trust of the child. In any case, the principle here is one of adhering to the essential.

The destruction of the ego is not meant to be the destruction of the self, but rather the deep *restructuring of the self*. Pluto-with-the-Sun individuals may be those who examine themselves very deeply. Pluto can often bring us a kind of psychological awareness, a desire to understand hidden motivations and causes. Ideally, we can renew by this process of inner examination. However, the examinations sometimes never stop and there is no rest from criticism to allow for growth. When expressed at its highest level, the Sun-Pluto person is not just someone who changes himself, but someone who changes the world.

The astronomer Copernicus was born with Pluto opposite the Sun. He transformed the way we viewed the physical universe by placing the Sun in the center. The center of gravity of our solar system was shifted, but not without considerable controversy and upheaval. Being a good Plutonian, though, Copernicus did not permit his theory to be published until after his death. He understood the power and danger of his ideas. His rebellion, then, was hidden during his lifetime so that he did not have to face its consequences personally. It is common for Plutonians to express their power in this indirect fashion.

Another astronomer, Galileo, was not so fortunate. He was persecuted by the Church for his scientific ideas. He was born with Pluto conjunct the Sun. Here we see the difference between the opposition and the conjunction. Oppositions may allow us a certain distance. But the conjunction for Galileo meant a more direct confrontation with the Plutonian forces. Galileo also had Uranus square his Sun which further emphasized his difficulty with authorities. Copernicus, though, had Uranus and Neptune trine his Sun, easing some of the possible confrontations. These multiple contacts from the outer planets may emphasize the potentially powerful role an individual can have on the world.

Perhaps the most symbolically appropriate contemporary Plutonian is Dr. Elisabeth Kubler-Ross who was born with Pluto conjunct her Sun in Cancer. Her book *On Death and Dying* was a major influence on the new understanding of death. By addressing this "forbidden" subject, she helped society to release some of its fears of the unknown. This is a very Plutonian thing to do. By opening up an area that is normally closed off, Pluto allows us to let go of a great deal of pain and suffering. The way through is not often easy, but the results can be exhilarating. This is shown, to some degree, by another Plutonian, psychologist/guru/social activist Richard Alpert (also known as Baba Ram Dass). Alpert was born with Pluto square (and Uranus conjunct) the Sun. Among the many paths he has taken—Harvard professor, LSD experimenter, meditator—has been his work with dying people. Alpert teaches that working with dying people is not simply a means to help others or to confront our own fears, but to stand at the very gate of life itself. It is a spiritual experience to be present with those in the process of dying. This Plutonian has shown us how to take what might be considered the worst possible experience and turn it into a moment of revelation and bliss.

If you were born with Pluto in hard aspect to your Sun, you may find yourself challenged by the battle between life and death. You may experience this in distrusting life's bounty or in a constant process of self-examination that may not allow you to find a level of peace and comfort. The Pluto tendency to dig below the surface can undermine self-acceptance leaving you overly critical or analytical.

A more subtle version of this is consciously to assure that you do not achieve a feeling of safety about yourself and your place in the world.

On a higher level, hard aspects from Pluto to the Sun indicate that you are here to change negative experiences of your father into transforming experiences for yourself. The net result can be healing for you as well as finishing old patterns of distrust or dissatisfaction in your father (and in his father too) enabling all of us to have a deeper understanding of life's mysteries. While the relationship of Pluto to the Sun is one of deep self-examination, it is important to understand that even this useful process can go too far. The constant turning over of a garden may keep the weeds out, but it will never allow anything else to take root.

Your inner spirit is the site of transformation. By focusing on the precise issues that are essential, you may change yourself and others without destroying the very ground of your existence. Understand that the issues of fear, power, and control are common to all human beings and that you are being given the chance to see these more clearly than most of us are. When you have Pluto with the Sun, be gentle with yourself so that the flowers are not destroyed with the weeds.

If power is something you consider negative, this shows you where you have to work. Plutonians *need* power and need to trust themselves in using it. Errors in the past do not mean that you can not have power now. The only way out is *through*, not around, this issue. It has been stated that "power corrupts," but we have also learned that powerlessness corrupts as well. Know that your purpose in life is neither to repeat the past nor to keep tearing it down, but to choose its most important aspects and to express them in new ways. Pluto returns us to the source so that we can renew ourselves at the deepest levels of our being.

When Neptune contacts the Sun in hard aspect, we have the paradox of egolessness and ego. It is as if the core self is not a solid point, but a shifting mass is sometimes nowhere and sometimes everywhere. Neptune-Sun can indicate the invisible father, the weak father, the sacrificing father, the escapist, magical, or idealistic father. In all of these instances, the challenge is to find oneself in the midst of this nebulous frame of reference for the ego. One can have the image of father as a wonderful human being, but somehow remain unclear about how to father oneself. Fathering is the capacity to project oneself into the world, to express and manifest will and creativity. While Neptune-Sun can often indicate creativity, the will or driving force behind it can be as shifty as a spring breeze, here one minute and gone the next. Confidence can quickly rise and fall as the core of the Sun becomes fluid and undefined in Neptune's realm.

Another image here is that of the individual who is in contact with the divine, the spiritual, or the universal. This is all well and good except that hard aspects between Neptune and the Sun can also lead to a loss of self in the process. When the self (Sun) is a bridge to the universal (Neptune), this combination can work effectively. Understanding the difference between being a channel and being that which is channeled is vital if one is to remain sane and centered.

Neptune can lead to that loss of center so that the self is lost. When one is a channel for creativity, visions, healing, etc., one is not the energy being channeled. Neptunians sometimes forget this and live their lives through their dreams, visions or fantasies. Without boundaries between self and subject, we can become so vulnerable that we will do just about anything to escape pain. We can numb ourselves through thoughts or actions, so-called healthy ones (spirituality, art, helping others) or unhealthy ones (alcohol, drugs, television). The healthy Sun-Neptune person is one who consciously moves between the worlds of I and the universal, keeping a balance between the individual identity and the collective experience.

Psychologist Carl Jung was born with Neptune square the Sun. His work included a mystical or spiritual dimension that was not then found in psychotherapy. He wrote about archetypes, collective universal forces, and their relationship to the individual. Each of us experiences these archetypal forces channeled through our individual thoughts and feelings. Jung's work was grounded in scientific training and scholarship that allowed him to move through Neptune's murky waters without losing his way. As a result, he broadened our view of the psyche and the human experience. While Pluto deepens, Neptune broadens; it is inclusive and able to find meaning without destroying or eliminating elements.

Dr. Albert Schweitzer is considered one of the great humanitarians of this century. He was born with Neptune square his Sun and conjunct his Moon. He sacrificed the comforts of the life of a Swiss doctor to heal the sick in Africa. This kind of sacrifice is typical of Neptunians and here, as is often the case, was supported by persuasive religious belief. By reminding us that we are part of something larger than ourselves, Neptune brings us that sense of grace or communion which can heal the soul. In effect, it is Pluto that does the surgery, but it is Neptune that allows us to heal by becoming whole again.

Mozart, a recognized musical genius of enormous importance, was born with Neptune opposing his Sun. His work enchanted millions in the past, and still does today (see the Introduction to this volume). Yet he lacked self-control and dissipated himself physically. Here we have the combination of Neptune's inspiration with a loss of boundaries which was destructive to the body. Neptunians are often capable of striking a universal chord which touches others while remaining lost to themselves.

If you were born with Neptune in hard aspect to the Sun, the challenge is to find this place of magic, of inspiration within yourself, *without becoming completely lost in it*. Saturn can help you with this as it is associated with both discipline and time. You can use the discipline of time to allow Neptune its periods of expression, but limiting them according to a particular schedule. Someone who wants to be devoted to the service of others, for example, could select a certain number of hours a week to do this so as not to burn out. A creative Neptunian should use a schedule so that food and rest are not forgotten for the sake of art. Remember that the secret is in finding *the right balance between preservation and loss of ego*. If the balance is lost, life is so tiring or painful that the wonderful inspiration, imagination, and compassion will not continue to be available to the rest of us. Forgive yourself for having limits and use them to channel your gifts for many years to come.

Uranus to the Sun may indicate a father who is radically different than the norm, experimental, nervous, brilliant, intermittently present or absent. Uranus with the Sun can also show radical shifts in one's sense of self. The revolutionary forces of Uranus to the Sun can lead to revolution against the self. We have here not the undermining of Pluto or the dissipation of Neptune, but the sudden overthrow of one's status, position or identity. That means that the Sun-Uranus person may find that the personal situation changes without notice. One can rise from the bottom to the top overnight and fall again as quickly.

When Uranus is in hard aspect to the Sun, we keep reinventing ourselves. The old self needs to be renewed from time to time just to keep life interesting. If not, we're likely to feel bored or caged up and will crack from the inside or allow outside events to throw us for a loop. The old model of father no longer applies for you; you need new forms of creativity and authority. You may have difficulty with authority figures and have a basic distrust in rules and the social order. When your sense of uniqueness is honored and acted on, there is less struggle with the outside world.

Psychologists Alpert and Freud were both born with Uranus conjunct the Sun. These revolutionaries of the mind broke from the traditions of their times and have played the role of trailblazers for the rest of us. Freud was a Taurus who established a body of work that is still with us today. The conjunction of Sun-Uranus in Taurus is particularly challenging as Taurus is very resistant to change. The struggles between new and traditional values show very clearly in Freud's work. Alpert, as an Aries, has found it easier to change names, identities and roles since this sign is more like Uranus than is Taurus. However, the impact of his work may not endure as long as Freud's. Alpert is the author of a book entitled *Be Here Now*, the perfect Aries/Uranus title, one which does not require our eternal attention.

When Uranus is in hard aspect to the Sun, we could say the lesson is that "we are not our fathers." When with the Moon, the lesson is "we are not our mothers." This may seem obvious, but the need to break off from our parents, to stop the patterns of reacting against them, and to discover our own path, is an essential Uranian process. The split with parents, on an inner or outer level, whether consciously chosen or not, is one that emphasizes the idea that Uranus is about both freedom *and* alienation. There are no old models to work from, and we are free to, and must, make new ones.

On its highest level, the Uranus-Sun person is one who can combine the personal (Sun) with the galactic (Uranus) so that we have something that is both new and warm and personal. In its extremes, Uranus can be very impersonal, adhering to revolutionary ideas, but far from the warmth of the human heart. Uranus-Sun asks that your inner spirit connect to new forms while retaining enough flexibility to remain human. In this way, the human heart remains vital as we explore new dimensions of creativity and expression.

Outer planet hard aspects to the Sun and Moon are direct challenges to our sense of self. While all aspects from the outer planets present certain issues, none comes so close to home as those to the

Sun and the Moon. This is because the Sun and the Moon have the most to do with who we are, as opposed to how we think, relate, act and so forth which are more connected with the other personal planets, Mercury, Venus, and Mars. So here we are not dealing with issues of form but with issues of substance. With the Sun, the challenges are more likely to be conscious. The Sun shines light on that with which it is connected. Furthermore, the Sun has the will to act, to create. This is not the case with the Moon.

☽ Psychologically speaking, the Moon may be the most important planet in a natal chart. This is arguable, but the hypothesis is based on the idea that the Moon is the essential matrix for life itself. It is the body closest to the earth and represents those forces which are closest to the self as well. While we may identify with the Sun, it can be said that the Sun is a work in progress, something that we are creating. The Moon, though, has been cast in the past, patterned, often passive and unconscious. The Moon is Mother, food, and nurturance. Perhaps we can survive with a chaotic father (ego); many do. But disruptions to the Moon are disruptions to the very forces that feed and sustain us.

When Uranus, Neptune, and Pluto make hard aspects to the Moon in a natal chart, ordinary ideas about family and emotions are absent. The most personal of planets, and the most personal of experiences, are touched by sudden change and excitement, reverie and confusion, fear and power. Here it is not the ego that is challenged, but our most instinctive responses. The old ways of the family no longer work; new models connecting us with larger families or more transcendant means of self-nurturance are present. On one level, any outer planetary hard aspect to the Moon creates "orphans," that inner feeling of being separate from or threatened by normal family experience.

Pluto and the Moon share qualities of feeling, although on very different levels. The Moon is derived from memory, personal experiences and family traditions. Pluto belongs to no family, but to nature itself, the raw forces of death and rebirth. Since the Moon is most frequently associated with our experiences of mother, Pluto with the Moon will add a dark tinge to our maternal experiences. Often Pluto-Moon people have been psychically invaded by mother, her fears are theirs, her desires are theirs. Sometimes she hovers close by controlling, directing, and manipulating. Sometimes her reins are invisible, but her power and fears are nevertheless felt.

The obsessive nature of Pluto comes from unfulfillment. When Pluto is with the Moon, we may always be hungry, always connected with mother's unfulfilled desires. We may distrust emotions or close relationships, a fear of intimacy. We may feel that to be close is to be devoured, just as we may feel devoured by our own emotional needs. To have Pluto in hard aspect to the Moon is to know forever what hunger is. This need not be negative if one learns how to use it. As always, Pluto is a reminder to look underneath the covers, to strip away the ordinary and discover the innermost levels of meaning. Therefore, those with Moon-Pluto can make wonderful therapists or healers. They can feel, in fact they need to feel, the most vital and tender points in others. Their desire, even need, is to live a daily life of transformation, and this works well for any kind of healer.

Another side of this, though, can be an addiction to crises. This element of unfulfillment can become so habitual with Moon-Pluto (or of restlessness with Moon-Uranus) that a comfortable life may not be possible. The emotional nature is one of seeking, moving deeply, and complicating ordinary life. However, when the individual with this position is able to create a daily routine that includes such intensity, a degree of calm and peace is available.

Pluto demands digging within. If we can create this consciously, then we do not have to dig up that which is best left alone. It is also important to consider that many of us want to deny Pluto completely. Outwardly, we may see no sign of this restless digging within. Those who deny Pluto may have greater difficulty in finding comfort because they are unwilling or unable to do the transformative work that is demanded. The dissatisfactions can be projected so that they come in the form of difficult circumstances or untrustworthy others. Owning up to that Moon-Pluto dimension suggests that helping others to transform themselves may allow you to be more comfortable with yourself and your own inner fears.

Pluto's relationship to the underworld indicates that Moon-Pluto people are very sensitive to the dark sides of themselves. They may feel that they are bound up in families in which suffering or unfulfillment is just punishment for their wicked ways. But, at its best, Moon-Pluto is about killing the old habits, the old family ways and mother's patterns, so that new ones can emerge. Those who show us the darkness must remember that they are not darker than anyone else. They are those trusted with dealing with humanity's psychic garbage. Plutonians (and Scorpios to some degree) need to learn that their contact with fear, negativity, and manipulation is not the same as being dark. Conscious working to transmute these dark forces enables the Plutonian to use his sensitivities for helping and healing.

The issue of manipulation is almost always present when dealing with Pluto. Pluto-Moon types do this instinctively and often don't even recognize that they are. Rather than denying or punishing such behavior, it is enough to identify it without judgment. Manipulation has to do with effecting the behavior of others. If one is doing this consciously and with a positive purpose, it can actually be helpful. Pluto understands that we are not islands; that each person affects every other person.

Working with Pluto is often about the descent into the underworld or our own private hell. Many Plutonians have experienced the dark night of the soul and have returned to the surface to tell us what they have learned. The drug addict turned drug counselor is one example of this type of person. The Pluto-Moon person, then, is often one who puts us in touch with those dark, mysterious, and often painful places within ourselves. Being able to help us contact that essential wound can be a first step in healing it.

Martin Luther was born with Pluto opposing the Moon and transformed Christianity by rebelling against the Mother Church. Betty Freidan, author of *The Feminine Mystique*, also was born with Pluto in opposition to the Moon. Her important book played a significant role in transforming the vision of women in modern society. J. Edgar Hoover was born with Pluto square his Moon and was the keeper of America's secrets as founder of the F.B.I. Investigation (of the soul, the psyche, nature or crimes) is perfect for a child of Pluto.

Neptune with the Moon is tricky business. We don't want to speak ill of mother, particularly if she was sacrificing, spiritual, or weak. But, Neptune-Moon is one of the more challenging aspects in that emotional confusion, a lack of clarity about one's feelings and needs, is often present. The Moon is, above all, personal. We all need to be loved and nurtured in a personal way. When Neptune is with the Moon, this is often not the case. The emotional connection with mother is diffused, filtered through illusion, idealism and sacrifice, which can lead to muddled feelings. There may have been moments of bliss when you, mother, and God were all joined as one. Perhaps it came through religion, or music, or the magic of stories and dreams, but there was likely not a great deal of clarity about your relationship. Mother's pains and joys may have been yours as Neptune dissolved the boundaries of the Moon. Those born with the Moon in hard aspect to Neptune are, thus, often highly sensitive, intuitive, and vulnerable. Their own needs and feelings can be lost or sacrificed under the relentless waves of Neptune, washing away individual issues for larger ones.

Mother-as-victim is one scenario here, a pattern that may continue with the individual playing out the victim role himself. This is certainly not the easiest placement for those who want to be clear about their needs. If we were bonded with mother, we may expect that others will be psychic or as intuitive as we are. We don't want to spell things out. We don't like the feeling of separation that comes from explanations. We may also feel that it is inappropriate to demand things of others (at least directly).

If our mother were not bonded with us, we may have connected with other people or images in which to lose ourselves, such as a church, cause, art form, or substance (food, alcohol, etc.). In any case, it is clarity that is missing, the unwillingness to be direct about feelings and needs. Of course, it is often the case that those with strong Moon-Neptune contacts are unclear themselves about their own needs. They are often so sensitive that they absorb the feelings of everyone around them. How can one sift out what is his and what is not?

The resolution on one level is in developing some kind of checking system, some way to know if what you are feeling is relevant or not. Ask someone who cares for you; "Do you think I'm being overly sensitive here? Is it important for me to have this job (person, food, etc.)?" This may be difficult for someone who doesn't feel comfortable sharing the personal burden with others. But, clarity is one way through it all. Recognize your fusional nature and balance it with some independence, if you can.

Since the Moon does represent essential needs, it is important for the Moon-Neptune person to have a daily life that includes some positive sides of Neptune. Is idealism or imagination a part of your routine? Do you have magic, compassion, or spirituality as a regular element in your life? If you can include these in healthy ways,then

Moon-Neptune can indicate a refined life of extreme beauty and creativity, caring, and compassion. When clarity is combined with Neptune's idealism, science combines with art, and good intentions manifest themselves in useful ways.

Marilyn Monroe is a prime example of a Moon-Neptune person. She was born with the opposition, the aspect of projection. People saw her as something she was not. She was a real, flesh-and-blood person on whom we projected our images of the fantasy woman, the screen goddess. This unreal identity was rooted in a very unstable childhood complete with a mentally ill mother and Marilyn's later abuse of alcohol and drugs. Neptune is associated with film, the giant illusion in which individual still-frames become moving images.

The danger of illusion on such a grand scale is loss of the individual. The other side, though, is one's ability to cast an image that is greater than life, one that touches masses of people. So today, we still have this greater Marilyn, the larger-than-life illusion, who smiles at us from photos and films now more than 30 years old. But, there was also the lesser Marilyn, the frightened, abused woman unable to get help in her most desperate final moment.

Shirley MacLaine is another version of Moon-Neptune. She was born with the conjunction in the sign of Virgo. The earth sign Virgo, along with her Sun in earthy Taurus, provides a solid contrast with Marilyn Monroe's Moon and Sun in airy Aquarius and Gemini, respectively. Shirley MacLaine, too, is a performer. Creating illusion is her business, but she has been able to combine this with another aspect of Neptune, spirituality. Shirley MacLaine is a very down to earth person who has written about some very unearthly subjects. She has made herself the subject of some ridicule by exposing her unconventional beliefs and experiences. But, she has done it with such solidity of character that she has opened a door to a non-material reality to millions of people. This is clearly a case in which Neptune has brought the personal elements of the Moon into a collective or public situation. In doing so, Shirley MacLaine has fulfilled some of the evolutionary potential of this aspect. It may well be that the grounded and disciplined parts of her personality have enabled her to do this successfully. If you want to build a tower to the sky it must be very well anchored to the ground.

Uranus and the Moon can indicate emotional volatility, a life of unexpected changes and an unusual or unstable family life. Mother could have been highly original, a genius, a freedom lover or a nervous wreck. In fact, you probably experienced her as quite different from the so-called normal mom. Of course, your own experiences are normal for you, so this kind of emotional intensity may also become normal for you. Sometimes Uranus-Moon means that the family moves a lot. Often there is the feeling that you don't belong to your family, that you dropped in from another planet or were adopted and nobody told you about it.

The essential point is that you are here to create new ways of nurturing, of caring, of feeding, and living your emotional and family life. Your rhythm and routine, your patterns of emotional expression may be very different. Getting close to you is not necessarily an easy thing to do. Sure, one part of you can jump in emotionally, but staying close can make you itchy. Experience may have taught you not to rely on others, to expect them to understand you or support you in consistent ways. So you can jump in and out of things before being tossed out, but the key is to remember that you don't have to relive the past, nor live your life like other people. You can invent your own ways and your own conditions for being close. Freedom is important—essentially the freedom to be yourself—and that can't be given up easily.

If life is full of surprises, it may be that you, too, are meant to throw some surprises. Uranians are here to wake us up. If you are a Moon-Uranus person, it is your job to *shake* us up, to make us re-examine our ideas of security. If you do this willingly and intelligently you will be called a genius. If you push this away and try to make a calm and ordinary life for yourself explosions can happen all around you. You can be the catalyst for change, so enjoy it.

Beatnik writer Jack Kerouac was born with Uranus opposite the Moon. His book *On the Road* expressed restlessness among many of his generation who were seeking new lifestyles, different from the safe norms of the 1950's. Bob Dylan was born with the Moon conjunct Uranus. This singer/songwriter has been one of the most influential popular musicians of the last 30 years. Dylan has always played the rebel, but in his Gemini fashion he has kept changing styles over the years. This is perfect, too, for a Uranian who wants to keep us off balance, to follow his own unique rhythms. Dylan is not known for his sentimentality, which is appropriate for Uranus-Moon. But, like a true Uranian, he has switched musical and lyrical styles many times.

☿ Outer planet aspects to Mercury indicate unusual patterns of seeing, thinking, and communicating. In each case, personal perception is filtered through the broader lens of collective vision and unconventional ideas. Mercury-Uranus indicates a great deal of nervous energy, unusual perspectives, the brilliant but erratic type. Off-the-wall ideas or radical visions typify this Mercury-Uranus profile. Lily Tomlin has Mercury square Uranus and has a brilliant and original mind. Her variety of comedic characters is one of her special gifts, perfect for the quicksilver mind of Mercury-Uranus. Astronomers Kepler and Galileo both had Uranus in hard aspect to Mercury (conjunction for Kepler, square for Galileo).

Individuals with Mercury-Uranus may be those whose speech and thought patterns did not develop rhythmically. The mind goes so fast that sometimes the tongue cannot keep up. Interruptions in communication are often experienced in childhood, meaning that time would not be given to allow you to express yourself. This can also lead to rebellious talk, unusual speech patterns, or impatience on a mental level. This combination can indicate that one is taking in a great deal of information, that the nervous system is being challenged to work quickly. Anything that strengthens the nervous system can be helpful here. When well integrated, the Mercury-Uranus person is not just a weirdo or the outspoken shocker, but the awakener, the enlightener. Given a particular problem, it is this person who is likely to see things differently than everyone else. While this can make ordinary communication more complicated, it is a perception that is valuable and should be honored.

Neptune with Mercury is the mind that tunes in all the stations at the same time. Mercury has to do with fine tuning, but Neptune prefers a broad-band approach to gathering information. The results can sometimes be fuzzy thinking or an inability to concentrate on details. Conversely, this person may be able to communicate in ways that touch the souls of others, to reach beyond the tangible and enter psychic realms. Many born with this combination were not taught to communicate directly. This indirectness can make ordinary communication more difficult. It is a poetic or non-linear mind that works well with images, but may have some difficulty with facts or practical matters. The challenge here is to be able to set the poetry aside when it's time to go grocery shopping. Learning to tune out the cosmic for the mundane is necessary for ordinary survival. On the other hand, there is the possibility to inspire with words or images, to evoke feelings beyond the limits of the literal and to pass on messages of faith and hope. You just need to learn how to sort out the useful information from the static.

Mystical philosopher Rudolf Steiner was born with Mercury conjunct Neptune in Pisces. This double dose of intuitive thinking was used in systematic ways to develop Steiner's Anthroposophical movement. Reformer Martin Luther had Neptune conjunct Mercury in the religious sign of Sagittarius. Musicians Bob Dylan and David Bowie both have Neptune square Mercury, emphasizing the poetic and musical sides of communications. Both are also known for a certain obscurity in their messages.

Pluto in hard aspect to Mercury brings us to the issue of communication in relationship to power and control. Generally speaking, these individuals were taught that communication is a medium of control and not a neutral means of sharing ideas or information. Distrust of the power of words, a sensitivity to being manipulated by them and the use of language in powerful ways is common here. On a deeper level, Mercury-Pluto means that communication can transform. It also means that the way in which a person communicates may radically change during the life.

Sometimes, those with Pluto in hard aspect to Mercury are sarcastic or use words in cutting or destructive ways. They likely experienced the same forms of communication when they were children. Withheld communication is another possibility, as the Pluto themes of nonexpression or going to the depths are both present. In any case, a key here is to remember that sometimes things are simpler; they are just as they appear and don't need to be ripped apart to find the hidden meaning or manipulation. It is useful to be able to see the intent behind words. This offers the possibility of a probing perception not taken in by the obvious. But recognizing that suspicion is not always warranted can reduce some of the secrecy and struggles here.

Here is a powerful group of people whose use of language has touched the masses: Abraham Lincoln and Nikolai Lenin had Pluto conjunct Mercury; Mao-Tse tung and Winston Churchill had the opposition; Goethe and Machiavelli had the square. This is a very potent group of communicators. All of them have helped direct the course of history due to their power to convince others with the power of their ideas. Those born with Mercury-Pluto can change the thinking of others. If it is done consciously, it can be helpful rather than a tool for petty manipulation.

♀ "Venus and the Outer Planets" sounds like the name of a 60's rock band. Venus, of course, would be the beautiful female lead singer. The Outer Planets would be the back-up band, a scruffy collection of weirdos, misfits, and magicians. The contrast between beautiful Venus and her band is considerable. She is calm, clear, and at ease with herself. The Outer Planets are jumpy, moody, and brooding. Since Venus symbolizes self-worth and attractiveness, her connections with the outer planets would indicate some unusual qualities in these areas. This also is going to show up in relationships, personal values, and tastes.

Venus and Uranus can indicate an intermittent love nature. This indicates a childhood in which love or approval was not given consistently. Behavior that would be rewarded one day would not be the next. Feelings of uncertainty as to worthiness or loveability are possible. Another view is that Venus-Uranus people are loved for being different and for being independent. Spontaneity in relationships and quick ups and downs are also common for this group.

Fundamental here is the idea that one is to be loved for being different. This can add independence and the possibility to create new kinds of relationships, but there is at the root a lack of commitment due to a distrust of love or approval. At the highest level, the Venus-Uranus person is the one who is searching for new forms of relationships, relationships in which both love and the individuality of each person are present. When dealing with Uranus, we are always challenged to create something new, without a model to work from. That is certainly the case here.

To protect oneself from unexpected rejection, the Venus-Uranus person can avoid commitments, or this person can attract partners who are really not appropriate, ensuring the rupture of relationship that is expected. This person needs to be able to recognize that relationships are not something that can be secured, but that they are *alive*. In this aliveness, each moment is unique and requires flexibility to be fully appreciated. Yet another element here is that Venus-Uranus means that one should be changed by love and that in loving others they too are changed.

It shouldn't be surprising to discover that Warren Beatty has Venus conjunct Uranus in Taurus. The combination of Uranian magnetism and Taurean sensuality have led to his reputation as a sexual libertine. Venus in hard aspect does not guarantee the kind of renown that Warren Beatty has but does suggest that the need is for a relationship that is based more on fascination than on security.

Venus with Neptune is about being loved for sacrifices. Here we have Neptune again as the carrier of self-abnegation. At its best, it is romantic beauty and spiritual bliss. But even such idealized endeavors as these can be wrapped up in illusion and ultimate failure. Since Venus describes how we expect to be loved, the Venus-Neptune person may find it hard to express needs clearly to others or to be realistic in relationships. The roots of this can be about being loved because you were not demanding, because you were invisible and put others before yourself. Ideally, this individual is one who is going to be able to combine personal and spiritual love. In this way, compassion for others, creative sensitivity, and idealism don't overwhelm your need to be respected and appreciated.

Musician Leonard Bernstein was born with Neptune conjunct Venus in Leo. He created beautiful music and presented it to the public in a dramatic fashion. Cutting a romantic figure, he represented American classical music for the world.

Pluto-Venus brings together an odd couple, somewhat like beauty and the beast! Venus is about love and pleasure and Pluto is about death and darkness. The Venus-Pluto individual is often someone who has been manipulated around love and relationships. In fact, you may have been left with the feeling that being loved is stealing or taking something you have no right to. This is due to Pluto's connection with underlying costs. Pluto is very adept at measuring the exchange between people. The Pluto-Venus hard aspect, then, can show a person who is *overly conscious of the cost of love.* If you are loved, perhaps someone else is being loved less. This can lead to feelings of guilt about receiving. Perhaps you will stay in a place of neediness or obsessive desire so you won't find the fulfillment or comfort that feels inappropriate.

Fortunately, the story does not end here. Venus-Pluto is the story of turning something dark into something beautiful. It's about finding the rusty old object and turning it into something beautiful and valuable. It is about finding treasure in the midst of tragedy. At its best, the Venus-Pluto experience is one of transformation, one that allows value and love to be found at the deepest levels of human experience. In the other direction, it is about the exploitation and perversion of love so that it becomes a medium of control, not one of sharing. Finally, Venus-Pluto, like Venus-Uranus, is connected with the idea that loving someone is *about being changed*. The transformative role of Pluto says that relationships are a means toward change and to being changed.

The notorious Rev. Jim Jones (Jonestown, Guyana) had Venus square Pluto and created a nightmare in which death and love joined in hideous fashion. Pornographer Larry Flynt was born with Pluto square his Venus, with Mars and Sun in Scorpio, revealing the sordid and potentially violent sides of sex and love. Elvis Presley was born with Pluto opposing his Venus and became an enduring symbol of male sensuality. (The projection, as with Marilyn Monroe, is shown through the opposition.) Here we find Pluto in the image of power. Marilyn Monroe had Neptune-Venus, which gives the image of vulnerability. In these cases, though, these individuals touched the world while losing touch with themselves. One other point with respect to Elvis is that he helped bring black music more into the mainstream by appropriating many of its elements. Here we have theft, seduction, and the discovery of art long hidden from view.

♂ Mars with the outer planets deals primarily with the forces of action and assertion. Anger, too, is often touched here as well as sexual intensity. Mars with Uranus suggests originality of action, an unwillingness to follow the rules and a capacity for inventiveness. Katherine Hepburn's conjunction of Uranus and Mars is one example of someone who has followed an independent path. Arnold Schwarzenegger has Uranus conjunct Mars and has turned his muscles (Mars) into fabulous success in films, doing it his own way. Jacques Cousteau has Uranus in opposition to Mars, accounting for his unique adventures. But he also has Neptune conjunct Mars which is perfect for his seagoing life. Radical professor Angela Davis has Mars conjunct Uranus and the Sun in Aquarius. She played the role of the Uranian, shaking and waking us perfectly, sometimes disturbing us in her desire to break down social barriers.

Neptune with Mars can often indicate someone touched by sensitivity of action, escapism, poetry, and fantasy. I think that it can correspond with a difficulty in focusing anger. Some people with this combination are strongly committed to non-violence. It can be based on spiritual values and accompany other actions of a spiritual or helping nature. Those with Mars-Neptune can be so sensitive to anger and aggression that they would rather sacrifice themselves than hurt others. Another expression of this is *indirect* aggressions. (Charles Manson has the conjunction.) In any case, the idea is that doing or pushing can be done or masked with compassion, intuition, and imagination.

Mystical expression of Mars-Neptune are shown in the chart of writer Carlos Castaneda, famous for his books on shamanism. F. Scott Fitzgerald was another Mars-Neptune, with the exact conjunction. Imagination as well as vulnerability are shown here. Another dimension is acting in ways which do not feel real. Neptune with Mars can indicate a lack of connection that makes fantasy more prominent in the life, for better and for worse. For those with Mars-Neptune, it is important to recognize your own expenditure of force. If you don't pay attention, you may easily tire yourself out or waste your energy. If you are overly protective you may not be able to get things done. Move gently, but with the confidence that spirit is guiding you.

Mars with Pluto is a potent combination, one that can transform through actions. This often indicates great power, but power that is frightening to the person who has it. Anger can be bottled up or directed with destructive fierceness. Pluto's contact with Mars can show the need to focus anger and aggressive energies in a very narrow band. When this is done a laser beam force is present that can be directed precisely. This allows force, energy, and anger to be used appropriately.

Karate king Bruce Lee had Pluto square his Mars. He was powerful, but ultimately destroyed himself, perhaps unable to trust this natural force. Psychologist R. D. Laing also had Pluto square his Mars. His barbs were intellectual and helped destroy old premises about the human mind. Mohandes Gandhi had Pluto in opposition to his Mars and was able to focus his intensity in non-violent confrontation which liberated the people of India. Here we have that precise application and connection to a higher cause which enabled Mars-Pluto to work effectively.

24 Briefly, the outer planets with Jupiter represent mutations beyond religious training of your childhood, and offer you the possibility to have unique visions and share them with others; and, as well, the potential to manipulate the environment for one's own justified philosophies.

The outer planets with Saturn challenge us to set boundaries and limits for the traditional approaches we have learned in life to preserve structure and security matters, and then to go on to freer, more knowing individual expression.

In every case, the outer planets remind us of the possibilities *to be more than that which we see around us*. Within each of us exists a unique individual who is trying to exist in a world of others. This outer world may seem dangerous or limiting, but it is not as overpowering as it might appear. The outer planets are our inner guides, enabling us to go beyond that which we have learned, that which we see around us and that which others tell us is possible. They can provide that bridge between our inner spirit and our highest potential if we are willing to pay the toll. That price is simply to trust ourselves to be more and to trust that we are part of something that is grander than we are. With these two keys, there are no limits.

Capel N. McCutcheon

Capel McCutcheon earned a B.S. in Engineering and an M.S. in Industrial Administration from Carnegie Tech. After serving in the Signal Corps during the Korean War, he worked in the aerospace metals and industrial rubber fields, finally becoming general manager of a Connecticut firm.

Along the way, Capel became interested in psychical research and learned water and medical dowsing. In the early 1960s, a series of mystical experiences led him to study metaphysics and theosophy. In the late 60s, he began studying astrology with Isabel Hickey, and in 1973 left industry to found the Astrological Bureau of Ideas, a counseling and computing service firm. He also taught astrology at three Connecticut community colleges for ten years.

Capel has lived at Olcott, the theosophical center in the U.S., and at the Findhorn Community in Scotland. He received his M.S. in Counseling Psychology from the University of Bridgeport, specializing in marriage and family therapy. For ten years he has been on the staff of Spring Hill, the home of "Opening the Heart" workshops. He is now in private psychotherapy practice and is writing a book on love during the recovery process from addictions.

Personal Expression of Archetypal Aspects

Capel N. McCutcheon

At rare times, the motions around the Sun of the great outer planets Uranus, Neptune, and Pluto bring them into angular relationships with each other in the sky that astrologers recognize as Major Aspects. Such relationships, from the point of view of the Earth, mark out times of important historic significance for our planet. From a personal standpoint, they seem to ask everyone in humanity to stretch and grow in consciousness in a particular way. From the perspective of cultures and nations, they create growth as well as changes of dramatic significance. For these reasons, we might say that their slow dance in the sky represents the particular Archetype to which the world, its nations and all of humanity therein, should aspire.

The Bible states that "The Heavens declare the glory of God!" The dance steps of the Archetype Aspects of these great planets signal to us the changes that are to be made within our world and ourselves.

First of all, each of the planets represents an archetypal drive or need within each individual. Let us look at some of the meanings of these outer three.

Uranus represents in each of us the need for independence, freedom, and individualism. It shows one's drive for progressiveness, one's innovativeness and inventiveness. It indicates one's need for and capacity to change, one's need for uniqueness or to be different. It represents one's drive to revolt or revolutionize or to do the unexpected, the need to change limits, to shatter barriers. It shows willfulness. It shows one's capacity for interest in the un-

91

usual. It is an indicator of one's intellectual intuitiveness, one's capacity for sudden mental insight.

Neptune, on the other hand, has a more subtle and gentle nature. It is an indicator of an individual's tendency in consciousness to dissolve boundaries or limits or to diffuse through barriers, to erode limits. It can represent one's need to go beyond boundaries, to go beyond the limits of intellectual logic to an ideal or to psychic awarenesses or mystical transcendence. It can indicate the capacity to go beyond the limit of personal selfishness to compassion or beyond the limitation of a single personality to the creativity of many dramatic roles, the talent of artistic imagination. Negatively, it can indicate one's tendency to go beyond the limits of responsibility to escapism. It can show one's tendency to be vague, confused or spacy, to be impressionable, vulnerable, or gullible. Or more seriously, to have illusions, delusions, or to be deceptive or dishonest.

Pluto represents one's need for control and power. It can represent one's ultimate obsession or compulsion to act, to accomplish, to renew, or transform. It indicates one's capacity to coerce, to push down the barrier, to push back the limit, to bring to the surface violently what one has hidden or repressed. More simply, it is one's capacity to force an issue, to bring something to a head, to go to an extreme. Pluto also represents in its passive mode the tendency to repress or suppress. It can show one's need to isolate, to be a loner, to crave privacy or secrecy.

Regardless of whether or not these planets are making major angular aspects with one another as they revolve around the Sun, they enter and leave the signs of the Zodiac without fail. For seven years, Uranus transits a single sign, returning to a starting place after traversing the entire zodiac only after 84 years. Even more deliberate is Neptune, spending 14 years in each sign and returning to bring again its influence to that sign only after 168 years. More erratic is Pluto, whose irregular orbit takes it inside the orbit of Neptune during its transit of Scorpio where it spends only 12 years. Pluto travels outward to the presently known planetary limits of our solar system, reaching its furthest limit in Taurus where it lingers in transit for approximately 30 years. In all, its whole orbit around the Sun measures about 249 years.

The characteristics of a sign best describe how, most typically, a person will express the planetary need or drive. Everyone born in that Uranus 7-year, Neptune 14-year, or Pluto 12 to 30-year period, will have an inclination to express themselves in similar ways with regard to the needs that planet represents.

With these three outer planets, their House position in the individual's natal horoscope will indicate a more personal expression of the drive or need than the generationally shared sign position. The House positions of these planets typically show the areas of life where the person is most likely to express the planetary drives.

In an analogous way during the long orbital periods taken by these planets to traverse the full zodiac, there are certain infrequent times when the three planets form major angular connections with each other. It is these rare aspects that we have called Archetype Aspects.

Some of these Archetype Aspects are even more rare than the time periods these planets remain in a sign. But some of these aspects remain in effect (orb) for time periods longer or shorter than the time one of the planets remains in a sign. For example, the conjunction of Uranus and Neptune occurs only once about every 170 years. The conjunction of Uranus with Pluto comes but once in about 115 years. The conjunction of Neptune and Pluto comes on the average only once in about 390 years. The irregular orbital speed of Pluto makes the forecast of intervals between aspects variable also: during part of its orbit, Pluto travels at the same speed as Neptune, so Neptune cannot gain on Pluto and whatever aspect is in orb at this time remains until Pluto's speed diminishes as it goes outside Neptune's orbit and Neptune can once again begin to catch up with Pluto.

The opposition aspects between any two of these planets time out about the same as the conjunctions. Since the squares, sextiles, and trines occur twice more often than the conjunction or opposition, the intervals between these aspects are less lengthy. The Archetype Aspects will occur but rarely and, when they do occur, they may last so long that they are as generational in their influence as the planets are in terms of their sign positions.

Getting Personal

However, there are important distinctions in the horoscope patterns of individuals that will make these patterns, these Archetype Aspects, extremely personal, and thus of decisive importance in an individual's life. When the Sun or Moon or any of the personal planets, Mercury, Venus, or Mars *are aspected with the Archetype As-*

pects of Uranus/Neptune, Uranus/Pluto or Neptune/Pluto, these individuals, as they mature, most often become key players in their community or in world events or changes of consciousness portended by the meanings of the particular Archetype Aspect.

Another way the Archetype Aspect is personalized in an individual is indicated by the House position occupied by the planets in the aspect. While any House position makes for some uniqueness, the 1st and 10th House positions are often as important as aspects from personal planets especially when conjuncting the Ascendant or Midheaven.

When there are no personal planets aspected to the Archetype Aspects, nor angular placements of Archetype Aspects, the individual still shares the attitude or consciousness of all those born during the time of the Archetype Aspect, *but he seldom acts out the Archetype in a key way.* It might be said of such people that they are the supporting rather than the principal actors in the drama of the times.

An example of this may be gleaned from the recent period of early 1940s births when Uranus in Gemini was trine Neptune in Libra. Upon maturing, during the 1960s and 1970s, many of the people born during that Archetype Aspect period manifested interest in esoteric matters including astrology. Most of these people at least gave lip service to the possibility that there must be something to these things, and spiritual or consciousness-changing techniques were widely explored. But when personal planets were closely aspected with the Archetype Aspect, such people did not just sympathize with things esoteric, *they personally participated.* They asked to be taught how to use the techniques and then went on and used the teachings in their lives. Those with personal aspects to the Archetype Aspect lived and epitomized and implemented the celestial archetype on earth.

The societal or cultural need or drive represented by the Archetype Aspect is a need or drive identified with by all persons born during the Aspect. In this chapter, I will show how persons who have personal planets involved in aspect with the Archetype Aspects did indeed epitomize the Archetype energy and brought it to practical expression in the world in some way; or in a field of endeavor that was special to themselves and the particular personal planet aspecting the Archetype in their horoscopes.

From an overall perspective, there are some important distinctions of a personal nature relating to the aspect relationship a personal planet makes with the Archetype Aspect. For instance, in the mid 1960s there was an Archetype conjunction of Uranus and Pluto in Virgo. Every two years during the approximately five years this conjunction was in orb, Mars joined these two planets in close conjunction, setting up a powerful personal connection for those born during these periods.

But how different was the challenge of life for those persons born say with their Suns or Moons in Virgo, Pisces, Gemini or Sagittarius compared to those born with Suns or Moons in Taurus or Capricorn, or Cancer or Scorpio. The latter have a trine or sextile personal aspect of Sun or Moon to the Uranus/Pluto/Mars personal Archetype Aspect in Virgo, suggesting showing innate talent or ease in assimilating and using this challenging pattern. The former have a conjunction, opposition, or square to this personal/Archetype Aspect, indicating a great dynamic in using it, and more stress in assimilating and using it than the former. The addition of more personal planets creating T-Cross or Grand Cross Aspects or Grand Trines with the Archetype Aspect in an individual's chart, heightens the expectation for that individual to feel stress or ease in expressing those needs.

In analogous ways, personal planets making such aspects to the Archetype Aspect as a quincunx, semi-square, sesquiquadrate, semi-sextile, quintile, etc. will also have personal effects. Depending on the whole orientation of the chart, aspects to the Archetype Aspect may be less or more important, but the major aspects of personal planets to the Archetype are generally the strongest or most important. In a more complex way, personal planets making major aspects to the Archetype Aspect may require more elaborate analysis. For instance, considering the Archetype Aspect Uranus in Gemini trine Neptune in Libra: a Sun in Aries might be sextile Uranus and at the same time opposition Neptune.

Let us first consider some meanings of aspects and then define some of the Archetype Aspect meanings: the conjunction of two or more planets creates a focus or emphasis of the planets involved, harnessing energies within a single sign and House of the horoscope. (Sometimes a conjunction can occur across two signs or Houses.) With such a common sign or House focus, if the energies of the planets are sympathetic or similar in nature, it may indicate a potential for an important talent or conversely, an excess of the combined energy. For example, Jupiter conjunct Venus might indicate a very loving nature or an excessively sensual one. If the energies are unsympathetic, it may result in the tendency to dilemma or effort. Saturn conjunct Neptune may indicate a nature to be torn between practicality and idealism or a capacity to express practical idealism. *Other planets aspecting the conjunction will contribute to the ease or difficulty in achieving the more constructive expression of the aspect.*

The opposition is a pulling in two different directions in the expression of two planetary energies. Here the challenge lies in the interaction of the individual with the outer world. The dilemma most often manifests in a challenge to the person from one or more external sources pulling the person in contrary directions. The person must resolve the dilemma through an inner awareness that produces a strategy such as developing both energies at different times. If they do not, the problem continues. For instance, Mars opposition Saturn may result in tendencies of paralysis by analysis, blocked expression, or starting/stopping with the result of poor timing. An awareness of these processes can result in separating the problem into smaller chunks and working to completion of these segments in spurts of disciplined energy.

The square also indicates a pull of two drives or needs in different directions. The dilemma of the square most often manifests as a *faulty expectation* within the mind of the person. The pulls are internal and the impossibility of the conflicting expectations is not apparent to the person until the expectation is projected upon an external object or person so desirable or fearful that, in order to have or avoid the object, the individual must alter or correct the expectation. In short, to understand the problem lies within oneself. For example, Saturn square Uranus often produces an unrealistic expectation that when the person with it wants freedom, the other person will not give it; and when the person wants security or closeness, the other person will not give it. "Hold/don't hold me" mixed messages often result. A solution often results from a gradual awareness of the need to negotiate each person's expectations to allow for differences in timing.

Of course T-Crosses and Grand Crosses containing both squares and oppositions combine or confuse the two issues but create tremendous dynamics to action.

The trine aspect indicates a natural harmony or momentum in combining the expression of the drives or needs represented by the planets involved. This ease of expression often manifests as a talent.

The challenge is inertia, an expectation most often that the person should not have to exert effort to achieve success. The antidote then is to exert the effort, to try, to cultivate, or practice the talent. For instance, Mercury trine Jupiter can indicate a talent for seeing large issues, for enthusiasm to understand. It may sometimes indicate a preference for not having to study in order to master details and feeling a disappointment with results that are below expectations.

The sextile aspect most often indicates a faculty or inclination or opportunity for a talent. Its challenge is also its advantage, similar to the trine, in that it requires effort to develop but includes the expectation of having an easy time with it all.

A Grand Trine or Grand Sextile greatly increases the talents of the individual so favored, but also increases the inertia, the expectation of success without effort. It follows that the individual whose horoscope contains some of both the challenging and the easier aspects combines the dynamic of effort with the faculty of talent for clear success. In such person's lives, we might expect a greater tendency toward accomplished significance. If part of such aspect configurations includes an Archetype Aspect, this achievement will be auspicious indeed.

Since all aspects have the potential for constructive and more challenging combinations of planetary drives, it is important to note that the opposition and square seem to create more of a challenge to find a constructive use for the energies: the energies seem pitted against each other. This stress often makes a person try harder to find a way out. While the trine and sextile aspects indicate talents that tend to find more constructive combinations more easily, they lack the stress motivation to action and may result in inertia or laziness while the person still "gets by." Whether the conjunction indicates tendencies to constructive or destructive combinations of needs/drives will be influenced strongly by other planets making easy or difficult aspects to the conjunction.

The Archetype Aspects

Positive potential tendencies of Uranus with Neptune include the following: an idealization of freedom or independence; a capacity to alter or change one's beliefs; a revolutionary imagination; the capacity to combine intellectual and emotional ideas or intuitions; sudden inspirations; unique creativity; innovative helpfulness; unusual ideals; the ability to project a unique image; an original or inventive imagination or creativity; combined compassion and altruism; a talent to combine science with mysticism; scientific exploration of psychic phenomena; compassion for all without prejudice.

Negative potential tendencies of Uranus with Neptune include confused rebellion; impractical inventions or innovations; unusual capacity for deception; sudden or unexpected confusion or delusions; psychopathic impersonalness; uncontrolled escapism; confusion of fact and fantasy.

Positive potential tendencies of Uranus with Pluto are strong willpower; a capacity for unusual control; an ability to transform ideas of science; forceful reform; discovery of new laws of science; capacity for individual self-transformation; defining occult laws; great self-control or self restraint.

Negative potential tendencies of Uranus with Pluto might include a tendency to force changes; an inclination to extreme progressiveness; a capacity for explosive rebellion; tendency to repress one's individualism; radical reform, revolt or revolution; an obsession with freedom; sudden, unexpected force, or violence; development of new forms of coercion or suppression; new forms of death or genocide; alternate repression and explosion; suppression of freedom or new ideas.

Positive potential tendencies of Neptune with Pluto are a capacity for spiritual discipline; a talent for psychological insight; an understanding of motives; the ability to inspire or motivate; controlled psychic powers; compassionate reform; a talent for controlled, disciplined creativity; a compulsion to help or save; a force for inter-racial harmony; subtle influence, hidden persuasion; spiritual power.

Negative potential tendencies of Neptune with Pluto might include a capacity for obsessive religious beliefs; enforcing beliefs through force, propaganda or lies; delusions of grandeur or dreams of power; deceptive or corrupt uses of power; a capacity for extreme deception; secret use of death as an instrument of rule or control; the confused use of force; emotional delusions; repressed fears; phobias; repressed desires; dissipation of power.

If the personal planets are now aspected to these Archetype Aspect combinations, there is a personal expression of the Archetype Aspect that reflects the nature of that personal planet's expression in the individual's horoscope.

For instance, if the client's Moon is aspected with a Uranus/ Neptune Archetype Aspect, one might look for an expression of an emotional idealization of independence, or less desirably, emotionally confused rebellion in the Houses represented.

When the Sun is configured with Uranus/Neptune, the person's deepest self-expression or drive for significance may show as interest in initiating new forms of compassionate service, or less constructively expressed, as having difficulties integrating scientific logic with spiritual beliefs.

When Mercury is aspected to this Archetype, one might expect to find a person with an original imagination and a capacity to change beliefs, an ability to create fantasy or sci-fi literature. Negatively expressed, one might expect the individual to express sudden confusion or be subject to unexpected delusions.

When we find Venus connected to Uranus/Neptune, we might look for unusual originality in imagination or a talent for unique creativity in original art forms, or an unusual love expression. Negatively expressed, we might find the confusion of newness within creativity, radical departure from the norms of good taste or style, deception or changeability in romance.

When Mars configures with this Uranus/Neptune Archetype, we might expect to find unusual physical prowess or sports talent or a significant talent for military strategy or innovation. Negatively expressed, we might expect a behavioral tendency to explosive defense of delusions or rebellious escapism.

Even Jupiter, though not technically a personal planet, when aspected with the Uranus/Neptune Archetype Aspect, contributes a personal tendency for optimism and enthusiasm in expression and more particularly for deeper faith; far away explorations to unusual places or increased idealism or delusions. Saturn, too, will add its special dimensions for disciplined expression or repression of Archetype expression.

In analogous fashion, the aspects of the personal planets with the Archetype Aspects of Uranus/Pluto and Neptune/Pluto will register personally very strongly. Combining the personal planets with the meanings profiled above for these Archetypes, for the Sun, look for the person's most significant self-expression; for the Moon, use the client's emotional or nurturing expression; for Mercury, use the mental or comunicative talents; for Venus, use the expression of art, affection, or appreciation; and for Mars, use energy or assertion.

So in summary, our thesis is that the more the Archetype Aspect pattern is incorporated in an individual's horoscope—the more personal planets or personal points such as the Ascendant are found to make aspects with these Archetype Aspects—the greater the probability that that individual will be unusual in a way expressing the combination of the Archetype, the personal planets or points involved, and the House in which they are found. Further, the likelihood will be greater that the individual will be destined to personally effect some form of the changes portended by the general meaning of the Archetype, in the fields indicated by the personal planet involved.

Horoscope Examples

[The birth data and sources for all examples are given at the end of this chapter, on pp. 122–123. It will be helpful to the reader to draw "in abbreviation" the aspect descriptions that follow in these 60 cases. Just a note or two on paper as you read will make the examples very clear and, indeed, amazing. —Ed.]

♅ ♂ ♆
○ △   First, let us consider the Uranus conjunct Neptune Archetype which occurs only every 170 years but is in orb for several years at that time.

In the horoscope of Sir Richard Burton, the great explorer, adventurer, and orientalist, the Uranus-Neptune conjunction in Capricorn squared his quadruple conjunction of Sun-Pluto (Pisces), Jupiter-Mercury (Aries) in the 5th House, and also squared his Moon in Libra in the 11th! This unusual world traveler explored Africa to find the source of the Nile, indicated by the Sun-Jupiter connection to the Archetype. His unusual interest in oriental cultures and literature and his writing and publishing about these can be expected from his Mercury connection to the Archetype Aspect. Among the writings he brought to the west was the *Arabian Nights*, pretty suggestive stuff for Victorian England. Burton had a Venus-Mars conjunction in Pisces in the 4th House which quintiled the Archetype, suggesting a sublimely passionate nature at the roots of his being, certainly appreciating the beauty of physical love.

And speaking of the Victorian Period, Queen Victoria herself had this Archetype Aspect in Sagittarius across the 7th-8th House cusp, trine her Venus-Mars conjunction in Aries in the 12th. From this we might expect an unusual love nature or even secret romances. How ever that may be (and she did have nine children with her husband), she had a Saturn-Pluto conjunction in Pisces that *squared* the Archetype. This can certainly be the indicator of the control or even the repression of the feelings represented by the trine when she felt them inappropriate. As monarch, this personal repression was transferred to protocol for an era!

Another example of personalizing this rare aspect can be found in Louis Pasteur. This extraordinary French scientist discovered the preventive health process of pasteurization still used for milk, etc. today. His unusual Mercury-Sun-Neptune-Venus-Uranus conjuntion in Capricorn in the 3rd House is certainly an indicator of genius, innovation, and compassion. Venus is also the ruler of his Ascendant and Mercury-Sun-Neptune-Venus are also square Pluto in late Pisces with Uranus also square Pluto more widely, creating two more Archetype Aspects, all with three personal planets interaspected.

Another innovator in the health care field with the Uranus-Neptune Archetype was the extraordinary Clara Barton, founder of the Red Cross. Her natal Sun-Uranus-Neptune conjunction in Capricorn in her 10th House conjunct her Midheaven and square her Aries Ascendant are indicators of her capacity for action in an unusual, compassionate way, focused as a career. Her Pluto conjuncts her Ascendant and not only squares her Sun-Uranus-Neptune-Midheaven but also squares her Mercury in Sagittarius in the 9th. Mercury also sextiles her Venus in Aquarius in the 12th. These other indicators of her idealism and compassion for all add to her capacity to initiate radical changes, not only in health care but in society's attitudes towards war and peace.

Karl Marx also shares this Uranus-Neptune conjunction Archetype, but he had it in late Sagittarius in his 10th House. His Mars quincunx Uranus, ruler of his Ascendant, indicated his potential for radical views or actions to achieve the unusual ideal in the world of the Archetype Aspect in the 10th. His Saturn-Pluto conjunction in the 1st House, square the Archetype, indicated the austerity involved with following the social ideal.

Another philosophical idealist, but one of a very different persuasion, was Henry David Thoreau of Walden Pond fame. This writer and transcendental thinker whose ideals anticipated the modern environmentalists, had Mercury, the ruler of his 4th House, in Cancer opposing the Uranus-Neptune conjunction. Mercury also conjoined the Moon, ruler of his Sun sign, and squared Pluto, thus participating in two additional Archetype Aspects. His thought, lectures, and essays show the idealism of the Archetype. Uranus ruled his Aquarius Ascendant.

Two unusually talented poets also share the Uranus-Neptune Archetype in personal ways. Walt Whitman had a Fire Grand Trine involving Mars in Aries in the Ascendant, Uranus-Neptune in Sagittarius in the 9th, and the Moon, ruler of the 5th House of creativity, in Leo in the 6th, showing the immense talent he displayed in his masterwork, *Leaves of Grass*.

Charles Beaudelaire, the famous French poet, with a darker nature pervading his "Flowers of Evil," has a Mercury-Pluto conjunction square Uranus-Neptune in Capricorn from the 7th to the 4th Houses. His Mars-Venus-Jupiter in Aries across the 7th-8th cusp also squares the Uranus-Neptune Archetype and conjoins Mercury-Pluto on one side and Sun-Saturn on the other. Mercury rules his Midheaven, again showing the connection to a pronounced literary fame.

Mary Baker Eddy, the chief architect of the Christian Science faith and a great prayer healer, had the Uranus-Neptune Archetype in her 1st House conjunct her Ascendant. It also was squared by her Pluto in the 3rd, an indicater of her speaking and writing skills (*Science and Health*). Her Sun in Cancer trined this Pluto giving a second personal connection to the three Archetype Aspects involving her Ascendant.

This great conjunction of Uranus-Neptune has begun to form again in our times here in the 1990s. All births throughout the period 1989–1995 will take on its influence. It will be fascinating to watch these children mature in the years ahead and to keep a special eye on those with many personal planets closely involved with archetypal aspect. Once again, there will *three* Archetype Aspects involved in these charts: The position of Pluto in Scorpio brings it into sextile aspects with Uranus and more widely with Neptune for part of this period. New changes in awareness are already taking place with the openness now revealing substance and sexual abuse as a means of suppressing feelings; new understandings and new therapies are emerging.

It is well to remember that, for these remarkable people of the past or future to express their role most effectively, there must be a humanity, a generation, a society that shares the Archetype. While whole generations born with these patterns express them most fully as they mature, everyone born earlier has received this influence of the Archetype by transits during the birth time of those who will express it, and will have, to the extent that they can respond to the transit, prepared the world to accept the new influence.

While we had to go back to the 1820s to find the last conjunction of Uranus-Neptune, we need go no further back than to the early 1940s to find a recent period of the trine between Uranus and Neptune, and the natural talents it represents.

The talented screen director, Stephen Spielberg, has had spectacular successes at the box office from films such as *Jaws, E.T., Close Encounters, Raiders of the Lost Ark,* and many more. His talent for imaginative innovation and leadership in his work is shown by his Sun in Sagittarius in his 6th House opposed to Uranus, his Uranus making the trine Archetype Aspect to Neptune in Libra, the ruler of his Pisces Midheaven. His Mercury in the 6th is sextile Neptune and trine Pluto in Leo in the 2nd, and that Pluto also sextiles Uranus and Neptune, creating, in effect, *three* beneficial Archetype Aspects. His Venus-Jupiter conjunction in the creative 5th House trine his Pisces Midheaven shows the potential for his financial success while the square of Venus-Jupiter to Pluto in the 2nd indicates his control of the budget and the macabre themes of some of his films.

There have certainly been some people who might be considered genius born well-aspected with the Uranus-Neptune trine or sextile Archetype Aspects. One would expect the Sun, that most powerful and important indicator of intrinsic being, to be strongly figured with the Archetype in such cases, and, as well, Mercury.

Leonardo Da Vinci, inventor, scientist, artist, author—truly a universal man—had his Neptune in Virgo at his Midheaven, both sextile Uranus in Cancer. His Taurus Sun in the 5th was sextile his Moon-Jupiter conjunction in Pisces in the 3rd forming a Yod aspect to the elevated Neptune in the 10th.

While his Sun squares Pluto and more widely squares Uranus, his Moon quincunxes Pluto. Neptune also forms a second Archetype Aspect with sextile to Pluto. Again, the signature of many personal-planet aspects to the Archetype is clear. Even his Sagittarius Ascendant sextiles Neptune and trines Pluto.

Another genius, Nikola Tesla, inventor of the Tesla coil, the induction electric motor and effective means of utilizing alternating current, which made transmission of electricity over long distances practical, had his Uranus in Taurus in the 1st, indicating a potential for invention of practical electrical devices. Uranus was sextile Neptune in Pisces and trined his Capricorn Midheaven. His Sun-Venus (ruler of Ascendant) conjunction on his fourth cusp sextiled his Uranus and trined his Neptune.

On a more modern note, Fritjof Capra , physicist and mystic, whose book *The Tao of Physics* attempts to bridge the gap between religion and science, has Uranus in Taurus conjunct his Taurus Ascendant trine Neptune in Virgo in the 5th, both forming a grand trine to his Capricorn Midheaven, with Mercury conjunct in the 10th. Mercury also opposes Pluto in Leo in 4th, which forms a second Archetype contact by sextiling Neptune. His Sun in Aquarius in the 10th also squares Uranus-Ascendant. He certainly upset the scientific materialism paradigm with his unusual insights and synthesis of ideals from two fields that had been antagonistic to one another for so long.

Politicians and statesmen with this Archetype Aspect achieve great accomplishments as well. Benjamin Franklin, one of the "architects" of the United States of America, as well as diplomat extraordinaire, writer of wise sayings in his famous Almanac, and an inventor, had both Uranus in Leo trine Neptune in Aries and more widely Neptune trine Pluto in Leo. His powerful Mercury in Aquarius opposed Uranus and sextiled Neptune, enabling him both to charm and surprise friend and foe alike as a diplomat. That he was both writer and revolutionary is indicated by that Mercury, which also ruled his Ascendant, and by his Mars in Sagittarius in the 3rd House square his Ascendant and trine Pluto. A Sun quincunx Pluto and a Moon quincunx Uranus complete the portrait of this remarkable human.

On a more somber note, another Capricorn political leader, Joseph Stalin, dictator of the U.S.S.R. had this Archetype Aspect in an Earth Grand Trine with Uranus-Moon in Virgo conjunction and Mars-Neptune in conjunction in Taurus. His capacity for practical success is clearly indicated. His dictatorial control is indicated by Pluto in Taurus in the 4th House opposing his Midheaven-Venus conjunction in Scorpio. The Mars-Neptune conjunction opposing his Midheaven indicates his skill in using deception and lies to rise in authority and against suspected enemies.

Traditionally, Moon and Venus configured with Neptune are signatures of musical talent in a horoscope and one would expect to find some of these connections to the Archetype Aspects in musicians' charts, especially during the times of great changes in musical art forms.

All of the Beatles, that well known musical group who not only brought their own unique form of Rock music to the world but also brought Maharishi Mahesh Yogi, the founder of the Transcendental Meditation movement, to the West, had the Uranus trine Neptune Archetype Aspect in their horoscopes. These men also helped bring in the change from "Sex and Drugs" type Rock and Roll to the more spiritual folk type Rock heralded by Neptune's transit out of Scorpio into Sagittarius.

John Lennon had Uranus in Taurus in his 1st House trine Neptune-Mars conjunction in Virgo-Libra in the 6th with an early Aquarian Moon completing a Earth Grand Trine. Mars rules his Aries Ascendant, and Venus squares his Uranus to complete the musical signature.

Paul McCartney's Sun-Mercury conjunction in Gemini squares his Neptune in Virgo, while his Moon-Pluto-Mars triple conjunction in Leo sextiles Uranus in Gemini and trines his Ascendant in Aries. His Venus in Taurus also trines his Neptune to complete the musical signature to the Archetype.

George Harrison's Pisces Sun in the 4th House squares his Uranus-Saturn conjunction in Gemini, which sextiles Pluto in Leo and trines Neptune in Libra. His Moon-Ascendant conjunction forms a Yod aspect with Venus in Pisces in the 5th *and with* Uranus. His Sun trines his Moon-Ascendant conjunction and forms a Yod with Neptune and Pluto which are in a second Archetype Aspect to each other.

Finally, Ringo Starr, the fourth Beatle has Uranus in Taurus trine Neptune in Virgo which conjuncts his Descendant and opposes his Ascendant. His Moon in Leo in the 5th is in conjunction with Mercury and Mars, and Pluto sextiles both Neptune and Uranus. His Venus in Gemini conjuncts his fourth cusp (and opposes his Midheaven) and also squares Neptune and the Ascendant, completing the musical signature to the Archetype.

Paul Simon has his Venus sextile Neptune and trine the Ascendant and Pluto as well as opposite Uranus. His partner in music in those days, Art Garfunkle, has Moon conjunct Uranus trine Neptune and Venus square Neptune and quincunx Uranus.

Finally there are the two great artists who met tragic ends through an overdose of heroin in the final days of Neptune's last retrograde dip into Scorpio from Sagittarius: the great innovative electric guitarist, Jimi Hendrix and the outstanding vocalist, Janis Joplin. Hendrix had a Sun-Mercury-Venus conjunction trine Neptune and sextile Pluto, opposed Uranus-Saturn. This triple conjunction extracted its toll despite the three Archetype Aspects figured within the musical signature. Joplin's late Capricorn Sun in the 12th made a grand trine with Neptune and Uranus-Saturn. Mercury conjoined Venus in Aquarius in the 12th and opposed Pluto in Leo in the 6th. Pluto formed two Archetype Aspects with sextiles to Neptune and Uranus.

♅ □ ♆   For Uranus square or opposition Neptune, one might expect to find individuals who express a more radical point of view or behavior than those with the trine or sextile. At least, the effect of their ideas or actions on the rest of mankind might be expected to be more abrupt or disconcerting. While this is often true in some area of their lives, very often, at least with the advantage of historic perspective, one finds that these individuals with many connections to Archetype Aspects are so remarkable that they are able to fulfill a synthesis of the competing energies and thus accomplish results of extraordinary note.

Henri Toulouse-Lautrec expressed an interest in what was, for his times, quite unusual subject matter. He seemed to delight in painting everyday people from the brothels, cafes, and theaters, as well as, of course, painting in the then radical art-style and colors of Impressionism. Lautrec had his Neptune in Aries in the 5th House square Uranus. His Venus in 2nd House squared his Neptune and opposed his Uranus, indicating a capacity to rebel from tradition in creative forms and yet earn a living through his unusual artistic talent. A Sun-Jupiter-Mercury conjunction in Sagittarius trine Neptune and a Moon in Libra opposed Neptune and square Uranus (while the Moon also sextiles Sun-Jupiter-Mercury) completes the remarkable number of connections to the Archetype aspect personalized for this pioneering artist.

With Salvador Dali, one finds the epitome of the art form known as Surrealism. This radical style shocked the tastes of the more conventional who, while acknowledging Dali's superior technique, questioned his relevance. Dali lived his life with much of the same flamboyancy expressed in his art. Dali had his Neptune in Cancer in the 12th opposition Uranus in the 6th. His Venus in Taurus in his 10th House sextiled his Neptune and trined his Uranus, while his Moon, ruler of his Ascendant, conjoined his Midheaven in Aries and squared both Neptune and Uranus.

In both these cases—Lautrec and Dali—we find the artistic signature of Venus closely associated with the Archetype Aspects. On the other hand, in the instance of two other great artists, Vincent Van Gogh and Pablo Picasso, the Archetype found is Neptune *sextile* Uranus for Van Gogh and *trine* Uranus for Picasso.

Joe Namath, professional football quarterback for the New York Jets and a star performer for his team, has *three* personalized Archetype Aspects: Uranus trine Neptune, Uranus sextile Pluto, and Neptune sextile Pluto. Namath's Mars, the significator of the athlete, is in Aries in the 1st House and makes important connections to these Archetypes. His Sun conjoins Uranus in Gemini in the 3rd and Mercury in Taurus in 3rd. All of these sextile his Mars in the 1st, showing his intelligence and ability to communicate energetically, important qualities in a quarterback. His Mars also opposes Neptune, showing a talent for deception necessary in this sport, while Mars trine Pluto in the 6th in Leo is an indicator of his physical strength and stamina (as well as supporting his highly marketable personal charisma).

Mark Spitz, the amazing Olympic swimming champion who won seven gold medals at the 1972 Olympics and had broken five world records by the age of 17, shows his control and stamina by his Pluto conjunction with his Ascendant in Leo opposing his Sun-upiter conjunction in Aquarius in the 6th House. Pluto makes the Archetype sextile to Neptune-Mars on the 2nd-3rd House cusp showing the athletic connection. However, Spitz's Uranus makes only a mundane square to Neptune, but Mars does make a legitimate square, tying together the mundane square. More to the point for swimming, his Moon in the 4th sextiles Neptune-Mars and trines

Pluto, tying the water indicators to Mars and the Archetype Aspects.

Charles Lindbergh, the first man to fly solo across the Atlantic Ocean, opening up the possibilities of long distance travel by air, had his Uranus in Sagittarius in his 1st House opposing Neptune and squaring his Virgo Midheaven, surely an indication of the capacity to do something out of the ordinary. His Uranus also opposed his Pluto, making a second Archetype Aspect from the personal 1st House, while Pluto in Gemini opposed his Sagittarius Ascendant, indicating a capacity for persistence in long distance endeavors. His Mars in Aquarius trines both Neptune and Pluto, which are not conjunct, and sextiles Uranus, tying in this planet of adventure. His Sun in Aquarius trines Pluto and sextiles Uranus, and his Moon in Sagittarius conjuncts Uranus and opposes Neptune. Again many connections to the Archetypes in the chart of this record-breaker.

The great psychiatrist, Carl Jung, placed emphasis on the spiritual needs and growth potential of his clients as much as on the developmental causes and basic drives of personality development. He used astrology as a diagnostic tool, and developed the concept of archetypes to explain concepts that urged human development. We would certainly expect to find personal planets aspecting Archetypal Aspects in Jung's horoscope.

Jung's Moon in Taurus conjuncts Pluto and squares Uranus in Leo by one degree. His Sun in Leo squares Neptune closely by a few minutes of arc. Between the two lights the second Archetype Uranus square Neptune are tied together. His Aquarius Ascendant completes and further ties together a T-Cross among these planets.

Jung's Sun and Uranus trine a Sagittarius Midheaven, and his Mercury-Venus conjunction in sensitive, nurturing Cancer sextiles his Moon and Neptune. The planets Pluto and Neptune are traditionally associated with psychology, and the latter with spirituality as well. His many personal-planet connections with the two of them in Archetype Aspects is a strong indication of his potential for influencing this then-new field of psychology in transpersonal directions.

Jonas Salk, whose work with virus vaccine development produced the first successful polio vaccine and who is presently working on a vaccine for the AIDS virus, has Uranus in Aquarius in the 1st opposing Neptune in Leo. His Scorpio Sun in the 10th forms a

Water Grand Trine with his Moon in Pisces and Pluto in Cancer, and links with the Archetype by a T-Cross square to the Uranus-Neptune opposition. The T-Cross shows his willingness to attempt to break "It can't be done" barriers and the Grand trine shows the potential for success.

The genius and universal man, Galileo, astronomer, inventor, writer and mathematician, had Uranus in Sagittarius in the 5th House opposing Neptune-Mars in Gemini-Taurus on the 10th/11th cusp and Sun-Mercury-Pluto in triple conjunction in Pisces in the 8th completing a T-Cross to the Uranus-Neptune opposition. This amazing grouping of three personal planets with three Archetype Aspects is a strong indicator of the mature genius. The overtones of rebellion also indicate that his discoveries would defy the accepted church dogma of the period.

Mohandas Gandhi, the great mahatma, whose doctrine of non-violent disobedience and spiritual integrity successfully brought India to freedom from British rule, had his Uranus in Cancer in the 9th House conjunct his Midheaven and square Neptune in Aries. His Sun in Libra opposed the Archetype Neptune while his Moon in Leo trined it.

Pluto also formed a second Archetype Aspect sextile Neptune. Gandhi's Leo Moon squared Pluto, and his Venus-Mars conjunction in Scorpio opposed Pluto and trined Uranus. His Saturn in Sagittarius completed a grand trine with Neptune and the Moon. Mercury conjuncted his Ascendant, which squared Uranus, while Jupiter conjuncted Pluto. Every planet in this remarkable man's horoscope *was connected to an Archetype!*

♅ ☌ ♇   Looking to the Uranus-Pluto conjunction, two philosophical iconoclasts and pioneers of the Theosophical movement stand out: Annie Besant, who served as the second president of the Theosophical Society worldwide, and William Quan Judge, a founder of the Society and President of its American section.

Besant was a remarkable woman of her day. She was a social reformer and leader of the movement for Indian autonomy even *before* Gandhi, a prolific writer and world lecturer on esoteric subjects, a clairvoyant and researcher, and an educator and pioneer in schools for Indian children regardless of class. Her Uranus-Pluto conjunction in the 1st House opposed Mercury in Libra in the 7th and squared Jupiter in Cancer in the 4th as a T-Cross. This configuration is a strong indicator of her writing and speaking skills with Mercury ruling her 3rd House with Gemini on its cusp. Her Moon in Cancer in the 4th conjunct Jupiter also squared Uranus in the Archetype Aspect and squared Sun-Venus which was conjoined with Mercury.

Uranus opposed Sun-Venus as does the Ascendant, forming still another T-Cross of Ascendant opposite Sun-Venus square Moon. With seven planets and her Ascendant in Cardinal signs, Besant was a veritable dynamo of activity, and with all these involved with the Archetype Aspect, these activities were not only of an unusual and pioneering sort but with her Moon-Jupiter in Cancer in the 4th, were also often highly compassionate. A second Archetype Aspect is formed by her Neptune in Aquarius in the 12th sextile Pluto in 1st, perhaps one of the signatures of her clairvoyant abilities.

William Q. Judge had his Ascendant conjunct his Sun-Pluto-Uranus conjunction in the 1st in Aries. What a spectacular indication of unusual leadership qualities! This conjunction also conjoined Saturn in Aries in the 1st, ruler of his Midheaven and in opposition with Jupiter in Libra, perhaps an indicator of the disappointment he felt when Besant succeeded Colonel Olcott to the presidency of the Society, to which office he felt promised.

Several hundred years earlier, we see Oliver Cromwell, a reformer of strong will who figured prominently in the civil war changing England from a monarchy to a parliamentary form of government who was Lord Protector of England. Cromwell had his Archetype Uranus-Pluto conjunction in his 1st House in Aries trine Neptune in Leo, forming two more Archetype Aspects: Uranus trine Neptune and Pluto trine Neptune, all together in a grand trine with his Sagittarius Midheaven What an outstanding pattern for talent and success of a remarkable sort! Out of his success grew the British form of government and later the United States republic.

In the mid 1960s Uranus again formed the Archetype conjunction with Pluto, this time in Virgo. It will be interesting to observe the extraordinary individuals this potential produces in our own times. Those then born are now in their mid twenties and will be making their mark felt soon.

Helena P. Blavatsky was one of the most extraordinary women of the 19th Century, or any century for that matter. Together with

Colonel Henry Steel Olcott, she founded the Theosophical Society as an instrument of brotherhood, ecumenism and esoteric research on behalf, she said, of the evolved men, Masters of Wisdom, who guide mankind's destiny. Her amazing exhibitions of psychic powers gathered attention, but it was the remarkable body of her writings covering and synthesizing science, religion and philosophy that earned her the respect of those prominent in these three fields—and the enmity of those rigidly holding to a world-view that kept them apart unreconcilably. Blavatsky managed to step on the toes of rigid scientists, religious leaders and spiritualists—all at the same time—with her documented criticisms.

Blavatsky's amazing synthesis of knowledge paved the way for the science of today, where physics and esoteric religion are more similar in paradigm than were religion and the old model of scientific materialism which disallowed the asking of metaphysical questions.

♅ ⚹ ♇   Blavatsky had the Archetype Uranus in Aquarius in the 8th sextile Pluto in Aries in the 10th. Her Leo Sun in the 2nd opposed Uranus conjunct Jupiter and trined Pluto, a strong indicator that she could have a personal role in changing scientific attitudes. Her Sun also quincunxed Neptune in the 7th in Capricorn, which opposed her Cancer Ascendant and trined her Pisces Midheaven, showing the potential for intuitive or psychic talents. Her Moon-Venus conjunction in the 4th in Libra opposed Pluto, indicating her capacity for discipline, as does Sun trine Pluto. Her Mercury in Virgo in the 3rd conjunct Mars-Saturn forms a Yod with Pluto and Uranus, a powerful indicator of her remarkable intellectual and literary skills.

Her partner in founding the Theosophical Society, Henry S. Olcott, a military lawyer, pioneer in promoting cremation, psychic researcher, life president of the Society, and a Buddhist saint in Ceylon for his remarkable healing work by the laying-on of hands, had his Sun and Venus conjunct in Leo in the 10th House opposing Uranus and trining Pluto, which formed the Archetype sextile to each other. His Neptune conjoined his fourth cusp opposing his Midheaven and squaring his Libra Ascendant.

John Glenn, the first American astronaut to orbit the Earth and later a United States Senator, had Uranus in Pisces in the 3rd House *trine* Pluto in Cancer in the 8th. Archetype Pluto is conjoined by Mercury and Mars in Cancer in the 8th, both of which also then trine Uranus. Jupiter, ruler of his Sagittarius Ascendant, conjoins his Midheaven, showing the potential for fame. Jupiter opposes Uranus and both square the Sagittarius Ascendant, indicating that fame might come via a far distant place, which is certainly true of space and orbiting the Earth. Mercury, ruler of his Midheaven conjunct Pluto-Mars trines Uranus and sextiles Jupiter, tying in the Archetype a second way to the career axis.

A favorite comedian of many, Peter Sellers, star of the *Pink Panther* movies and many other films, had Uranus in Pisces in the 7th trine Pluto in Cancer in the 11th. His Sun-Mars conjunction in Virgo in the 1st opposed Uranus and sextiled Pluto in the Archetype Aspect, an indication of the unusual energy he expended to create his comic effects and his capacity to do the unexpected, to the delight of audiences everywhere. Mercury, the ruler of his Sun sign, Ascendant, *and* Midheaven, is in Leo in the imaginative 12th House conjunct Neptune, both of which quincunx Uranus and square his Midheaven. This is certainly a signature of high potential for a talent in film of a special sort. Finally, his Moon in Taurus elevated in the 9th conjunct his Midheaven trined his Sun-Mars conjunction, sextiled Uranus, squared Mercury-Neptune and widely sextiled Pluto. The remaining two planets Venus and Saturn also aspect the Archetype.

The brilliant World War II general, George Patton, who vanquished Rommel on the African desert and raced across Europe to defeat the Germans, had Uranus in Libra in the 5th trine Pluto in Gemini in 12th. His Pluto also conjuncted Neptune, adding *two more* Archetype Aspect contacts. Patton's Mars in Virgo in the 4th conjunct his fourth cusp and opposing his Midheaven squared Pluto-Neptune indicating his innate warlike nature and capacity to use force in deceptive and unusual ways in his career. Mercury, ruler of his Gemini Ascendant and 4th House, opposed his Pluto and completed a T-Cross with Mars opposite his Midheaven and also sextiled Uranus. His Scorpio Sun made a wide square with Mars to complete the signature of a warrior.

♅ ⧠ ♇   One of the more frequent Archetype Aspect patterns is Uranus square or opposition Pluto. I have this pattern personally, with Sun-Uranus square Mars-Pluto.

Though no personal comparison is intended, let me begin my examples here with Albert Einstein. Einstein had his Uranus in Virgo in the 3rd House square Pluto in late Taurus in the 11th. Uranus was also trine Neptune, ruler of the 10th, in *early* Taurus also in the 11th, adding a second Archetype Aspect. His Pisces Sun in the 10th House sextiled Pluto and Mars in Capricorn, which also trined Pluto. His Mercury in Aries in the 10th conjoined Saturn, squared Pluto and quincunxed Uranus in the 3rd, indicating an extraordinary mind. Jupiter, ruler of the 6th and co-ruler of the 10th is in the 9th, opposing Uranus and squaring Pluto, indicating the potential for a university profession and a capacity for independent and original thinking. His revolution upon the ideas of the nature of reality in theoretical physics heralded the coming atomic age and the end of scientific materialism as a viable philosophy.

Some extraordinary statesmen have also had this so-called " afflicted" aspect between Uranus and Pluto as Archetype. Sir Winston Churchill, Prime Minister of Great Britain during World War II, had Uranus in Leo in the 11th House in a Grand Cross square Pluto, square Mercury in Scorpio in the 2nd and opposing Saturn in Aquarius in the 5th. This legendary speaker and writer of a history of England had his Sun in Sagittarius in the 3rd House *trine* Uranus and sextile Mars in Libra in the 1st. His Venus, ruler of his Ascendant, was in the 3rd, sextile Mars-Jupiter in the 1st, making a Fire Grand Trine with the Moon in Leo, ruler of his 10th, and Uranus and Neptune in Aries in the 8th. All are indicators of the success that earned him knighthood and a Nobel prize in literature.

Franklin D. Roosevelt, contemporary of Churchill, as President of the United States in the war years, was a rival for the claim to great oratory. He was also the creator of the Liberal ideal of the so-called New Deal to end the United States' great Depression of the 1930s. In contrast, he had Uranus in Virgo conjunct his Ascendant, making the Archetype trine aspect to Pluto in Taurus in his 9th. Uranus also made a second Archetype trine to the Neptune-Jupiter conjunction in Taurus in his 8th House. His Sun-Venus conjunction in Aquarius in the 5th squared Neptune-Jupiter, and his Moon in Cancer in the 10th sextiled the Neptune-Jupiter-Saturn triple conjunction.

Depending on your point of view along the liberal-to-conservative axis, his 8th House use of tax money was wonderful and idealistic (Neptune-Jupiter) or fearfully unrealistic (Neptune-Saturn). Perhaps it was a bit of both, but few would deny that Roosevelt changed the economic system radically. His Mercury in Aquarius in the 6th is the ruler of both Ascendant and Midheaven. It's square to Pluto, quincunx with the Ascendant, and trine to Mars-Midheaven and his Moon, are indicators of his unusual success and the trust he enjoyed from the people who elected him to four terms as President.

The remarkable clairvoyant and trance medium, Edgar Cayce, had Uranus in Leo conjunct his Ascendant and square to his Pluto-Midheaven conjunction in Taurus. His Moon in Taurus also was conjunct his Midheaven, and Neptune squared Uranus and widely conjoined Pluto. This, with his Sun in Pisces in the 8th sextile the Archetype Pluto and quincunx Uranus, is the profile of an unusual career and personality. His Mars-Jupiter conjunction in the 5th trine the triple conjunction of Neptune-Moon-Midheaven in the 9th, sextile Venus in Pisces in the 8th, which is the ruler of the 10th, are indicators both of his psychic talents and his career as a photographer.

Helen Keller was born blind, deaf, and dumb. She rose above her handicaps as a pioneering inspiration to handicapped people everywhere. She has this Archetype Uranus conjunct her Midheaven, and square Pluto and square her Ascendant.

Shirley MacLaine, dancer, actress, and author of many biographical books on channeling and contacts with extra-terrestrials, has this Archetype in touch with her Sun-Mars-Uranus conjunction. Her Moon-Neptune conjunction in Virgo also trines her Sun-Mars, an indicator of psychic interests and talents.

The Dalai Lama, spiritual leader of Tibet and winner of the Nobel Peace prize, has Uranus in Aries in the 7th square Pluto in Cancer in the 10th. His Mars in the 4th, opposing Pluto and squaring Uranus, can indicate his forced departure from his homeland. His Sun in Sagittarius trines Uranus and quincunxes Pluto. His Moon, ruler of his 10th house, is in Capricorn conjunct his fourth cusp and trines Neptune, an indication of a spiritual profession.

It is interesting to note that the Dalai Lama's Venus, ruler of his Libra Ascendant, is conjunct Saturn in Aquarius, the brotherhood sign, trine his Ascendant. He uses this aspect with modesty and confidence rather than with fear. It is an example again of rising beyond the negative of a difficult aspect, as was his Archetype T-Cross. I think that astrologers do a great disservice to the profession when they predict *fatalistically*: not only are they often wrong, but they offend scientists and the thinking public alike by not seeing that atti-tude and effort can make a difference in destiny.

Finally, let us look at the great humanitarian, medical mission-ary, musician and also winner of the Nobel Peace prize, Albert Schweitzer. His Mars in Scorpio in the 2nd, indicating a potential for medicine and surgery, opposed Pluto in Taurus in the 8th and formed a Grand Cross in fixed signs to the Archetype square Uranus in Leo in the 10th, square Saturn in Aquarius in the 4th. A Moon-Neptune conjunction in Aries in the 7th formed a T-Cross in Cardi-nal signs with Sun-Mercury in Capricorn in the 4th and Jupiter in early Scorpio in the 1st. Who says one cannot rise above the chal-lenge of a difficult chart? (With a little help from his Fire Grand Trine, with Venus in Sagittarius in the 3rd to Uranus, and more widely on to the Moon.)

$\Psi \, \sigma \, \text{P}$ To introduce the very rare Archetype Aspect of the Neptune-Pluto conjunction, who better have we than the excep-tional film director of mystery and suspense, Alfred Hitchcock. Hitchcock had Neptune-Pluto conjunct his fourth cusp in Gemini, opposing his Midheaven conjunct Saturn in Sagittarius. His Leo Sun in the 6th House sextiled the Neptune-Pluto Archetype Aspect and trined the Midheaven-Saturn conjunction. Neptune also trines his Pisces Ascendant. Hitchcock's Moon-Jupiter in Scorpio in the 8th was quincunx the Archetype Aspect Pluto, an indicator of murder and mystery as a personal interest.

Jeddu Krishnamurti, the extraordinary philosopher and edu-cator, who renounced the pressure to claim leadership as avatar of the Aquarian Age to lecture and teach a doctrine of seeking enlight-enment within oneself, independent of any religious creed or group, had the Neptune-Pluto conjunction in Gemini in his 4th House trine his Aquarius Ascendant. Pluto ruled his Midheaven. Avatar or not, his doctrine or non-doctrine was Aquarian in ideal. His Uranus in Scorpio conjunct his Midheaven opposed his Sun-Mercury in Taurus at his fourth cusp and quincunxed his Neptune and squared his Ascendant very closely. Krishnamurti's teaching revolutionized attitudes. He is one of the 10 persons most often mentioned as influential in changing thought in the 20th century.

The famous pioneer of parapsychological research in America, J. B. Rhine had the Neptune-Pluto Archetype conjunction in Gemini in his solar 9th House trine his Sun-Mars conjunction in Libra. A Moon in Aquarius completes an Air Grand Trine, a mark of the open and curious intellect and the investigative talents he demonstrated. Further evidence of a personality capable of playing an important role in radically changing the way science views consciousness was his Uranus in Scorpio quincunx Neptune in the Archetype conjunction and Venus, ruler of his Sun sign, square Neptune-Pluto. Telepathy, telekinesis, precognition and survival all were treated seriously in research in a university setting for the first time.

Harry Truman, the United States President who made the momentous decision to use the nuclear bomb against Japan to end World War II, had Neptune in Taurus, Pluto in Gemini in a wide conjunction in his 8th House. Uranus in Virgo in his 12th formed two additional Archetype Aspects. His Sun in Taurus conjoined Neptune while his Mars in Leo square that Sun/Neptune in the 8th. This combination is suggestive not only of his no-nonsense approach to presidential responsibility but also to his potential connection to death in archetypal proportions. (We recall that he first gained the presidency through Franklin Delano Roosevelt's death. Truman was Vice President.)

In a similar manner, Adolph Hitler, the Nazi dictator of Germany whose aggression precipitated World War II with its high death toll on all sides, had this Archetype Neptune-Pluto conjunction in Gemini in his 8th House. His Moon in Capricorn in his 3rd quincunxed Neptune-Pluto. He wrote of his plans of conquest, which included genocide of the Jewish people and a superiority of whites to people of color, whom he would enslave or exterminate. Neptune and Pluto are associated with races by many authorities, and this lethal potential is indicated in the Archetype's 8th House placement. Venus, his 8th House ruler, conjoins Mars and squares Saturn as further indications of violence; his Mercury-Sun opposes Uranus-Ascendant, with Mars quincunx Uranus, showing unexpected mood changes and fits of temper.

Perhaps the best all-around baseball player of all time, Babe Ruth, used the Archetype in quite a different manner, for athletic achievement rather than violence. His Sun in Aquarius trined his Neptune-Pluto conjunction and formed a T-Cross with Mars opposite Uranus.

Fred Astaire, the suave and debonair ballroom dancer of films for four decades from the 1920s onward, and a fine actor for two more, had the Neptune-Pluto conjunction in Gemini in the 7th with his Moon in Gemini in the 6th conjunct Pluto on his Descendant. His Uranus conjoined his Sagittarius Ascendant and opposed Moon-Pluto, while Saturn in the 1st conjoined his Ascendant and opposed Neptune. Again, three Archetype Aspect tie-ins with Personal Planets and points. His Venus, ruler of his Libra Midheaven and Taurus Sun sign, conjoined Mercury (his suave manner and speech and grace in movement) in Aries in a Fire Grand Trine with Mars (his athletic dancing) in Leo and Uranus, Ascendant, and Saturn (unusual personal discipline). Venus-Mercury was also sextile Neptune-Pluto.

♆ ⚹ △ ♇ Another outstanding athlete, world heavyweight champion Cassius Clay (Muhammad Ali), had, instead of the conjunction, the sextile Neptune in Virgo in the 2nd sextile Pluto in Leo in 12th. As would be expected of a violent professional, his Mars in Taurus in the 9th is conjunct his Midheaven and squares Pluto. His Uranus/Saturn in the 10th forms an Earth Grand Trine with Neptune and his Sun in Capricorn in the 6th. Uranus sextile Pluto makes the third Archetype. An amazing athlete who made and lost it via Neptune in the 2nd.

The inventor, Thomas Edison, had Neptune in Aquarius in the 4th House sextile Pluto in Aries in the 6th. His Aquarius Sun-Mercury conjuncted Neptune and sextiled Pluto, and his Uranus in the 5th also sextiled Mercury and trined his Leo Midheaven. These patterns show his potential talent for scientific imagination applied to his pioneer effort for new developments in the field of electricity. He was the inventor of the electric light, the motion picture projector, and Gramophone.

The chief author of the United States Declaration of Independence and third President of the United States, Thomas Jefferson, had Neptune in Cancer in his 5th House *trine* Pluto in Scorpio in the 9th conjunct his Midheaven. His Uranus in Capricorn in the 12th also trined his Pluto-Midheaven conjunction, adding another Archetype Aspect. His Uranus was conjunct his Aquarius Ascendant. His Aries Sun in the 2nd was square Uranus showing his independence and formed a Fire Grand Trine with Mars-Saturn in Leo in the 7th and Moon in Sagittarius in the 10th, an indicator of his many talents. Venus in Taurus, ruler of his 9th House in his 3rd opposed Pluto while Mercury in Pisces trined his Pluto-Midheaven, indicating the connection of the Archetype patterns with writing of a moral or philosophic nature.

Martin Luther, the leader of the Reformation in Christianity, out of which came the creation of Protestantism, had Uranus-Neptune conjunct Mercury on the 4th/5th House cusp, sextile Pluto-Jupiter in his 3rd. His Moon in Aries in the 9th trined Mercury-Neptune-Uranus indicating his potential for creating a new form of religion. However His Venus in Scorpio conjuncted Saturn and both quincunxed that Moon which also opposed Pluto to show his tendency to shut down feelings and affections.

Ψ □ ♂ P   As we complete our survey of Archetype Aspects with Neptune square or opposite Pluto, we find that some of humanity's most celebrated beings, if you will, have this so-called "affliction." Isaac Newton was the genius English physicist whose formulation of theoretical mechanics of light and astronomy and gravity defined our reality until Einstein. He was an astronomer, mathematician, and writer on astrology. Newton had Neptune in Sagittarius in the 2nd opposing Pluto in Gemini in his 8th. Venus, ruler of his Libra Ascendant in late Aquarius in the 4th formed a T-Cross with the Archetype. His Uranus in Scorpio in the 1st opposed Mars, which trined his Sun in Capricorn. Uranus formed a Grand trine with his Midheaven in Cancer and Jupiter-Saturn in the 5th. The personal connections indicate not only scientific talents but fine intuitive powers.

One of Newton's predecessors in science and the person credited with founding modern astronomy was Nicolas Copernicus. He was also an astrologer. In contrast to Newton, his Neptune in Scorpio in the 3rd made a sextile to his Pluto in Virgo in the 1st and more widely conjoined Uranus in the 3rd indicating his unusual mind. His Pisces Sun in the 7th opposed Pluto and trined Neptune and Uranus. Finally, his Mars in scientific Aquarius in the 6th squared Neptune indicating an intuitive talent, trined Saturn in Gemini indicating disciplined thought, and quincunxed Pluto showing investigative abilities. His Mercury in Pisces in the 8th opposed Pluto and trined Neptune repeating the signature of unusual mental capacities.

Another scientific pioneer whose theories in the biology of natural selection and evolution were an anathema to rigid Church theologians had Neptune in Sagittarius conjunct his Ascendant and square Pluto in Pisces in his 3rd House. Charles Darwin's personal connection indicates his ability for radical/imaginative theorizing and the potential for the controversies he aroused among religious fundamentalists and scientists alike. His Mercury in Pisces was conjunct Pluto and trined Uranus in Scorpio. The Uranus trine Pluto is again an additional Archetype. Venus, ruler of his Libra Ascendant, in Aries trines Neptune-Saturn-Ascendant in Sagittarius, which squared the Mercury-Pluto.

Finally, to summarize our thesis again, when the great Archetype Aspects form in the heavens, *they announce the arrival of a time of high purpose and change in the world.* Those fortunate enough to be born at the time of such an Archetype Aspect, or even more especially a time of several simultaneous Archetype Aspects, will share the attitudes represented by those Archetypes. Those individuals who have personal planets or points intimately aspected with these Archetypes, as they come into maturity and according to the frequency and numbers of these contacts, will play out roles of greater importance, for better or worse, in bringing the Archetype's expression to the world.

Of course, there were many other people born in the world on the same days as these remarkable people. Perhaps some, perhaps none had exactly the same degree and sign, Moon and House cusp positions. Regardless, *they* did not change the world, or at least did not change it in ways of which we are aware.

Why? As astrologers, most of us would admit we do not yet fully understand why. Perhaps it is that those others did change the world, but in ways we do not notice or in ways we do not value enough to record. What importance have we placed on good parenting or proper schooling in a society that values garbage collection above teachers monetarily, and cheap dog food above saving the whales from extinction?

And, I can add, "circumstances," whether determined by karma or chance, *do* make a difference in terms of opportunity at times. Being born a king vs. born a commoner; being born in a jungle tribe vs. a developed nation; born in a slum vs. a wealthy suburb. Indian Chief Seattle, for example, spoke more eloquently and morally to world ecology than any peer, but was regarded as a savage by his conquerors. Timing plays a factor. Seattle was ahead of his time and his truth is only today coming to be appreciated.

Some astrologers, fascinated by this problem, are working with the charts of twins to try to uncover the mysteries of small differences in charts and great differences in lives. It is both a wonderful and a humbling realization that, though we, as astrologers, are privileged to remove a few of the many veils that shroud the wisdom of the workings of our universe, we see but partially the magnificence, the mystery, and the majesty that manifests as our vision of reality.

Birth Data (in order as appears in text)

Sir Richard Burton 3-19-1821 9:30 pm LMT Hertford, England A2
Queen Victoria 5-24-1819 4:15 am LMT London, England PW
Louis Pasteur 12-27-1822 2:00 am LMT Dole, France A3
Karl Marx 5-5-1818 2:00 am LMT Trier, Germany
Henry D. Thoreau 7-12-1817 9:00 pm LMT Concord, MA A2
Walt Whitman 5-31-1819 1:45 am LMT Huntington, NY A2
Charles Baudelaire 4-9-1821 3:00 pm LMT Paris, France A2
Mary Baker Eddy 7-16-1821 5:38 pm LMT Bow, NH PW
Leonardo da Vinci 4-23-1452 9:40 pm LMT Vinci, Italy A2
Nikola Testa 7-9/10-1856 midnight Smiljan, Yugoslavia A2
Fritjof Capra 2-1-1939 10:55 am MET Vienna, Austria A4
Benjamin Franklin 1–6–1706 11:00 am LMT Boston, MA PC
Joseph Stalin 1-2-1880 8:15 am LMT Gori, Russia A2
Stephen Spielberg 12-18-1946 6:16 pm EST Cincinnati, OH A3
John Lennon 10-9-1940 6:30 pm GWT Liverpool, England A2
Paul McCartney 6-18-1942 2:30 am DBST Liverpool, England A2
George Harrison 2-25-1943 0:05 am GWT Liverpool, England A4
Ringo Starr 7-7-1940 0:05 am BST Liverpool, England A2
Jimi Hendrix 11-27-1942 10:15 am PWT Seattle, WA A2
Janis Joplin 1-19-1943 9:45 am CWT Port Arthur, TX PW
Henri Toulouse-Lautrec 11-24-1864 6:00 am LMT Albi, France A2
Salvador Dali 5-11-1904 8:45 am GMT Figueras, Spain A4
Mark Spitz 2-10-1950 5:45 pm PST Modesto, CA A2
Joe Namath 5-31-1943 ? time Beaver Falls, PS PC
Charles Lindbergh 2-4-1902 2:30 am CST Detroit, MI A2
Carl Jung 7-26-1875 7:26 pm GMT Kesswil, Switzerland A2
Jonas Salk 10-28-1914 11:15 am EST New York, NY A2
Galileo Galilei 2-25-1564 3:14 pm LMT Pisa, Italy A2

Mohandas Gandhi 10-2-1869 ? time Porbandar, India A2
Annie Besant 10-1-1847 5:29 pm LMT London, England PW
William Quan Judge 4-13-1851 5:07 am LMT Dublin, Ireland A2
Oliver Cromwell 5-5-1599 3:00 am LMT Huntingdon, England A2
Helena P. Blavatsky 8-12-1831 2:17 am LMT Ekaternislav, Russia
    PW
Henry S. Olcott 8-2-1832 11:15 am LMT Orange, NJ A2
John Glenn 7-18-1921 4:00 pm EST Cambridge, OH A2
Peter Sellers 9-8-1925 6:00 am GDT South Sea, England A2
George Patton 11-11-1885 6:38 pm PST San Marino, CA A2
Albert Einstein 3-14-1879 11:30 am LMT Ulm, Germany A2
Sir Winston Churchill 11-30-1874 1:30 am LMT Woodstock,
    England A2
Franklin D. Roosevelt 1-30-1882 8:45 pm LMT Hyde Park, NY A3
Edgar Cayce 3-18-1877 3:03–3:30 pm LMT Hopkinson, KY PC
Dalai Lama 12-18-1933 12:41 am zone-7 Sining, China A2
Helen Keller 6-27-1880 4:02 pm LMT Tuscumbia, AL A2
Shirley MacLaine 4-24-1934 3;57 pm EST Richmond, VA PW
Albert Schweitzer 1-14-1875 11:50 pm LMT Kayserburg, Alsace A2
Alfred Hitchcock 8-13-1899 8:00 pm GMT London, England PC
Jeddu Krishnamurti 5-12-1895 12:18 am LMT Madanapalle,
    India A3
J. B. Rhine 9-29-1895 ? time ? place Circle
Harry Truman 5-8-1884 4:00 pm LMT Larmar, MO A2
Adolph Hitler 4-20-1889 6:30 pm LMT Branau, Austria A3
Fred Astaire 5-10-1899 9:16 pm CST Omaha, NE A2
Muhammad Ali 1-17-1942 6:35 pm CST Louisville, KY ABC
Thomas Edison 2-11-1847 3:00 am LMT Milan, OH PC
Thomas Jefferson 4-13-1743 1:54 am LMT Shadwell, VA PC
Martin Luther 11-10-1483 11:00 pm LMT Eisleben, Germany PC
Isaac Newton 1-4-1643 1:00 am LMT Woolsthorpe, England A3
Nicholas Copernicus 2-28-1473 4:48 pm LMT Torim, Poland A2
Charles Darwin 2-12-1809 3:00 am LMT Shrewsbury, England A2

Sources

Astro Data 2, 3, 4; Lois Rodden, AFA, Tempe, AZ, 1988. – A2, A3, A4
American Book of Charts; ACS, San Diego, CA, 1980 – ABC
Penfield Collection; Vulcan Books, Seattle WA, 1979 – PC
Profiles of Women; Lois Rodden, AFA, Tempe, AZ, 1979 – PW
Circle Book of Charts; Circle Book, Ann Arbor, MI, 1972 – Circle

Jayj Jacobs

Jayj Jacobs has had a full-service astrology practice in San Francisco since 1972, counseling businesses, couples, individuals, and politicians. He also designs and sells complete computer systems, primarily to astrologers. He became interested in astrology in 1964, at age 15, and his initial training was with his father, Don "Moby Dick" Jacobs, with whom he developed an innovative approach known as "Experience Astrology."

Jayj has co-led The Annual Prediction Seminar since 1971, with accuracy always better than 90 percent. He has lectured on a wide variety of subjects for AFA, AFAN, Aquarius Workshops, ISAR, NCGR, NORWAC, SWAC, UAC, and numerous local organizations in the U.S. and in Canada.

Jayj's articles have appeared in *Astrology Now, Aspects, Welcome to Planet Earth, The Sun-Sign Astrologer*, and others. He writes a monthly column—Star*Light—for *Smoking Singles Magazine*. Jayj has revised the series of 10 "Moby Dick's Matrix Charts," and distributes his father's works as well as his own, notably "The Experience Astrology System," The Transit Dial, and his Graph Kits.

Jayj is an AFAN co-founder, on the Steering Committee, and is Chair of AFAN's Legal Information Committee.

Relating Through the Outer Planets

Jayj Jacobs

Once a horoscope consultation moves beyond the realm of character analysis and development to current issues and personal interests, clients invariably ask about sex and money. They may phrase it as an inquiry into "love and work" or "relationships and success" or even "satisfaction and accomplishment," and they may emphasize one over the other, but the basic request is always for insight into "who will join me on what journey, and how will that be, for me?"

Incorporating the outer planets, Uranus, Neptune, and Pluto, within an interpretive or counseling session is crucial to both understanding the dynamics of any relationship and to enhancing the compatibility between any two people. It is not an exaggeration to state that without sufficient outer planet contact, a relationship is not one of significant or lasting impact! It may be fun, exciting, even joyous, but it won't be greatly consequential.

While the Ascendant and the inner planets will indicate impression, awareness, connection, communication, affinity, desire, growth, and responsibility; *revelation, inspiration, and empowerment* are the province of Uranus, Neptune, and Pluto, respectively. So are shock and rejection, confusion and deception, manipulation and dominance. The range of expression for each of the outers will be presented later in the interpretive section of this chapter.

To analyze the interpretive content of compatibilities, we need a viable context in which to examine relationships. That requires looking at relationships themselves. Since astrology is about life and how people live it, our techniques as well as our interpretations need to match the facts; they need to correlate with what actually occurs in real life.

What actually happens when two people interact? What categories of interaction can we discover or establish to analyze the interplay of personality, character, and behavior between two individuals? Who does what to whom? And what exists as a framework before they even begin to relate? What is the context for our discussion of their experience of each other?

Astrologically, we look at relationships as they occur in life, through four frameworks, four ways of organizing and analyzing, experience; each is a separate matrix of information and interpretation. These matrices are: Reality, Roles, Response, and Process.

In the astrological model of life, the horoscope is a diagramatic representation of a person's mechanisms and processes for creating reality and interpreting experience. The major components are Signs on Houses, Planets in Signs, and Houses and Planets in Aspect to each other. *The process by which life unfolds and relationships develop is shown by transiting planets through Houses and in aspect to natal planets.*

Life looks different to each of us because our points of view differ. Everyone stands on a unique point in the circle of the Zodiac. We filter the input we receive through receptors that are individually calibrated. We interpret our circumstances in our own way, based on our own frames of reference, values, and expectations, which we have constructed throughout our personal history. The distillation of all this that we term our experience is our reality. Where there is agreement we call it Reality, or cultural norms, or community standards. Nevertheless, our Life is in our personal experience of it.

As people relate to each other they confront *each other's reality*. In doing so, they discover the extent to which they share common values, complement or contradict, and whether or not they appreciate, tolerate, or disdain the other's standards, preferences, and expectations. For example, if one person believes in technology and the other believes in magic (Uranus in the 9th versus Neptune in the 9th), it's likely to become an issue between them. Or, if one's idea of a good time is watching "Dances with Wolves" on the VCR, and the other's is dancing the night away in clubs, it may be difficult to date together (Neptune in a Libra 5th or in a Scorpio 5th).

People interact with each other from a variety of *roles*, archetypes, or positions. We see ourselves—or put ourselves—in roles based on our own horoscopes, but others see us based on *their* charts. The role catagorizes the communication and channels the interaction (through the filters that operate there) into a particular arena where it is concentrated. For example, everything your mother says or does is seen as being presented to you by your mother in her role as "mother" and is filtered by your history of experience with her. When your boss and your best friend tell you the same thing, even in the same words, you hear it differently because you listen to them through different "ears" that focus on the role they have in your life.

All relationships exist within an individual's experience, totally, and nowhere else. There is no object, no thing, no "The Relationship" that exists out in the physical universe so you can point to it or touch it, or measure it *separately from the people who are experiencing it*. The concept exists, but the reality doesn't. There is only each person's own *experience of relating to another*. Their experience of relating to you is their own separate and distinct experience. It may be totally different from your version. You and the other person are different "experiencers," experiencing a different other "experiencer." Just as attraction may be all one-directional (they're hot and you're not; you're keen and they're mean), joy and pain may begin or remain in one person's experience, alone.

People react and respond to each other. People in a relationship don't average out: relating generates a synergy and produces more than an average or even a sum. One person stimulates the other who experiences that stimulation and responds; the other person stimulates (in the same, a similar, or a different manner) and then the first person responds. The stimuli interact with each other, reinforcing, balancing, and even counteracting each other. The realities, roles and responses dance together to the music of time's passage.

You are the Gift:
Be Careful What You Bring to the Relationship

Reality is "the way life is" for each of you, as shown by your birth charts. The charts are compared House by House: one person's signs on Houses and planets in Houses are juxtaposed to the other's so that the similarities and differences between each person's reality—relative to that specific area of life—is revealed. Some of the differences will be experienced as complements, others as contradictions. Some of the similarities will be experienced as reinforcements, and others will be interpreted as interferences.

Each of us has an inherent way of being in life, a way of operating with others that we bring to *every* relationship we have. Each attitude, behavior, consideration, desire and demand, expectation, fantasy, friendship, generosity, hope, humor, idiosyncrasy, invalidation, judgment and justification, kin, knack, love and longing, motivation and maturity can be an asset or a liability to ourselves, and the same or the opposite to the person with whom we are in relationship. So can our needs, opinions, promises, preferences, questions, responses and reactions, requests, tastes, upsets, values, wants, wisdom, x-rated ideas, yearnings, youthfulness, and our zaniness.

The outer planets in an individual's natal (and solar) Houses are but some of the indicators of what someone brings to a relationship, of what they bring to the table for barter. Unlike most other chart factors, these outer planets are specific to zodiacal signs and to generation: only certain Ascendant or Sun Signs can have the Outers in particular Houses, and the signs that hold them are indications of the evolution of generations. For example, *only* Cancers and Leos can have Pluto in Leo in the 1st House, and only half of them do. If Pluto is in a Leo's 1st, it's in either Leo or Virgo. Virgos can have Pluto in the 1st House only when Pluto is in Virgo or Libra. Here are some Outer Planet/House interpretations that show up as issues in relationships.

1st House Placements

Uranus in the 1st says you're more unique than most, but it isn't a license to ignore the specialness of others. You're one-of-a-kind, self-determined, and self-sufficient; your independence will be an issue. You're not the exception to every rule. If you're intractable, the relationship will soon be over.

Neptune lets you be a chameleon to your sweethearts, and charm them with compassion and acquiescence.

Pluto's obvious sexuality attracts people like bees to a flower for honey, but they may miss your other attributes. The threat of your determination drives some people away but draws those who respect or lust for power and can handle it.

2nd House Placements

Uranus (even more so if also in Taurus) gives an odd set of values and tastes and an insistence on financial independence that can frustrate security. Take it your way, but let them have it *their* way.

Neptune can't count, so the books aren't balanced, nor are the bills paid on time. Expressing no preferences (Keyword: "whatever") confuses those who would be suitable for you or seek your approval.

Pluto's financial fixations and fluctuations can drive a wedge of worry between you and panic your partners. Absolutism is difficult to deal with.

3rd House Placements

The paralogical ricochets of Uranus from one idea to another can baffle people and make for awkward conversations. Did they ask you to make them feel stupid? Remember: opening Pandora's box also "seemed like a good idea at the time," and don't speak all you think. Brilliance means that they do "get it."

Your Neptune may know what they're going to say, but you can still let them finish their sentence. Using your ability to inspire and motivate will evaporate your own tendency to confusion. Look for facts as well as for meaning and omens.

Pluto gives the ability to dominate the conversation and dictate their opinions, but even if that strength gives you the right, it may not be the right thing to do. Let strategy decide tactics and remember that they're on your side.

4th House Placements

Uranus here makes you feel like an outsider. You don't even expect to fit in or belong. Having had no example or practice in co-operation makes you difficult to live with.

Neptune will most often wash away security and leave you the child of wanderers, drifters or grifters. Parental drunks, druggies, and dreamers give you no basis for trust. You float on your own. If you happened to grow up ministered to with compassion, keep sharing the acceptance with others.

Pluto here says you grew up amid battles for dominance (and learned determination or destructiveness) or survived in spite of death or desertion (but you still expect abandonment). Let go of it, transmute it.

5th House Placements

Uranus knows that variety is the spice of life (especially in

Gemini) and wants its seasonings fresh, yet aged to perfection. Your insistence on the new, better, and different can interfere with development and ripening. Neptune longs for someone with whom to dance on the clouds and ride rainbows. The trick to seeing beyond Reality is not to step off the edge and fall into an unworkable fantasy. *Acceptance* of who you're with works wonders.

Pluto here desires good, clean, wholesome, recreational sex and knows its favorite sport (especially in Leo). Preoccupation with the prurient or (possessive) obsession with the playmate breeds crisis.

6th House Placements

Uranus in the 6th is used to doing things its own way and doesn't listen well to suggestions or requests. Take some input and get clear on other people's perspectives before suggesting "a better way."

Neptune's service orientation needn't be subservient: inspiration is valued higher than sacrifice. Paint a happier picture.

Pluto's life and death employments may thrill or terrify your intended. Look beyond danger for purposeful pursuits *and* your partner's co-participation.

7th House Placements

Uranus doesn't do the ordinary, conventional, or traditional in either agreements or partners. Only the exceptional is acceptable. Enroll others in the ideal, but don't insist. Your rights aren't as important as your aims. Try making allowances for other people's foibles.

Neptune seeks a soulmate and hopes to find it on the first try, or on the next one (especially in Libra). You may find someone who needs more fixing than you can fix before you're through.

Pluto desires a sexy dynamo who's willing to empower, but *you* may get overpowered instead. You expect the relationship to accomplish a purpose greater than itself. Don't obsess or stay just for the sexual excess.

8th House Placements

Uranus in the 8th expects sex always to be exciting and won't settle for Yankee pot roast. It needs fancy French sauces and nouvelle cuisine but will also grab a burger on a bun or a taco on the run, with a friend or two. It takes two to tango, but maybe you can teach them to dance to your tune.

Neptune assumes sex will be a spiritual experience that results in the blending of beings or the reunification of souls, which is cosmic when it occurs. Give it time.

Pluto in the 8th is driven by desire, empowered by passion, and resurrected by sexual release. Great sex is priceless. Does anything else matter? How much of what will you (or they) put up with or without for it? (Cancer and Libra cusps on the 8th create a paradox for Uranus and Pluto there, but amplify the Neptune manifestation).

9th House Placements

Uranus in the 9th rewrites the world's philosophies by extracting a piece-from-this to combine with parts-from-that. The consistent element is the belief in free choice: remember to grant it to others.

Neptune believes that reality is for people who can't handle fantasy or haven't yet found a good one, and that science is just another religion. Distinctions are blurred and there may be no right or wrong, except what's convenient or what's too much of a hassle. Easy come, easy go with the flow.

Pluto's 9th House drive is to bring knowledge to the surface. You will commit piracy on others' privacy to get at the buried treasure chest of truth. Wanderlust may become a euphemism for homelessness.

10th House Placements

Uranus in the 10th is a law unto itself; nobody can tell you anything. (Stronger in Leo or with Leo on the cusp). Pretty soon, they'll stop trying if you can't turn independence-as-the-price into innovativeness-as-the-payoff.

Whatever your occupation, Neptune in the 10th makes contribution your true career; your path through life and your public reputation. Remember, charity begins at home, so give some of it to your other.

Pluto's drive for authority and dominance in the world may make you a top provider, but beware of dictating to your life partner, or of treating them as a competitor.

11th House Placements

Uranus in the 11th, with its strange aspirations, makes you difficult to follow into the future. If you insist on going it alone, you'll be home alone. Stand for freedom for everyone.

Neptune's dream of service will inspire your partners if rumor and deceptive friends don't have at them first. Be sure to share your spiritual aspirations early on, and be sure that your partner gets the message.

Pluto's 11th House aim to find and fulfill a purpose adds meaning to life, as its attention to climactic events adds excitement, but your penchant for playing around with your friends may rub your sweetheart the wrong way.

12th House Placements

Uranus in the 12th gives you a sense of the future, and of your partner's objectives. They might object to the revelations, but they will certainly be shocked by the consequences of ignoring things spiritual.

Neptune's psychic ability and spirituality make for acceptance and service unless you buy the cultural bias and drown the light in drink.

Pluto's sense of danger keeps you both out of trouble, and its intuition about intimate connections is consummate. Being half tuned-in makes for a tragic hero, a miss-the-mark martyr.

Relating Through the Outer Planets in Each Other's Houses

Roles are a matter of perception. Your point of view about them, and others about you, determines which roles you assume with them. You perceive people in their interaction with you, *according to which of their planets are in which of your Houses*. Others also see you as belonging or being important to them in particular arenas, through the "windows" of their Houses. You relate to a person through the filter (i.e., assumptions and expectations) *of the role you put them in.* You affect each other's Houses according to the nature of the planets your chart places there. Each person's experience of that part of life is changed by the other person's planetary influence in that house.

Horoscope charts divide life into Houses, arenas of activity, domains of experience. Each house is the way it is for you (and that part of life is how it is) from the signs and planets in that House, *until you begin to interact with someone else*. Then *their* planets begin to operate in that House (and all your other Houses) bringing you new experiences, new attitudes and new ways of being that reinforce, amend or contradict your ordinary way of operating.

When their outer planets fall into the same Houses in your chart that your outers are, the effects, results, and manifestations of your own planets are reinforced, but new levels, directions, and styles of expression for that planet become available. You do things with *their* Uranus, for example, that you wouldn't do with your own!

When their outers land in Houses different than the Houses holding your outers, new possibilities arise, new visions appear, and new commitments surface. While these new indications truly can be opportunities, they are often experienced or evaluated as distractions, invalidations, or contradictions. You choose how you interpret them.

House interpretations of the effects or experiences of the outer planets in each other's Houses that follow here in the text will work as well as anything does with the House system you use. I use Equal Houses for compatibility analysis and enhancement. For an added (and necessary) dimension to your understanding of the dynamics of the relationship, I recommend that you also work with all the planets in each others' *Solar Houses*. Use the Sun's birth-time calculated degree, sign and minute as the cusp of the 1st House, and use that same degree for the following Signs on each successive House. Solar Charts, being from the Sun, show life and relationships as they flow out from character, identity, and the essential nature of being. Don't work without them.

NOTE: One mundane manifestation of Uranus and Pluto transits through Libra (1968–1975 and 1972–1984) which changed the rules of relationships, is that more people are willing to date and relate outside their age group, and farther outside it as well. Pluto's increase in speed also makes it more common for one person's outers to be Houses away from another's. New relationship dynamics have been discovered and more are on the way.

The Other's Uranus in One of Your Houses

• *Their Uranus in your 1st House* incites you to discover a new individuality, a fresh sense of yourself, separate from society's socialization and beyond parental prohibitions. You become more independent and maybe a little obstinate as the real you stands up. Experimentation excites you and leads to changes in appearance and presentation. Sometimes you move toward an ideal, at other times you resist or change just for the hell of it. Their differences, oddities and ideals spark new insights into your self, and into others.

• *Their Uranus in your 2nd House* disturbs your values and preferences in unpredictable ways. Their message is that you could have better values; theirs, or *really* your own. New tastes arise from fresh insights on values and value. Old tastes are rekindled by the spark of renewed idealism and individualism. Finances fluctuate as you spend from both your usual habits and from your new hopes. New and/or odd income sources are attractive; the beacon of freedom beckons you to independence.

• *Their Uranus in your 3rd House* sparkles new thoughts and odd ideas for you. You begin to think differently about thinking, learning, and speaking. This person edits your statements and may alter your meaning. A new talent for distinctions develops as does one for listening between the lines. Your speaking startles others and even yourself. Your writing gets odd, and you may communicate into left field. If your own Uranus is already here, the two of you can feed ideas to each other like electric dynamos.

• *Their Uranus in your 4th House* disrupts your home environment and your family dynamic. Rebellious breaks from the family are likely as you become adamant about your rights. This Uranian says you can't be treated like that. Later, security in your independence may allow a treaty between equals, as adults. Their customs, preferences, choices and ideas startle you into seeing your home ideals as possibilities. If Your Uranus is here your odd taste in unusual homes and domestic lifestyles is supported. But, there will still be some conflicts over moving, destinations, lifestyles, traditions, and in-laws!

• *Their Uranus in your 5th House* changes your idea of fun and allows you to engage in new activities and recreations. You often discover that what you formerly disdained is a new delight. The romance won't get stale; there will always be a new way to play together, a new something to do. But it may not become stable, either. The independence allowed may permit flirtations and even affairs (especially if your Uranus already lives here). Their independence (or aloofness) may add to your flirtatiousness; which their idealism would find hard not to accept.

Special (brilliant) and/or unexpected offspring are more likely, and adopting or fostering becomes a more viable possibility.

• *Their Uranus in your 6th House* produces a different work ethic; you want to do different work, and to do it differently, your way or not at all. If self-employment were a possibility (your Uranus here), it becomes a probability as long as the relationship lasts. Odd attitudes toward work develop and lead to strange behavior. Indifference, rebellion, and occasionally enjoyment show up on the job. The other shows you the way to new jobs and new skills.

• *Their Uranus in your 7th House* indicates anything in relating *except* what you expect or what's expected of you! You create your own relationship agreements, which are idealistically unique. You adopt new roles and role models or try having none at all. You surprise yourself, shock your friends and family, and either flaunt convention or ignore societal norms. If your own Uranus is here, this is what you've hoped for; if not, you're either willing to give it a try or feel pressed into it, depending on the cuspal sign and other planets in this House. This cross-placement may produce separations and reunions (and re-separations) with independence often the issue between you.

• *Their Uranus in your 8th House* indicates that their differences excite you and entice you into doing something out of the ordinary.With this one, trying new things, new places and new positions is intriguing. So-called "unnatural acts," or behaviors with a socially acceptable level of kinkiness, seem perfectly natural and turn you on more than before. You even enjoy mistakes and accidents that produce pleasure. You'll never be bored, but you may end up frazzled. Your insights (often from shared ideals or sharing aspirations) trigger transformations.

• *Their Uranus in your 9th House* creates a willingness to re-investigate life from new perspectives. Your beliefs will be challenged and re-designed, or discarded. Life won't look the same or be looked at the same way before you're too far into this relationship. This person will interest you in strange philosophies; old, new, odd, accepted and not, until you invent your own. Someday, when you least expect it, you'll be invited to travel to strange new places, at the spur of the moment.

• *Their Uranus in your 10th House* indicates that their choices, chances, and changes affect your career. Their decisions—and your resulting dilemmas—cause you to change companies, positions, even careers. You could be a casualty of their consciousness and contrariness, or inspired to incredible innovation and advancement. You may at times work temp, be self-employed, or become an independent contractor from their ideas or actions.

• *Their Uranus in your 11th House* encourages your individuality and aids in realizing your ideal selfhood. This person promotes your true aspirations, and does so by assisting your selection of them. He or she rejects assumptions, proposes options, questions answers, and insists on the clarification of objectives. People who bring you this position also bring you strange people, and unusual groups, with weird ideas. They allow you a new view of the future, one of your own design (with a little help from your friends).

• *Their Uranus in your 12th House* turns on an inner light that sparks intuition and triggers insight. Spiritual inspiration is available as this person and this placement opens you to psychic channels and abilities. You open up especially to them and this results in great empathy between you—or explosive disruption, which depends on your acceptance or not of what you uncover and how they go about attempting to edit your vision.

The Other's Neptune in One of Your Houses

• *His or Her Neptune in your First House.* Their Neptune in your 1st House confuses you; you don't know who you are or whom you are relating to. You may see an ideal person who isn't really there, even when they con the shirt off your back. You are likely to forget who you are, or who you were trying to be, and adapt yourself to them. Alternately, this may be a person who truly supports, accepts, and inspires you. You become awakened, illuminated and even enlightened. In the process, you become a more giving and more receptive person, but retain the ability to say "no."

• *Their Neptune in your 2nd House* takes the pressure off money. It also takes *your* attention off it! They may deceive you about their values and about your finances; If the acceptance or tolerance level is too high you could merely say "so what?" "Oh well," or "Oy vey" until the next time. Your judgments relax, your acceptance expands and your preferences become less precise. When an elevated Neptune inspires you together you seek happiness from creativity, sensuality, and spirituality.

• *Their Neptune in your 3rd House* reinforces your imagination and intuition and telepathy. One sends thoughts, and the other receives them, but which is who? You may not be able to tell, and it may not matter. You (often) may not even need to converse, since it seems unnecessary. When beings commune do they need words to communicate? Their Neptune in your 3rd may move you beyond reality, clouding observations with fantasies, leaving you confused, bemused and amused.

• *Their Neptune in your 4th House* tends to dissolve any urge for home ownership or stability. Relating with this person may take you on a relocation odyssey through many dream homes and, eventually, to your own personal Bali Hai. The gift is mellowness: permission to accept the lack of family, roots, and territory or the grace to acknowledge family as-it-is.

• *Their Neptune in your 5th House* brings you the opportunity to find your own perfect blend of the sensual, romantic and spiritual. You may find yourself dancing the night away or chanting the night away, or both. You may have found the ultimate love-affair, or you may think so only to have it, or them, slip away and disappear. With their Neptune here, their romantic interest may not actually have the same reality for them that it appears to have for you. Resistance and resentment either evaporate or else they drive Neptune away. You're in awe of their inspiration, and they of your expression.

• *Their Neptune in your 6th House* moves you to serve and help them, and then to do so for others. What you gain in compassion, you lose in rigidity. They inspire you to effective contribution, which may remain personal and social, but can lead to service jobs where you are doing "good works" and doing them well. You may nurse them through job and/or illness crises and maybe drug or alcohol issues.

• *Their Neptune in your 7th House* suggests an other-worldly or unreal pairing: a spiritual bond or a fantasy con. You think your names are written together in the Akashic records or in The Book of Love!

You intuit and suspect your "Soul-Mate." There is a strong risk of hopeless marrying in hope of reform, even if *your* natal Neptune isn't here.

• *Their Neptune in your 8th House* promises a sensational sensual experience and delivers on the promise. This position is a sexual fantasy looking for a time, place, and manner to manifest. You imagine the consummate lover, but this one may remain a cherished, unconsummated fantasy. If it gets physical, give this inspired lover their lead and turn-about when you're done. Blissful, magical, mystical sex can turn into love and spiritual union. Their Neptune here eases your rebirth-regeneration process and smoothes crises.

• *Their Neptune in your 9th House* inspires prophetic insight, intuitive knowing. You know you know, and they accept that you do. Your beliefs become more mystical and your philosophy more spiritual. Rigid dogma disappears, and the knowledge of peace comes forward. Traveling becomes a means to fulfill a fantasy, to perform a service, to inspire, or to be inspired.

• *Their Neptune in your 10th House* manifests as their strong faith in you. This soon translates to faith in yourself, trust that you will win greatly in the end, or sooner than that. Drink faith like tequila: with the salt of practicality and the sweet/sour lemon of doubting. Temper it with knowledge of your limits and abilities. Failure to do so will send you tilting at windmills or off to conquer the world without inviting your army to the battle.

• *Their Neptune in your 11th House* makes your ideals and aspirations more spiritual, but perhaps too ephemeral to realize. Hope blurs the distinction between wishes and attainable goals. Blind faith may make beautiful music, but you'll find that you can't find your way home. They introduce you to mystical, supportive friends and make compassion a component of connections. Some of your new "friends" will be fiends and fantasy fanatics or space cadets.

• *Their Neptune in your 12th House* shows someone who knows you well (you may wonder if they know you *too* well). You'll also be confused about what's real when you disagree about the way you are. They anticipate your thoughts and requests and provide before you can ask. This is cozy and comfortable and you're content if you relax into it. It's annoying if you resent being transparent or resist being totally accepted. Or if you don't think you're acceptable.

The Other's Pluto in One of Your Houses

• *Their Pluto in your 1st House* transforms your self-image and self-expression: you feel empowered and enabled. Some recognize and validate your personal power (especially with your Pluto here) or grant it to you. With others, their attempts to dominate you trigger metamorphic empowerment and, no matter who wins this round, you're more able to stand your own ground the next time you're surrounded. Their Pluto in your 1st House also means you are emboldened and may become brazen. Your energy and sense of self are sexualized. A new, sexy, powerful presentation and appearance arises from the ashes of a former self-image.

• *Their Pluto in your 2nd House* forces fluctuating finances down and up, again, to great extremes of both. Totally new values arise with the changes in fortune in a chicken and egg paradox. They want control of the money in the relationship and may resort to tricks or tantrums to get it. Their Pluto can purify your values, to your everlasting satisfaction, but most people will only attempt to impose their own values on you.

• *Their Pluto in your 3rd House* demands you change your wrong opinions (to them, those opinions of yours are, at best, "undeveloped"). These people try to force *their* opinions on you and they do make convincing arguments. They attempt to make you talk, and to drive you beyond a conversational level to reveal your "real" thoughts, to realize what you're actually thinking. Sharp probing and a commitment to completion get you both to your bottom line truth, but domination destroys communication.

• *Their Pluto in your 4th House* stimulates the recall of past memories (early years or past lives), unsettling to you, to say the least. A total break from the past, and often from your family may result. They give birth to a new life for you, mostly through their life commitments, but also through their commitment to you.

• *Their Pluto in your 5th House* makes fun sexy and sex fun (maybe even a sport). It galvanizes your urge to play, to create, and to recreate; now you gotta go out (or get out the paints). Their Pluto intensity absolutely alters your pleasure pattern; it can bring dangerous liaisons and hazardous recreations. They may be possessive, even obsessive in this love affair; you could be too. But be loyal, to avoid Pluto's onslaught, and committed, to access its passionate power.

• *Their Pluto in your 6th House* shows that they push you to work and drive you to excellence. They may launch you into new fields and plant new skills. Your resistance or their domineering insistence may bring health crisis; their intention and intensity might also generate remission. You can matter-of-factly use them to relieve your tensions, with neither of you objecting to that (especially with Pluto in Virgo).

• *Their Pluto in your 7th House* makes relating so vitally important it seems necessary, even demanded (the more so with a Cancer cusp). The relationship is very intense; considerations, crisis, and commitments collide, yet "marriage" is still desired. Their possessiveness is a certainty; and obsessiveness is very likely. Emotional violence is a possibility from frustration, jealousy, etc. (especially if in Cancer). Eventually a totally new way of regenerative relating replaces old patterns, and old loves.

• *Their Pluto in your 8th House* delivers (the ultimate) catalytic sexual experiences: enough to overrule many negatives, if not all of them. You may get caught between a rock and a soft place.

Empowerment entices, transformation tantalizes, and sexual excess exceeds expectations. This placement intensifies crises but adds restorative impact to the outcome. You find yourself risking resources, even danger or death for rebirth.

• *Their Pluto in your 9th House* may alter or intensify your religious tendencies as your convictions are challenged and you are forced to construct new conclusions. It deepens your philosophy, broadens your understanding, and strengthens your desire to know and prove that you do. Worn-out, life-shaping beliefs are shredded to compost in your new reality. Wisdom awaits you.

• *Their Pluto in your 10th House* makes both of you career-compulsive. They may be set on defining a new domain of endeavor for you or be dedicated to your current designs. Pluto creates a committed drive to reach the top, to control the game, to reap the rewards (and fuels your own fire if your Pluto is here as well). There is a real danger of going too far to reach where you're going. Pyrrhic victories may cost you more than either of you is able to pay, if you don't play by the rules.

• *Their Pluto in your 11th House* focuses their, and then your own, firm intention on distilling, refining, purifying, and then reaching your aspirations. Whatever else, they may involve you deeply in social causes or humanitarian concerns, being friends of mankind, to fulfill the purpose of having an impact (especially if your Pluto resides here). You also get new, sexy or powerful, and possibly dangerous friends.

• *Their Pluto in your 12th House* will envelop you in tragedies together: perhaps even the tragedy of being together. Alternately, it may resurrect you from suffering your own sorrowful catastrophes. Your ascension to helping other victims and transforming their lives as well as your own culminates in rewarding service and potential enlightenment. Their Pluto also intensifies your psychic insights and redesigns your spiritual blueprints for life and reality.

Cross-chart Aspects

Response always contains stimulus and, astrologically, is shown by planetary *aspects* across charts. You affect the other person by your planets that aspect their planets. In turn, you are affected by and respond to their planets' aspects to your own planets. The effect is in keeping with the nature of the planets involved: each planet "does what it is" to what the other planet is, does, and represents in that person's chart. These stimulations may be enjoyable or painful; each may be advantageous or detrimental to you, whether you like it or not.

Aspects and Orbs

Gone are the days when all trines were good and all squares were bad, thanks to the astrologers who looked to their clients and their experience rather than to the archaic tomes of the astro-curmudgeons of old. As with birth charts and transits, *the actual planets involved in the relationship aspect are much more important in determining what occurs, than is their angle of approach to each other*. Of course, the aspects will be different in strength and level of tension if the other's planets make major or minor aspects, hard or soft, but the effect is primarily different in degree rather than in kind. *Which* planets are involved is primary: what the aspect is, in most cases, only a modifier.

Quite often planets in soft aspects attract each other while those in hard aspects both attract *and* resist each other so that the person involved feels a push-pull or love-hate energy with that portion of the other's make-up. Since relationships show their colors in conversations, it may be useful to think of most soft aspects as producing dialogs and discussions, while the hard ones often manifest in alternating monologues and in debates.

Difficulty with an aspect in a relationship is often a function of the level at which, or the way in which, various natal chart factors are *expressed* by the person sending or *interpreted* by the person receiving the aspect. The entire scale over which two planets in aspect can manifest is higher (in terms of satisfaction and workability) with soft aspects and lower with hard ones, for most people most of the time. Sometimes you beat the odds, sometimes you don't.

For example, if their Mars is always expressed as hostile or impatient, then almost no contact with it will be useful or enjoyable, and similar, if their Saturn always expresses itself as disdain and invalidation. However, if they generate Mars as initiative and eagerness, then you're excited by it. Or, with Pluto, if you interpret their honestly intended and well delivered thrust toward your empowerment as a crass attempt at manipulation, you'll retard your regeneration. And, if you refuse to be contributed to you'll never be filled by the etheric light of a positive Neptune. It's not just what the other does that matters, *it's what you think it means, that makes the difference.* And you can change your interpretations, which might be all it takes to save your "marriage."

Other compatibility contacts can have an effect on the aspect in question: your Jupiter aspecting their Saturn (or Pluto), for example, will elevate it as it returns aspects to your chart.

To see all the ramifications of a relationship, full natal aspect orbs are important in compatibility as well, even for the Outer Planets. I use 10 degrees for the Conjunction, Square, Trine, and Opposition (and 12 if the Sun or the Moon is involved). I allow 6 (and 7) for the Sextile and 3 degrees (3:30′) for the Semi-sextile and Quincunx. I don't use any other aspects in relationship analysis.

Closer cross-chart aspects will be stronger, of course, and those that are within 4 degrees, and the more so 2 degrees, will be the strongest because *the planets will be simultaneously triggered by aspects from transiting planets throughout the relationship.*

As an illustration: A former business partner and I have a Mars-Mars Square from 24 Scorpio to 22 Aquarius, so there was always an element of competition present, either with each other or, as a team, with everyone else. Whenever anything transited those degrees we would both flareup with the heated words of argument or the slow burn of resentment. Read some of the aspects below (like

Mercury or Mars to Uranus) as if they were oppositions, and then imagine what would happen if, say, Mars or Mercury transited Square to both planets, or if Saturn or Uranus hit them Trine and Sextile. You'll get the feel of the way transits kick-start the relationship and bring it to life. And the way they kick it when it's down.

Aspects To and From Uranus

• *With your Sun*—you illuminate and encourage their unconventionality, while you identify with their iconoclastic independence. Your awareness of their ideals and aspirations lets them see the way to achieve them. They spark you to be yourself and to change to become who you can be. You invite, or in hard contacts, dare each other along, being naughty together, to your mutual delight. A great friendship.

"I know who I was when I got into this relationship but I must have changed several times since then." "You're welcome."

• *With your Moon*—you enjoy the free spirit in this one. If you like being surprised, this aspect's for you, but you'll also be startled, shocked and stunned on occasion. Emotional upsets strike like lightning, but last much longer. Most people will come to resent getting their fingers plugged into the wall socket when it looks deliberate or callous. Even if the excitement cools, friendship can remain.

"I'm more upset at her for getting upset with me than she was upset at me to begin with."

• *With your Mercury*—your fascinating differences of opinion energize original thinking and creativity on both sides, if you can stand being made wrong, or at least being edited and corrected. You'll change your mind and discard old opinions and prejudices, or they will do it for you. You can articulate their ideals and may make plans to implement their aspirations. Together you're a genius.

"We've had to invent a new vocabulary to capture the meanings of the concepts we've discovered together. Grok?"

• *With your Venus*—you love their originality and uniqueness; you've never met anyone like them and are absolutely fascinated by their brilliance and specialness. They insight you to flaunt convention with them. In hard aspects, or with rigid placements, you'll have conflicts over moral codes and advanced ideas, as they attempt to liberate you. They didn't ask you if you were free, they just assumed you wanted to be. And you will be.

"Are you for real? God, I hope so." "I could never do that, no I couldn't . . . well, okay, just this once . . . again?"

• *With your Mars*—you energize the independence and assistance in this one. But you'll activate obstinacy if you attack their ideals or threaten their rights. A challenge leads to fun but (frequently) fierce debates: any assault precipitates explosive quarrels and fights. Delightful, unconventional sex and strange sensations fascinate. Hard aspects, rigid signs and some placements tend toward insistence and resistance. A serpent and bird relationship.

"You want what put where?" "Oooh! I never would've put a hammock in the hot tub"

"Over my dead body!" "OK, if that's how you want it!"

• *With your Jupiter*—you not only give them permission to be unique, you may boost them to be bizarre. A tendency to tolerate (or enjoy and even promote) outrageous behavior can make it sexual. A Svengali hypnotic fascination with a real character, or between a pair of oddballs. Usually a one-sided mentor-disciple relationship. There can be friction over who's at the head of the class, or you can take turns teaching. Philosophical differences and discoveries draw you together.

"By George, Higgins you did it, you did it. You passed her off as a lady, as royalty. Marvelous!" "Just you wait Henry Higgins, just you wait."

• *With your Saturn*—you want to curb their contrariness so you can concretize their calling, but they can feel like they're being fitted with cement overshoes when your attempts or aspects are too hard. They'd like you to lighten up and see beyond your considerations, and you say the problems are real and they aren't realistic. A tendency to play mental S&M games with each other, like "take-away," "withdraw" and "so what."

"If you don't quit that tinkering and get a real job, I'm going home to mother." "Ask me if I care." (See "The Outer Limits"later in this chapter, for aspects between Uranus and the other Outer Planets.)

• *With your Ascendant*—you treasure (and sometimes endure) the fascination with each other's oddities and individualism. This relationship gives you permission to be yourself. In hard aspects, you wish they wouldn't always insist on authenticity.

"After they made you, they broke the mold" "What mold, I

thought I was just putty in your hands?" "Putty? Marble, maybe." "Don't mutter when you call me a marvel."

Aspects To and From Neptune

• *With your Sun*—you bring their dreams to consciousness and may vitalize them into vibrancy. High-level connections inspire you, with an infusion of spirituality, and bring out your best. Deep understanding through empathy and identification may render most conversation unnecessary. You've got a psychic hotline or a metaphysical fax between you. Confusion creeps in when you're not paying attention. Harsh contacts can make this a relationship of exploitation and disillusionment. If you're too easy now, you might resent and regret it later.

"69 * $?" "!"

• *With your Moon*—in easy contacts, or with well integrated planets, this pair produces extreme (even eternal) trust. You understand their hopes, dreams and fears and nurture them. They intuit your needs and wants and accept them. In hard aspects, you question the reality, completeness and constancy of it all. Since Neptune both believes you and confuses you, chances are you'll both be deceived. The trust may be abused but *probably* can never be permanently damaged.

"Of course you can borrow my new car. Here are the keys I had made for you. You can toss the old keys to what used to be my car into the trash."

• *With your Mercury*—this one turns the lights on so you see colors or hear voices: however your imagination and intuition work, they work better here. Your faculties are elevated and inspired; you clarify theirs. But your "best friend" bit may appear to them as if you're their severest critic. This cross aspect is excellent for a writing team or artistic collaboration. Hard contacts and denial produce confusion and misunderstanding that continually threaten and may eventually destroy the connection.

"See the green dragon in the palm of my hand?" "Of course, don't you?"

• *With your Venus*—you love the way the spirit moves them, and the way they dance with their imagination. A dream of love; the love of your dreams. A tender vision of sharing and cooperation that may be realized in reality; at least, a sweet relationship or a loving friendship. With stress in life, or from aspects and placements, the acceptance may slip or get dragged into such eager gullibility that it almost demands deceit; it certainly presents the opportunity, and seems an invitation.

"If I built you a castle in the clouds would you live there with me forever?" "Isn't that where we are, dear?"

• *With your Mars*—you encourage their faith and dreams and urge them to act on them, which is what they call support. They inspire you to contributory action, and you know you've got charisma in their eyes. This may also be the desire of your dreams. It's easy to visualize making love with them. If you put a little energy into the vision, it can happen, and become inspired passion. Faith and care make it like magic. With the push-pull of hard aspects, they shimmer or shimmy in front of you and when you move in too fast, they back off, teasing; often imagining sex, but not realizing it.

"I didn't think I could do it, then I remembered that you knew I could, so I did. Now, how can I possibly show my deep and lasting gratitude?"

• *With your Jupiter*—they've never (or seldom) been so intuitive or so clear in their inspirations as they are with you. You understand what they see and what it means: maybe better than they do! They'll take your word for it, as they've given you the authority to interpret their vision. The interaction is mystical, spiritual, philosophical, an alliance of service that can become romantic, adding pleasure to the joy that bonds you.

"OH, I see now, love is an attractive force, just like gravity." "Yah, and gravity is the love every part of the universe feels for every other part."

• *With your Saturn*—you want to help to manifest their dreams, or at least get their feet on the ground so they can get a steady view of what their dreams might be. They feel that what you consider a kite string is a ship's anchor, and you're a wet blanket, too. You could begin by asking if they want coaching, then ask what they think they need. Accept a a small infusion of unused space. Harsh placements indicate intuitive suspicion, misunderstanding, and incompatible realities.

"Did you read that book I gave you on how to follow your bliss to the bank?" "No, but I slept with it under my pillow."

(NOTE: Neptune's aspects to other Neptunes, Uranus and

Pluto are in "The Outer Limits" later in this chapter.)

• *With your Ascendant*—you're in tune with their imagination and are sure it's special, even if it's a little "off." Your acceptance of and praise for their psychic ability may be a bit much. You tend to see them as potential victims, and will either rip-off or protect them according to *your* nature and *their* expectations.

"Okay, tell me where I'll be in five years, in 10 and in 20 years." "Right here with me." "Wow!"

Aspects To and From Pluto

• *With your Sun*—you get shot full of sexuality by this one, unless you don't like it, in which case you feel threatened and intimidated. You will get stronger, either through their empowerment or through their attempts to dominate you. They remind you of someone you've forgotten in infancy or seem to remember from a past life. You feel you've always known each other, and it might be true. There is a strong, strange attraction which frequently contains a paternal element. Your reactions tend to be compulsive, theirs sometimes intimidating.

"Excuse me, don't I know you from a past life?" "Know me? Do you mean that in the biblical sense?" "Whatever turns you on..." "Would you help me make a list?"

• *With your Moon*—love at first sight. Not necessarily the kind that strikes your eyes, but surely the love that strums your heart. You feel as if you've found a family member, friend, or lover from somewhere in time; very often there is a sense of Karmic past lives and an urge to nurture their purpose in this life. Extreme emotional depth and turgid turbulence. At times, the certainty that you can't live without them, and that you can't live with them either. There is concern over what it will cost you to be with them. There can be a fierce final rejection.

"I said I'd come back for you." "But I've been waiting since the second Crusade and I'm on my second marriage."

• *With your Mercury*—you had your own mind and your own opinions before you met this person. Now, their subtle pressure pushes you to re-examine your processes and re-think your opinions. If you can overcome the natural guardedness and (mild) suspicion, this deep sharing of ideas and speculation can lead to powerful revelations. With hard hits or between crude communicators, others attempt to force their conclusions down your throat and bend you to their will. Icy suspicion, frigid fear, or scathing scatologies kill communication.

"Are you saying that when you want my opinion you'll wring it out of me?!" "No, just that I'll tell you what it is."

• *With your Venus*—you've fallen in love at first sight, with the package, with the persona and mostly with the power within. This is pure, permanent fascination; you will never forget each other; Karmic lovers caught in a silken web of debt and favors. Hard Pluto contacts can extract exorbitant interest and you feel like a victim. Pluto cooks your values in their smelting furnace, eliminating the dross.

"Excuse me, my prince, but is 'Charming' your first name or your last name?" "It was my middle name, but it will be exactly and entirely 'as you wish,' Beauty, my love."

• *With your Mars*—you've found the eternal flame. This one turns you on, works toward permanence, and keeps you burning with desire. Thankfully, the feeling is usually mutual. This is pure passion; lust at its best. If the game's not at first willing, it can become a matter of conquest. Hard contacts and harsh charts turn this into an intense sexual (dominance) relationship, likely to express as exploitation, but which may still be wildly enjoyed on both sides. If frustrated, it can turn to enmity or spitefulness like Karmic rivals; if not lovers, then enemies, competitors, or crusading colleagues.

"What's love got to do with it?" "Who cares. Let's do what we have to."

• *With your Jupiter*—a liberating relationship of abandon, unrestrained excess and divine decadence, if the rest of your charts let it be. This is also a Karmic teacher-pupil relationship in which you (and they) have lessons to learn. The relationship may fail spectacularly from your resentment or rejection of the teacher's dominance, or because of sexual tension. It may also open you both to new worlds of wisdom and experience. There are conflicts of opinion and belief, especially about teachers, trainers and gurus, workshops and worship.

"I'm not getting into that, so if you're going there I'm not coming with you." "Will you, if we stay home and play together?"

• *With your Saturn*—your sense of authority and propriety confronts their sense of purpose and commitment. You could build empires together, but your fear of dominance (or rejection of regenerative empowerment) may abort this relationship. Otherwise the domination/resistance can develop into master-slave attitudes and altercations. Hard hits from harsh placements: instant, instinctive, intuitive distrust or dislike, even hatred. The temptation to harm each other gets extreme and may manifest mentally, emotionally, even physically

"You could be doing great things with your life. When are you going to quit slumming, and get on with it?" "As soon as you lighten-up and get off my back."

• *With your Ascendant*—you're sexually enticing to Plutonian partners, partly from their transferred energy. You bring out the sexual directness and straight-forwardness in them. They seem sexy, strong, and dominant to you, irresistible rather than just attractive.

"We'd be great together, if you weren't so shy." "Try me."

The Outer Limits

• *Uranus with Uranus*—in the conjunction, your insight into each other's ideals and the insistence on the rights you share ties you and your sub-generation together. In the Semi-Sextile and Sextile, the awareness of other banners clarifies your own commitments, but there may be some contention over the relative importance of targets for rebellion. In the square, the contradictions cause conflicts over causes and concern over what's worth fighting for and the weapons to be used. There are odd, strange relationships involved, with unpredictable side issues.

"Okay, we do the 'save the rain forest' rally together. Then while you're arguing for astrologers' rights, I'll do the school prayer march, then meet you at 'save the whales'."

NOTE: Natally, Uranus and Neptune are trine each other for most people born during the '40s, square for most of the '50s, and sextile for many '60s births. If you were born with these two in aspect, and are relating with someone close to your own age, you'll have this aspect across charts, and may have it both ways.

• *Uranus with Neptune*—your orneriness and radical ideas disrupt their dreams and shock them out of their futile fantasies. Their acceptance of your insights into their vision and your editorial suggestions for alteration and enhancement help them get it together again. Occult discussions and mystic experiments; a possible psychic synergy or spiritual alliance; frequent exploitation, victimization, and mutual mind-warping in off balance contacts.

NOTE: Pluto and Uranus are conjunct in the charts of people born in the mid to late '60s. Many of the Uranus in Cancer "runaways" sub-generation will have a conjunction with their parents and others of the 33-year-long Pluto-in-Cancer generation.

• *Uranus with Pluto*—you rattle their cage, challenge their commitments and shock them out of their resignation, complacency or inconsistency. If they don't retaliate by raining on your rally and burning your banners, you could find your ideals invigorated by their commitments, or even their obsessions. No one said it would be comfortable: catalytic, yes, even potentially monumental, but not easy. Intense, explosive sexual escapades or exploitations may only threaten, might actually happen, but will seldom persist, without other strong indications. A fascinating weirdness; hard and harsh contacts that may produce antipathy, intense dislike, threats of harm, irrevocable rejection.

"What you do is absolutely inconsistent with what you say, so, from now on, I'm ignoring both." "Ignore this."

• *Neptune with Neptune*—in the conjunction, you strongly share, accept and support each other's hopes, dreams, fantasies and illusions as well as your generation's common societal phobias and social solutions. In soft aspects, their generation mystifies you. As you begin to understand their dream, you're glad you've got your own. With hard aspects, total confusion, disbelief (and sometimes disdain or distaste) obscure communication other than inspirational or artistic.

"How can you believe that? Why would anyone believe that when they could believe what I know?" "Works for me."

NOTE: Pluto and Neptune were Sextile in the charts of everyone born from the early '40s through the middle '80s. If you're one of these people, relating to someone born within about five years of you, you'll have this aspect in one or both directions. Many of the "Baby Boomers" of Pluto-in-Leo/Neptune-in-Libra fame have Pluto conjunct their parents' (generation's) Neptune. Also, their Neptune is often squared by their parents' (generation's) Pluto, thus The Generation Gap.

• *Pluto with Neptune*—in soft contacts, you accept their preoccupations and nurture their commitments. You may even be tolerant of their obsessions. You spiritualize their sexuality and welcome it, when it has been sufficiently elevated by your Neptune. In less positive circumstances or with other chart conflicts, you will probably use each other and wind up both resentful at being shortchanged. Rip-offs are possible and likely in special situations. Pluto intensifies Neptune's holy image so you dazedly follow its blinding light in a daze into unreality. Pluto's manipulation or obsessions can also pervert the dream and bury it, if not actually destroying it.

"Did the earth move for you, too?" "Yes, right into another dimension where rainbows walk and unicorns talk, where brooks babble, and the wind whispers, where..." "Uh Huh, Home."

• *Pluto with Pluto*—in the conjunction, your personal versions of your generation's obsessions, preoccupations and commitments are intensified, catalyzed and regenerated through involvement with those who share a similar commitment or controlling force. Your determination drives the other's desires as well. The whole generation plays a part in the process, but those with close aspects play a major role in the design and direction of your life. Soft aspects with Pluto indicate a Karmic connection, as if you've gotten together (again) to empower each other. Possibly an intense (even explosive) relationship, sexual revitalization, developmental breakthroughs, and new levels of influence are probable. Hard aspects indicate powerplays, struggles and confrontations, even conflagrations or awkward, resentful empowerment.

"What'll it be, Tennis to Led Zeppelin with Coke, or balling to Sgt. Pepper on the grass?" "How about Die Walkuere on the balcony with tea, after both?"

Final Notes

Process is the way life is unfolding. It is what is happening in your experience of living; what you are involved in, or going through; what your circumstances are, or are becoming. This is shown by the position and movement of the *transiting* planets. We examine the transits through Houses for each person and look at what is available for, and important to, one person as compared to the other. Analyzing aspects from transiting planets to both person's natal positions shows what each of them is going through and how they are developing out of the House placement dispositions of each person's planets in the other's horoscope. Transiting House positions and aspects then indicate the process of dealing with life and realizing potential in relationship time.

Living is a dynamic process. A person's interests, activities, opportunities, even emotions, affections, and relationships change over time. Discovering to what degree and in which areas the two people are—and will often or always be—operating in sync, or out of sync, is important to understanding and enhancing their experience of coordination, participation, and co-creation: their compatibility.

The willingness, intention and commitment, of *both* people, to create and enjoy a satisfying relationship—and the competent, responsible behaviors that arise from that—are what's required for any relationship to flourish. This grand intent may or may not be sufficient; but the thrust is essential, no matter what the charts indicate. Nothing is more essential than open, honest, complete communication. The quality of the relationship is determined by the *quality of the communication.*

The *necessary* ingredients in a satisfying life and in a satisfying relationship are the right mixture of *harmony and excitement.* Some measure of each is essential to every person and every relationship. The particular blend or proportion of these is individually determined. It will most likely be different for each person in the relationship.

Every relationship or personal interaction is a combination of price and payoff, or perhaps better stated, price *versus* payoff. It costs you something, if only time and attention, to be with someone. There are no free lunches or free relationships. Also, there is *always* a payoff, even if you don't recognize it consciously, at the time. There are no interactions out of which you get nothing at all, although you may not truly appreciate or respect the payoff.

The payoff is what you're in the relationship for, what you gain from being involved. If the payoff is worth the price, you pay it. If it is not, then you don't. People have their own standards, preferences, tolerances and requirements in a relationship. They always decide to participate, or not, based on their own values, never on yours.

All of us have an "Unpayable Price," something we will not give up, or put up with, no matter what the payoff. For many people there is a "Priceless Payoff," something so valuable or so essential to them that they will pay *any* price for it.

You bring to any relationship your own Assets and Liabilities, shown by your horoscope; so does the other person. These are your combined strengths and weaknesses, pluses and minuses, gifts and lacks, talents and debilities, knowledge and ignorance, etc. Each of you, in the relationship, gets to work with and/or play with the other's assets and liabilities, as well as your own. The assets may combine, and they may balance or counter each other's liabilities. Conversely, the liabilities may combine and work counter to each other's assets.

If we conceive a "Relationship Scale," at the top there would be unity. Then, we would regress through harmony, complement, duality, dichotomy, paradox, contradiction, conflict, and antithesis. The outer planets dramatically help to position relationships within the spectrum of this scale of interaction dynamic and degree of fulfillment.

Mary E. Shea

Mary E. Shea, M.A. Psych., is the writer/co-editor of a yearly electional astrology datebook called *Good Days Action Planning Guide*, a book that can be understood by the general public, yet has the technical information professional astrologers need. This guide helps you plan activities for the desired outcome. She calls this "masterminding the world." Mary also wrote *Planets in Solar Returns: Yearly Cycles of Growth and Transformation* (1991 ACS), about yearly birthday horoscopes. This book was written specifically for astrologers.

Mary does astrological counseling for clients across the country via phone and tape. Her readings are psycho-spiritual, as well as practical.

Mary is an international speaker and a lecturer at many astrological conventions. She is on the faculty of the Princeton Astrological Society and a teacher of the Gilbert Navarro Correspondence School of Horary Astrology.

Besides teaching astrology, Mary also runs workshops on experiencing and balancing the chakras, opening the heart (Heart Journey), and spiritual paths to consciousness.

Making Choices with Outer Planet Transits

Mary E. Shea

Uranus, Neptune, and Pluto in transit represent three very different processes for change, growth, and the breakdown of established structures. It is important to remember that these three heavenly bodies are trans-Saturnian planets. For a long time astronomers and astrologers thought Saturn was the outermost planet in our solar system. It was considered the limit, the symbol of the end of our immediate awareness. Saturn is the last planet we can see unaided with our own eyes. But with the invention of the telescope, the discovery of Uranus, Neptune, and Pluto followed. We broke outside the limits, physically, mentally, psychologically, and also spiritually. Together and individually, each in its own way, these planets are associated with *breaking barriers*.

Saturn rules structures that have stood the test of time and laws that were developed to rule the masses. It is the planet associated with setting the limits that condense energy into matter. Uranus rules modernizations. It breaks barriers by calling for improvements on what has been built and established. Uranus also signals a desire for freedom from all restrictions. It is the only planet which spins on its side while in orbit! For this reason, Uranus is associated with the rebel, the person who does not conform. Laws might be alright for the masses, but what about the individual test case. Those with impulses for Uranian freedom want to understand how a broad-based law applies to their particular situation. They want to be the exceptions to the rule. In this way, Uranian methods chip away at Saturnian structures.

The principles associated with Neptune go beyond Saturn by testing for the spirit of the law. The question becomes, "what is the intent of this rule?" The law is only a reflection of the original purpose behind it. It is the Neptunian design to penetrate to the deepest meaning. Increased sensitivity is the mode by which this is done. Those who are sensitive to the spirit of the law, do not need the law at all. They innately do what is best by adapting the spirit-purpose to the specific situation. In this way, Neptune indicates timeless principles that go beyond outdated Saturnian rules and rigid structures.

Pluto represents the next step in human development— *empowerment*. Pluto symbolizes the force needed to empower the lifestyle envisioned during the search for individual freedom and spiritual purpose. Saturn at its worst can be the "herd mentality" with everyone thinking the same. Uranus is the ability to break away from the standard to think for oneself. Neptune indicates comprehension of Universal principles brought about by increased sensitivity. Pluto, the planet of power, represents the strength to live the new system created in the mind. Without Uranus, one can get bogged down in the norm. Without Neptune, one becomes a rebel without a cause. Without Pluto, one becomes a spiritual wimp, knowing and understanding certain beliefs, but unable to act on them.

For the next few years, these three outer planets will be traveling together. Pluto in Scorpio will be transiting sextile to the Uranus-Neptune conjunction in Capricorn. This makes for a very powerful combination. Those people experiencing the transit of one of these planets will probably experience the transits of all three. Developments will be complex, and growth will be accelerated.

Sensitivity to Outer Planet Transits

All of us are different in our sensitivity to the outer planets. You might be very sensitive to Pluto and not notice the passing of Uranus and Neptune. The best way to discern your sensitivity and response pattern is to look at the natal chart itself. For example, if you have a prominent and strongly aspected Uranus in your chart, you will probably experience strong change as a mode for growth. If Neptune is strong in your chart, you should be very sensitive to change on a more subtle level. You may not need external change in your life to be aware of a shift in consciousness. If Pluto is strong in your chart, you are more likely to respond with power to intense situations. Individuals are very different in their awareness of the processes associated with these planets. By watching your pattern of response, you can discern which planets are especially meaningful for you. Go back over important events and turning points in your life to see which transits were occurring at those times.

Timing

The transits of the three outer planets can last for a couple of years, especially when a "triple transit" occurs. In this situation, the transiting planet passes in aspect to the natal planet three times: first direct, then after turning retrograde, and finally as it moves ahead direct for the last time. This process may take as long as three years for Pluto. The outer planet can have an effect on you for that entire period of time.

Because we differ in our sensitivity to the outer planets, we cannot talk about a definite orb. It is different for different people. The process usually begins slowly, getting stronger as the transiting planet draws near and then fading out after the pass. Almost everyone will notice changes occurring when a planet is in orb by less than one degree.

Work with your transits positively rather than waiting for them to happen to you. If you can, create an avenue of expression by planning an *appropriate* experience during contact. For example, one man planned his first Kundalini Yoga class around his Pluto transit. That night he had his first out-of-body experience. A conscious choice such as this helps to focus and release your personal energy in a controlled way.

Uranus Transits

Uranus indicates the need for change. While Uranus is transiting so closely with Neptune, you have to wonder if some people need to be anesthetized to make changes. Either major transitions or incessant fluctuations emerge as the pattern of manifestation depending on how the individual copes with the personal push for freedom. Transformations may occur quickly and require a long period of adjustment, *or* progress slowly, possibly occurring late in the transit and only after a long period of anticipation or restlessness. As a rule, most changes are expected, predicted, and initiated by the person. Many changes are carefully planned and well-executed, involving a minimum of tension and anxiety.

With Uranus transits, you cannot stay with old structures. You must modernize and create more freedom in your life. By studying the transiting placement of Uranus and the natal planets it aspects, you can see where changes are more urgently needed and more likely to occur. Conditions associated with the House position of transiting Uranus are likely to evolve significantly over the year and the focus of change will be directly related to the planet being aspected.

Increasing restlessness is the early psychological warning signal for this transit. The desire for change will increase as situations are outgrown. You will feel unsettled. If you wish to work with the process, *welcome* the opportunity for adjustment and make all the necessary preparations. Start by asking questions. Consider alternative ways of handling those issues facing you. Do not lock yourself into one pattern of growth. Allow changes and insights to develop naturally during the transit.

Generally, it is only when the individual thwarts needed changes or controls situations tightly that tensions manifest in the form of anxiety. These emotions result from ambivalent feelings in those who resist their own process. These people get caught between a fear of change and a strong desire for the very change they fear. A dual mind-set takes over, one built on an approach to, and also an avoidance of, change. When one is unable to affect needed changes, the mind splits between two mutually exclusive goals. Anxiety results. Eventually, mental ambivalence and erratic commitments to two very different paths are reflected in fluctuating external conditions. Long overdue, yet still avoided changes, manifest in the environment as disruption caused by others, or by areas of neglect. Adding to the anxiety is a perceived loss of control over external situations.

Eventually, the restlessness and tension rise to a feverish pitch until one finally agrees to make changes, or can no longer prevent their occurrence. When conditions reach this intensity, people usually make reactionary changes, without careful consideration or adequate preparation. They do not have the tools to handle a process they have been avoiding all along. Instead of welcomed transitions, sudden upheavals occur. If you would truly control your own destiny, you would listen to the need for change and respond to the earliest hints of restlessness. You would give yourself the freedom to work toward a conscious transition before a crisis arose.

Consistent with the desire for change is the need for freedom. You cannot maneuver if you are locked within a restrictive environment. The push for freedom is a common precursor of change, but at other times, the change itself is the motivating force behind the process. Sometimes, *both* mechanisms are operating and intertwined. Freedom allows the process of change to develop smoothly. Freedom is also a frequent by-product of the changes that occur.

When you are functioning at your best and working positively with Uranian concepts, you move easily through a series of questions and alternatives, eventually making choices and taking independent action. You learn and grow from all encounters. Your desire for options, answers to questions, and alternatives to problems leads you to many different situations, persons, or concepts.

At this time, it is important to watch what experiences you are drawn to. Observation is a necessary step before choice. Do not resist the insights that follow. Take in fresh information. Learn to value all experiences. You will see that no one person, place, or idea is perfect. The same is true for your existing circumstances—those you hold to so tightly. This realization brings you to the door of choice, aware of the changes that need to be made and the possible options for the future.

The arrival of insight signals the beginning of the period of decision. You start by reassessing your involvements and commitments, and then choose to detach either internally or externally from those situations, persons, or concepts which restrict your growth or no longer have anything to offer you. You learn as much from defining what you *don't like* as you do from defining what you *do like*. The changing environment—comparisons and contrasts—accentuates what is important and what is not. Take corrective action and adjust circumstances to your needs. Separations might occur, but not always. Detachment is a more accurate word, and you can detach internally while maintaining the external experience. But freedom and choice must arise on either the inner or outer plane. You must choose, otherwise the choices will be made for you.

Remember that this process of question, decision, and independent action is an ongoing one, occurring on many different levels simultaneously. Events might be sudden and complete, or reoccur in numerous small steps.

All planets represent a creative process. Uranus is the creative process experienced through change. The exposure to various ideas, situations, and people stimulates original thought and sudden insight. One becomes accustomed to looking at life from different perspectives. The multifaceted approach encourages working with new ideas. In this way, the individual begins to participate in the process of change by creating options.

Uranus Transiting the Sun

Uranus aspecting the Sun suggests a time when egotistical forces of the conscious personality must be released or transformed either internally or externally for growth to continue. This transit is like spring-cleaning for the ego. Even though you pick up your house daily and keep it clean, sooner or later you must do spring-cleaning. The windows need washing, the rugs need beating, and the walls need scrubbing. You clean the closets and throw out what is no longer useful while you reorganize what you wish to retain. The same is true of the ego. Eventually, you outgrow your present "beingness" and find that certain behaviors are no longer useful. This excess baggage needs to be eliminated or transformed. Uranus transits to the Sun indicate a time when this is most likely to happen.

It is natural to latch on to what works and to stay with it. Familiarity breeds security, even when what is familiar is also burdensome. We all get "snagged" by a particular idea, fear, or mode of being. We put blinders on and refuse to see the major or minor changes that need to be made. We are afraid to let go of our positions, unaware of options. We fail to see beyond the needs of a snagged ego, desperate to maintain a passé position, fearful of what the future might bring, frozen in time and space.

Uranus is the planet which symbolizes freedom, desired or not, from a stalled position. The more resistant you have been in the past and the longer the forces of tension have been allowed to build up, the more powerful and less controllable is the release. The more options you have available, the more likely you are to channel the changes in a productive manner. Certainly, the search for alternatives is crucial to assuaging fears, releasing tension, and directing results. You can move on to something better during this transit, or you can simply move on.

During the time of the Uranus transit to your Sun, significant life changes will occur, either externally or internally. Possible events include pregnancy/birth, career switch/job transfer, marriage/divorce, relocation, or illness for you or someone close to you.

Internal psychological transformations are just as likely to occur, even more so for those who have created the options. Included in the inner process are movements from boredom to originality. Freedom replaces restriction. The final outcome, whether external or internal, is associated with the amount of pent-up personal energy to be released, and the range of options created. Resistance tends to lead to externalization. If you are in touch with your masculine side, the process is more likely to be internal and generated by you. However, if you are not in touch with your masculine side, and especially if you are a woman who resists her more assertive urges, the period of growth is most apt to be focused externally on a significant man in your life.

> **Sun at 13 degrees Capricorn in the 12th House, sextile to the Midheaven at 15 Scorpio and trine to Jupiter and Saturn in the 3rd House at 5 and 7 degrees Taurus respectively.**

Jean was a middle-aged woman who was having trouble in her relationship to her husband. With her 12th House Sun, she wanted him to take the lead in most matters, but he refused. He rarely took the initiative and resisted most changes. Jean, on the other hand, had many ideas about what could or should be done, especially with regard to the house. She was the motivating force behind the decision to put an addition on their small home, and the construction and renovation took over a year. During this time, Jean consulted with her husband on everything, but he offered more resistance and negativity than input. Jean wanted companionship in the building process, something her husband didn't offer. He objected to everything, making the process much more arduous. They fought repeatedly. Jean hated working alone and having to make decisions. She also hated having to push to get the smallest thing done. Jean was in a dilemma and stalled.

The push-pull situation went on until Uranus contacted Jean's Sun. At that point, her husband became seriously ill and could offer no assistance or resistance whatsoever on any decision, even those associated with his care. Jean was forced to take complete responsibility for all decisions. With Neptune also transiting her Sun, compassion rose. She saw her husband for what he was and understood what he could not be. She stepped back from trying to change him and assumed the very power she had avoided. *She stopped asking for permission* and *he stopped giving her resistance.* Because of his illness, she accepted the freedom she had avoided.

Uranus Transiting the Moon

Probably the most common external manifestation associated with Uranus transits to the Moon is a change in domestic situation. Either you move from one place to another, or someone else moves in or out of your home. A "musical chairs" routine can occur in the home as occupants move from one bedroom to another or change the house around to suit personal needs or preferences. Renovations, additions, repairs, and redecoration may be included in the grand plan for change.

A disruption in the home or family can lead to an *emotional* reorientation. On the other hand, emotional changes can be the motivating force behind modifications to the home. It's a question of which comes first. Changes occur on more than one level. Emotional transformations go hand in hand with events occurring on the physical plane. While Uranus transits to the Sun indicate house cleaning for the ego, Uranus transits to the Moon indicate *emotional* house-cleaning. Nonproductive patterns of response need to be eliminated from your repertoire so that true intimacy can occur. Feelings of rejection, guilt, fear, and anger snag your development and lock you into stalemated conditions.

Uranus transits to the Moon indicate a time when you can break away from patterns holding you back. The process of emotional release might be easier for women than men. A male who is not in touch with his emotions will tend to have a difficult time with a woman during this transit. She might be more in tune with tensions occurring in their relationship and create the necessary changes. Females who are equally out of touch will tend to have trouble with their mothers. Though the purpose is always internal growth, the triggering events can be external.

Relationships are bound to be affected by all this internal and external coming and going. You could become involved in a new relationship, or an old one might go through a period of transition or separation. Strong attractions are also possible at this time. If you feel caught in an emotional rut, dramatic changes are more likely to occur.

As your situation and emotional needs change, you face new issues and problems. Changing scenarios accentuate your ability or inability to handle emotions and relationships effectively. Negatively, emotional control is difficult and feelings are erratic. You are overwhelmed one day, or detached and cool the next. You say or do things without considering the emotional consequences. But then, off-the-cuff reactions might be necessary to give you the freedom needed to make internal or external changes.

Positively, this can be a time of emotional potential, full of new feelings and greater intimacy. You could circumvent negative or debilitating emotions by creating new emotional patterns.

Moon at 11 degrees Capricorn conjunct Mars at 7 degrees Capricorn all in the 6th House. Ascendent is 14 degrees Cancer.

Karen became a new mother as Uranus transited her Moon. She had waited a long time for this. She was in her thirties when she married and wanted to start a family immediately. The role suited her well. Although it was a major change for her, she thrived with the new responsibility. In the early months, her days were very hectic, but after things quieted down, Karen grew restless. Her husband was frequently away on business. His new company was doing well, but required much of his time. Karen missed seeing him, but knew not to dwell on negative feelings. She was used to working full-time, so she decided she needed a project to occupy her days. Since money was not a problem, she began to design a new home for her family. She drew up the plans with an architect, hired a construction crew and oversaw the building process. The house went through many changes while under construction and is still not finished, but it has given Karen an outlet for her restlessness. Meanwhile, she is still encouraging her husband to spend more time at home. She wants him to enjoy their good fortune. The Moon symbolism for home, house, family, and feeling all were challenged and intensified by the Uranus transit.

Uranus Transits to Mercury

Uranus transits to Mercury suggest a time when you are open to new and different ideas, methods, and ways of thinking. Insights arise from what you are learning and studying, or from concepts you are developing on your own. Your thoughts grow more complex and profound as you learn to see things differently, viewing situations from many points of reference. Thinking becomes holographic with multifaceted connections into other areas of life and many levels of interpretation. Straight-line thinking becomes passé.

A mental shift occurs from left-brain critical processes to right-brain creativity and understanding. Some find this shift difficult to make, but most make it easily. As facts become interconnected, the ability to learn, understand, and remember increases. Sudden realizations are the order of the day, and psychic openings are possible as intuition is heightened. Creativity grows, and you are wise to take advantage of these impulses. Strive for originality by investigating new ideas and brainstorming with others. Open up to new possibilities by eliminating left-brain resistances and favoring insight over rational thinking.

Implied with this transit is an increase in problem-solving ability. You are able to approach problems from a variety of perspectives and need not get locked into one way of thinking or being. Alternatives help you to break stalemates and negative thought patterns that hinder growth. You become mentally versatile, adapting to situations as they arise or modifying circumstances to suit your needs.

The freedom to investigate many ideas occasionally leads to a very unfocused mind. Concentration becomes difficult if you constantly run from one project or concept to another. Thinking is interrupted by erratic impulses and insights. It becomes difficult for you to stay with one thought. New information is more exciting than reorganizing what you already know or concentrating on what you have to learn. If you must work on a lengthy project requiring a sustained mental effort, take frequent breaks and rotate tasks. Keep your interest level high by being very creative and spontaneous in your approach.

Some individuals experience psychological strain during this time. Increased nervousness can usually be traced back directly to a stressful situation. Investigate the sources of tension. If possible, withdraw from situations which tax your mental and physical health. Practice relaxation techniques and avoid stimulants. Work on calming and nurturing your nervous system.

Mercury at 6 degree Virgo in the 7th House. Midheaven at 2 and Mars at 8 degrees Sagittarius.

Debra took a job as an executive secretary for the head of a large company just as Uranus squared her Mercury. Soon after she started working, she learned that her job would involve some travel. At the time, Debra had a tremendous fear of flying and was incapable of getting on a plane. She would have panic attacks just thinking about it. She had to overcome her fear or lose her job. It was time to free herself from this debilitating phobia.

Debra decided to see if hypnosis would help her. During her weekly visits with the hypnotherapist, she learned to relax her body and reprogram her mind. She also learned about dream analysis and past-life regression. Things started to make sense to her as she began to work with her fear. Her intuition grew, and she had great insights into her own healing. After a year, she was ready for the big test and flew across country for the first time. She is now a regular (though admittedly sometimes reluctant) air traveler.

Uranus Transiting Venus

Uranus transits to Venus usually denote changes in relationships. For some people, this will mean a sudden attraction and the excitement of a new love. Involvements can be very strong and very quick, but may not have staying power. It's easy come, easy go and extremely exciting in between. Intense attractions might lead to marriage, but short-term affairs or loose associations are more likely. Turn-arounds occur as friends become lovers and some love relationships seem more friendly than intimate. Less conventional arrangements are also possible. These include clandestine or extramarital affairs, homosexual contacts, May-December romances, and long-distance love.

An already existing relationship can go through a period of adjustment. Difficult associations will most likely end or become on-again, off-again erratic involvements. Permanent or temporary separations are likely, especially when commitments are lacking or never kept.

But for those in healthy associations, changes will occur within the relationships themselves. The Uranus transit will not indicate a break in ties or a loss of dedication between lovers; bonds can strengthen. Changes will be discussed and agreed upon by both parties. One person might need the freedom to pursue a personal, career, or educational goal. A partner might be totally supportive of this move. Changes that affect both parties are likely, and issues of fidelity and open marriage are sometimes topics for discussion. External factors such as pregnancy and health also lead to change.

A general mood of disruption and restlessness permeates all partnerships, whether old or new. Expectations and behavioral patterns which were once taken for granted may now be nonexistent. New patterns emerge, and you can expect the unexpected. While the necessary adjustments are being made, the continuing disruption can cause conflict and temporary distancing between the people involved.

Financial changes will also occur when Uranus transits Venus. There may be a break or fluctuation in income because of commissions, incentives, lay-offs, or part-time hours. Financial windfalls in the form of gifts and inheritances occur, but shortages and large expenses are just as likely. During this transit, some people become self-employed while others dispose of excess possessions.

Venus at 11 degrees Libra in the 4th House square the Ascendant at 18 degrees Cancer.

Joan had been divorced from her husband John for five years. It was a very bitter divorce and the fighting had continued without stopping. Joan was always suing her ex-husband, and he was always harassing her or counter-suing. Joan worried about money. She was dependent on John for support and had to pinch pennies to make ends meet. The support checks were generally late since John delayed every transaction. So Joan went back to court to have her husband's salary garnished and the check deposited automatically.

Things were quiet for a while, but then John retaliated. Using the account number for the automatic check deposit, he was able to withdraw all Joan's money leaving her penniless. He did this the day Uranus transited square Joan's Venus for the second time. Joan is now back in court suing her husband for return of the funds and also suing the bank for wrongful conduct and damages.

Uranus Transiting Mars

Strong changes, usually self-initiated, are associated with Uranus transits to Mars. Freedom of action is the motivating force behind these changes and any restriction will be met with assertiveness, if not anger. You refuse to get trapped in a situation without options. You need room to maneuver. Anything boring is out. Anything new and exciting is accepted and encouraged. You reject tired routines and repetitive conflicts.

Changes range from a constant stream of minor adjustments to dramatic and sweeping transformations. Either change can be beneficial or detrimental, depending on individual differences and the manifestation. Delays are unlikely, since speed is of the essence. Once the process has begun, matters tend to move forward quickly. During this time, you may become more assertive or more detached. You may set concrete goals for the future or retreat from an unrewarding path. The tendency is to abandon situations that are no longer productive or comfortable. The amount of control you have over these changes depends on the choices you make or refuse to make.

Changes in relationships are common with this transit and are most apt to occur in those associations which involve sexual activity or require an assertive or aggressive demeanor. New and powerful attractions are possible, since sexual energy is heightened in those who are experienced, or is awakened in those who are not. Sexual experimentation increases as you investigate different forms of stimulation and diverse techniques. Occasionally, preferences change, as one is more likely to meet people with different sexual orientations.

During this transit, behavior patterns might be somewhat erratic, and on-again, off-again situations will exist. Partners come together, relationships break up, and change is the order of the day. A need for greater freedom is usually the cause.

Mars at 9 degrees Cancer in the 4th House opposed Saturn at 6 degrees Capricorn in the 10th House and square Mercury at 0 degrees Aries in the 1st. Transiting Uranus in the 10th House.

When Uranus transited in opposition to his Mars, Ted was in his early thirties and very unhappy with his situation at home. His marriage was not stable. Although he loved his wife and they were still good friends, they realized that they were not happy together as husband and wife. They had numerous fights which left Ted feeling drained and withdrawn.

Ted was also dissatisfied with his job. He had worked for a wonderful company for many years, but now, with the recession, the company was in financial trouble. His boss, who was normally pleasant to work for, succumbed to stress and took his anger out on anyone available. Job security was nonexistent. Ted felt trapped. He did not have the education he needed to get ahead. Nor did he have the time to go to school or even a quiet place to study on his own. Tension at home was high, and his wife was constantly making demands on him.

Finally Ted made some decisions and took action: he cut back his hours at work, dropping to 30 hours a week. He refused to fight with his wife and moved out of the house into an apartment, sharing expenses with a roommate. As he and his wife both began to calm down, their relationship got better. With his wife already working, they were able to budget their incomes and share the expenses of raising their daughter equally. This left Ted with enough money to pay for school and enough time to study. He is now continuing his education and dating his wife.

Neptune Transits

Neptune has been interpreted as many things on many levels: confusion, deception, spirituality, and creativity (just to mention a few). But when Neptune transits a natal planet, there is a common theme that occurs over and over again and is consistent with the psychological transition taking place. First and foremost, the Neptune transit is a *call to understand and work with subtle and not so subtle human and Universal principles and energies*. These forces are brought to your attention by an increased sensitivity on one or more levels:

- You might develop allergies as your body becomes more sensitive to certain foods or environments. You learn to avoid those substances and situations which make you ill. Sometimes you have to work to identify the offenders.

- You may become more sensitive to those who are wounded, whether they are emotionally upset, spiritually in need, physically ill, or disabled. As sensitivity increases, compassion rises, and you find a way to help. But if you are commonly taken advantage of and weakened by self-sacrifice, Neptune will herald a time when you must eliminate the activities which drain you.

- Your increased sensitivity may call you to express yourself creatively in new ways. This can be a time of great insight through symbol and metaphor.

- Spiritually, you may be drawn to a religion, philosophy, or thoughts which have great import to your understanding of life and the world you live in. Unfortunately, what you understand and try to live may not be understood by others. If insights do not fit your present life situation, you can get caught between two worlds, not sure of the next step to take. Disillusionment can follow if your beliefs prove false.

- For some people, the increased sensitivity will become too much to bear. They will seek to withdraw from raw perceptions or drown their senses in drugs, booze, or addictions. Finding it difficult to accept, understand, and grow with their new sensitivity, they will feel compelled to retreat from it.

It is the increased sensitivity and the need to direct these sensations and subtle forces in a meaningful way that are the hallmarks of the Neptune transit. As the protective shell which keeps you immune to external influences sheds still another layer and your awareness grows a little more, *you are offered a choice.* You can either develop with, and learn from these new sensations, moving to a higher understanding, or you can try to block out or ignore the new influences, staying with your old pattern of behavior. Sometimes the process is frustrating and arduous. You are often asked to give more when you have already given everything you have to a chain of events you do not fully understand. But there are rewards for those who stick with the progress and try to get an overview of the big picture.

Choices are not limited to the spiritual plane alone, but can occur on the emotional, mental, and physical levels also. For example, Neptune on the *spiritual level* is associated with the Universal Oneness, Karmic Laws, Ideals, a strong trust in God, and higher beliefs which form the backbone of spirituality. The growth process on the spiritual level has ramifications on the other levels as well. Each level of experience supports and triggers the others. It is all the insights on all of the levels which eventually help you toward a more rewarding and fulfilling lifestyle.

The lower manifestation of a Neptune transit on the spiritual level is disillusionment with beliefs. The individual becomes entangled in despair, or in fanatical concepts and outright fantasy. Distortions at the spiritual and philosophical level eventually cause distortions in perceptions on all levels of awareness as the trickle-down principle takes effect. Spiritual despair is the result rather than enlightenment. Hopelessness sets in, and the support needed for growth is thwarted.

The same dichotomy of choices is present on the other planes also. At the *emotional level*, the individual is capable of great compassion and sensitivity towards others. This is a time when empathic understanding strengthens the bonds between loved ones. You are called to give more than you have in the past while expanding your circle of concern to those you might not know.

The more difficult manifestation of a Neptune transit on the emotional level is a susceptibility to anxiety and worry. The sensitivity which is meant to foster understanding instead heightens one's vulnerability to life, others, and the future. Fear prevails. There is no trust in God, Higher Self, or the Universal Plan emanating from the spiritual level to support your decisions. You feel lost and abandoned, lacking both spiritual and emotional connections. In very negative situations, real relationships are not established and emotional deception and fantasy occur.

At the *mental level*, creativity and inspiration help to expand the individual's intellectual capacity. Neptune is more closely associated with right brain activity than the left. New abilities and insights can develop in those willing to let go of preconceived notions and thought patterns. Observation, free-floating awareness, and an openness to seemingly irrational insights can lead to brilliant realizations.

Difficulties at the mental level involve confusion and deception. What you are told is different from what you intuitively feel. Changing beliefs and thought patterns leave you without a point of reference. You flounder because you are unable to make good decisions. New insights contradict old ways of thinking, and you are unable to discern the truth. The development of right-brain processes breeds distrust. Creativity is thwarted, experimentation restricted. The child never gets to play. Without an understanding of the big picture, mental energy is wasted through a lack of cohesiveness. One focuses on insignificant details. There is no system, no rhyme, and no reason to thought, no purpose to the course you have set upon.

And finally, Neptune on the *physical level* is service to others. Principles filtered down from the spiritual, emotional, and mental levels begin to flow into daily practices on the mundane plane. There is a consistency; as above, so below. It is possible to physically manifest the spirituality you aspire to. You are able *to do that which you believe, feel, and say.* Neptune at its highest level of manifestation on the physical plane is a direct reflection of the enlightened promise made at the spiritual level.

When things start to go wrong on the other levels, it seems that only difficulties filter down to the physical level. When it rains, it pours! Confusion, disorganization, and exhaustion are most apt to occur. You lack a total concept necessary to unify your actions and prioritize tasks according to their importance. You are overly sensitive on all levels without an understanding of how to handle that sensitivity or respond to outside pressures.

During Neptune transits, any of the above mentioned insights or difficulties can occur. Sometimes, actions are a confused mixture of ambivalent responses. This contributes to the confusion. The more focused the individual is on a search for answers and the need to understand the newfound sensitivity, the more cohesive actions will tend to become. A unifying principle at the spiritual level structures responses, focuses energy, and promotes understanding right on down the line.

Neptune Transiting the Sun

Neptunian transits to the Sun indicate that the ego of the native is being challenged. Lessons in humility and vulnerability are common as egotistical responses to life are thwarted and denied. Personal identity is questioned, especially if you identify more with *what you do* than *who you are.* You cannot "play a role" during this transit, you must be real. Role-playing leads to anger. Personality inconsistencies result in confusion. A personality crisis is likely for those who lost touch with self somewhere along the way. For these individuals, stripping away the ego and the personality facade results in an unstructured response to life and a temporary loss of control and direction.

During this time, you are more likely to be confronted with your own human frailties or those of someone close. Awareness of personal shortcomings opens you to understanding the shortcomings of others. Empathy becomes easier when you are no longer perfect yourself. We all suffer from a pandemic disease called humanness, and we all eventually die from it. But that does not mean we have to stop living now to accommodate someone else's character flaw. Martyrdom and victimization are an exaggeration of the issue if you give to the point of losing your sense of self. Your ego becomes so identified with a self-sacrificing role, you forget who you are. In these situations, personal or second-hand involvement with alcoholism, drugs, addictions, or co-dependent situations is possible. Physical tiredness follows.

This transit is meant to arouse understanding and compassion. You are asked to give to those less fortunate and truly deserving. It is a time to be less concerned with self-oriented interests and more concerned with the needs of others. But you cannot ignore the true self when setting standards for behavior. Wise giving is more intelligent and more beneficial than giving from guilt without purpose or understanding. Sensitivity leads to a stronger sense of self and an enlightened ego which chooses according to the needs of all those involved.

Sun at 16 degrees Cancer conjunct Pluto at 17 degrees, both in the 7th House.

Carol is a sixty-two year old woman who has been taking care of her mother all of her life. Her mother is now eighty-five years old and senile. She has been living with Carol and her husband for forty years. Carol feels overwhelmed by guilt whenever she entrusts the care of her mother to someone else. She will not hire a nurse to watch her mother, nor will she take her to a senior citizen day care center. Placing her in a home is out of the question. Though her mother has periods of poor health, she could easily live another ten years. Carol feels physically drained and mentally trapped by her mother's need for around-the-clock care. She feels she has given up much of her own life to care for this woman who might now outlive her and/or her husband. Her husband is past the age of retirement, but has refused to stop working. They had always hoped to travel in their senior years, but with Carol's mother around this seems impossible, and he does not wish to quit work and sit home all day with nothing to do.

As Neptune transits opposite Carol's Sun, she realizes that her ego has become so identified with the caretaker role that she has sacrificed her own needs and those of her husband. For years, she has put off plans until her mother would pass away. Now, time seems to be running out while her mother's care becomes increasingly more demanding. Carol is being asked to "give wisely." Sacrificing out of guilt is draining away her energy. She has to look at the overall pattern of her responsibilities to make appropriate choices for herself and her family. She and her mother have had a co-dependent relationship for years. During this time, her mother had rejected the assistance of anyone other than Carol. Years have gone by, and regrets won't bring them back; but with compassion and firmness, Carol *can make changes* that will balance the scales of giving and help her discover the part of herself ignored over the years.

Neptune Transiting the Moon

Neptune transiting in aspect to the Moon indicates a time when intuition and compassion arise from a greater sensitivity to feelings not openly expressed or owned. While the ego and self-identity are challenged when Neptune transits the Sun, the emotional and intuitive nature is the point of focus when Neptune transits the Moon. Emotional vulnerability increases as the unconscious, feminine and receptive side of the individual is sensitized by subtle experiences that defy immediate identification and/or comprehension. Vague sensations and intuitive glimpses represent the initial intuitive or emotional input, and you don't know what you are picking up. What is this emotion? Are you sensing another's sadness? Is this vague perception an insight? Or is it all just your imagination?

Uncertainties leave you hanging as you wait for further information and developments. During this period, emotional situations cannot be controlled or structured, so you learn to accept what is offered. You also cope with emotional uncertainty, agreeing to relationships which are not clearly defined, giving without a guarantee of return. You view insecurity as a natural by-product of your situation and trust that things will eventually work out, one way or another.

Compassion and empathy are very much a part of the intuitive process and the movement towards acceptance. Here is a transit which really pulls at the heart strings because you identify so strongly with what others are experiencing. Sometimes this cognition clouds your perception of your own feelings. Emotional connections are made because you rise above judgmental attitudes and truly understand another's situation. You readily offer assistance and give more than you normally would. You let your nurturing nature flow and allow others to become dependent on you or you on them. You accept people as they are, weaknesses and all. During this time, you might care for someone who is ill or disabled, or you could simply care for another person more than you care for yourself and your own welfare. Neptune-Moon transits are a sign of *self-sacrifice*. It is common to see this transit in the charts of new parents and those with elderly relatives to nurse.

Spiritual or emotional idealism lifts your understanding to a new level. But putting someone on a pedestal leads to disillusionment and diminishes the possibility of the genuine progress that could have been accomplished through recognizing and dealing with human weaknesses. Idealization is a blindness that creates unrealistic expectations and distorts perceptions, while blocking out human faults. You deceive yourself when you avoid a truth more threatening than mystery. Situations remain clouded. Inconsistencies go unchallenged, and deception is likely. When much is left unsaid, false assumptions take over. You fill in the gaps, seeing things not as they are, but as you hoped they would be. This continuing lack of accurate information is usually compounded by emotional estrangement. You become estranged from the person/truth you wish to avoid and your own emotional state. Anxiety and excessive worry grow. You miss the opportunity to use your intuitive insights in a constructive way.

Neptune transits to the Moon call us to recognize our emotional commonalities. We are all one, and we can use our new-found sensitivities to foster understanding and emotional connections to others.

The Moon in 13 degree Aries in the 4th House opposed to the Sun at 16 degrees Libra and Neptune at 9 degrees Libra, both in the 10th House. Transiting Neptune squares from the 2nd House.

When Neptune transited square his Moon, Peter was middle-aged and married for 25 years. He and his wife had drifted apart. Although they remained cordial with each other, they were no longer sexually or emotionally intimate. This left Peter in a state of limbo, neither married nor single. He did not know what to do about this, but avoided addressing the problem and acted as if nothing was wrong. This left his imagination free to create scenarios of rejection regarding his wife and fantasies of attraction about other women.

Peter displayed a temper and was easily provoked, but he never admitted his anger, only his annoyance. He frequently stated that he could not control his emotions. For years, his wife would compensate for his outbursts by "fixing" everything. But now, because of the estrangement, she was withdrawn and he was left alone to cope with his own moodiness and to identify his own feelings. He found this process difficult.

During this time, Peter was forced to begin to comprehend his own emotional nature. He started to pay attention to how people reacted to his words and began to see why they withdrew. He learned to think before he responded and was able to be gentle with his words, especially to his daughter. Though still troubled by his homelife and still unsure of his relationship with his wife, as Neptune left his Moon and went on to square his Sun, he began to work with his situation in a more sensitive way.

Neptune Transiting Mercury

Neptune transits to Mercury suggest development of the right-brain processes through studies of a spiritual, intuitive, or creative nature. It is a signal that a search has begun for subtle truth, possibly of a higher nature. Information of this type is not necessarily taught or given, but must be felt and experienced. Mental sensitivity increases as the native learns to work with those less clearly defined pathways to knowledge. Intuitive insights and psychic flashes are common during this transit.

Dealing with subtle truths can lead to some uncertainty and confusion in the thinking process. Increased intuitive or psychic awareness can precede the ability to weigh this information for its accuracy and symbolic content. It is sometimes difficult to discriminate between what is really an intuitive perception and what is more closely akin to worry, fear, or false hope. Symbolic dreams are sometimes mistaken for foreboding premonitions if a teacher is not available to guide the way. It is also hard to find practical applications for the increased sensory input. Idealistic concepts and insights can be unrealistic given your present situation. Mental stress and worry result from trying to integrate two different worlds (the practical and spiritual), and two very different forms of knowledge (the factual and intuitive).

Important facts (left-brain data) that you receive may be partial, inaccurate, or vague. Some people will be the victim of intentional secrecy or deception. Without adequate information, you could be left hanging. Your normal points of reference for evaluating situations have changed. You easily become confused or misled, especially if you do not listen to intuitive perceptions and warnings. It may not be possible for you to assess your circumstances accurately and make an informed decision during this time. In older people, this transit might signal the beginning of senility. Medications can create a befuddled mental state regardless of your age. Neptune's most negative interpretation is a loss of mental capabilities through drug and alcohol use. This manifestation is more closely associated with an individual history of abuse, but problems can begin during this period. Those who normally turn to chemicals to help them cope with problems will find their rations escalating.

This transit is meant to foster great insight to lead to learning of a less obvious nature. Those who heed intuitive impressions, have the option of growing in their right)brain sensitivity and creative expression.

Neptune Transiting Venus

Neptune transits to Venus are associated with uncertainty surrounding financial situations and relationships. Changes occurring in these areas assist you in becoming more sensitive to inner qualities of beauty. You will be able to anticipate the shifting sands if you are conscious of subtle signals and messages.

Financially, this is a time when you can live without fiscal guarantees. You may have to if you are starting a new business or investing money in a new venture. Anxiety over money will not stop you. Those with a steady job will have paychecks affected by commissions, incentives, profit-sharing revenues, lay-offs, or leaves of absence without pay. Salaries can also fluctuate because of part-time work, second jobs, or on-call hours. Under these conditions, you never know exactly what your salary will be until the check arrives. In rare situations, you could be unemployed and not know where your next dollar is coming from.

Changing living circumstances (i.e., relocation, divorce, illness, large purchases, or major sales) also affect the amount of money available to you. Many times, it is impossible to predict the effect these changes will have, especially when several variables are involved. If you expect money from others in the form of a loan, gift or inheritance, you cannot be sure how much you will receive and when you will receive it. Regardless of whether or not the financial uncertainty is job-related, monetary uncertainty exists in some form or another. This is a good time to foster a strong appreciation of the non-material side of life and allow your appreciation of the inner qualities to grow.

Neptune transiting Venus can indicate the growth of unconditional love. Significant emotional relationships become more supportive as partners become sensitive to each other. The subtleties of unspoken preferences are made known. You yield to your partner's needs, sometimes neglecting your own. Empathy and compassion increase as inner beauty is appreciated and allowed to blossom. External trappings are devalued, and what you materially own and share is not as important as what you are willing to give emotionally.

If you are not already married, you or your partner may not wish to make a commitment at this time. New or less stable love relationships tend to lack definition and clarity. The situation may be such that you can't even label your relationship or give it a name. In any relationship, your partner's intentions may be unclear or actions contradictory. He or she may come and go, appear and disappear, say one thing and do another. One minute you know you are loved and the next minute you are not so sure. It's difficult to know where you stand. While in this limbo, the relationship remains suspended in time, without a guaranteed future or a present reality. Clandestine relationships are common with this transit.

No relationship comes with guarantees to begin with, but with Neptune-Venus contacts the security can be even less evident. A persistent sense of confusion can cause you to misinterpret what is actually occurring. You don't always see the truth. This is most likely to happen when one or both partners are ambivalent or deceptive. At worst, there are lies to contend with. Because of the lack of clarity, idealization and deception might occur, making partners seem too good to be true. Aggrandizement of this sort can only lead to disappointment.

The best relationships breed compassion and sensitivity. Lovers who are honest and open with one another deepen their commitment and grow to appreciate each other's inner qualities.

Venus at 10 degrees Capricorn conjuncts Mercury at 13 degrees Capricorn in the 12th House. Neptune transits these two planets and opposes natal Moon at 11 degrees Cancer in the 6th.

Gloria was a divorced, middle-aged woman who lived with a man named George for 15 years. During much of this time, George had a series of second mistresses. As time went by, Gloria felt less and less loved and more and more insecure. But Gloria was afraid to leave George. She had never been on her own and she was afraid she could not make it financially. Although she earned a good salary, she was heavily in debt and lived rent-free with George.

Life continued like this until Neptune began to transit Gloria's Venus and Mercury (by conjunction) and Moon (by opposition). She met Larry, a very wealthy man whom she grew to both love and loathe. The two made plans for a business and life together. After only two months, Gloria left George, agreeing to marry Larry. They contracted to have two houses built, one for investment and one to live in. They made a bid on a restaurant. But even before the wedding, problems began to emerge as Larry's checks began to bounce. He was about to close on a $7 million deal and had cash flow problems. Gloria borrowed money and covered thousands of dollars worth of checks.

Immediately after their August wedding, the check for the two houses bounced, and Gloria began to suspect that her husband was not the millionaire he purported to be. She caught him in one lie after another. She confronted him with the evidence she had gathered; only then did he admit the deception. Gloria had enough sense to get out quickly. She filed for an annulment.

Gloria was evicted from her new home after only two months. Now she was without a place to live and was in worse financial shape than before. Unable to depend on anyone but herself, she started to take control and make some decisions. She rented an apartment in a building with security guards and friendly neighbors who watched out for each other. She went to garage sales and filled her apartment with beautiful furniture. She closed all the accounts she had with Larry and wrote all the creditors. She sued him for the money she had lost.

Gloria is thankful that Larry got her to leave George. But she realizes that if she had been braver, she could have left on her own. She was used to George's deception, but she had not trusted her intuition when it came to Larry. There were many clues along the way about the deal that was "too good to be true."

Neptune Transiting Mars

As we will see, Pluto transits to Mars imply actions that are *unconsciously* motivated, Neptune transits to Mars imply actions that have *no obvious motivation at all*! There is a great deal of uncertainty as to the direction you are headed and the goal you intend to reach. You ad-lib life with no definitive need or desire directing your course of action. In some situations, careful planning is not feasible. Surprise events or unexplained twists of fate can occur, disrupting your schedule and leaving your previous course of action hanging and incomplete.

Uncertainty and confusion seem to go hand in hand with this combination, and contradictory actions are possible. It is easy to stray from your original purpose when goals are not clearly defined. Some people might view your actions as confusing or inconsistent. It is easy for others to misinterpret what you are doing when your direction is unclear. This is a time when you can keep your plans secret, but if you are open to suggestion, objective feedback will help you remain well-grounded and consistent with your stated goals. Take time to listen to what others have to say.

If you do follow a specific plan of action, there are probably no guarantees that your actions will pay off. For example, if you are working on a project that is a long shot, it's questionable whether or not you will see a practical return on your investment of time and effort. Employment might be unpredictable, with rumors of layoffs, or changing company politics and office procedures. Despite bleak predictions, you might decide to trust things to work out and continue on the course you have set.

You have the ability to function despite uncertainty. Inner guidance is especially strong, and projects can become almost effortless if you are sensitive to the universal flow of energy. You can be correct in assuming success even when the odds are stacked against you. But if you idealize your situation and miscalculate the results, you will be disillusioned when your efforts are unrewarded. Misguided endeavors are consistent with Neptune transits to Mars, especially with the more difficult or stressful aspects such as the square and the opposition. Therefore, you must carefully consider your intentions and actions. Be ready with an alternate plan if matters do not progress. Humanitarian pursuits and volunteer efforts are also associated with Neptune transits to Mars. You willingly give your time and energy to a worthy endeavor and are able to sacrifice your own needs and desires.

The spiritual aspects of sexuality can awaken in you now. Perhaps it is time to be more careful with your body. Whom you have sex with affects what you think of yourself and what you believe about others. New, subtle, physical and nonphysical energies can be felt by those most sensitive. You may wish to investigate Tantric or Taoist sexual practices (Eastern traditions) and become more versed in the exchange of energy taking place during love-making.

Mars at 27 degrees Pisces in the 2nd House squared by transiting Neptune in the 11th.

Jan was in her mid-thirties, working full-time and attending graduate school, when she became pregnant unexpectedly. She had planned to continue her education, but now did not know what to do. She had recently remarried, and her older husband did not wish to have any children. He had three from a previous marriage. They had just purchased a new home and the mortgage required two incomes. Jan's husband pressured her to have an abortion, and she was very torn. She did not want to threaten her new marriage, but she did not want to abort the child either. The decision went back and forth for weeks. It was during this time of turmoil that Jan began to feel that the unborn child was a comfort to her. She sat talking to the baby, sang it songs, and read it books. She felt a gentle mixing of energy within her body. This was her first pregnancy, and it was a time of discovery. She decided to take the chance, school or no school, job or no job, husband or no husband. She rearranged her schedule so she would have time off when she needed it most. Reason might have indicated a different behavior, but Jan went with the subtle feelings she felt.

Pluto Transits

When Pluto transits a planet in the natal horoscope, the balance of power begins to shift, and you might gain or lose power during this time. You want to gain so that you will have the option of living your life according to the principles set down during Uranus and Neptune transits to your natal planets. Without empowerment, you will be forced to live by someone else's rules. You can strengthen your position naturally or use force. The growth-oriented response is to empower both yourself *and* others, internally and externally. There is much to be gained here from a kinetic human exchange.

Unfortunately, many find the empowerment task difficult to accomplish under the best of circumstances. Fears from the unconscious magnify threats to personal power causing defensive or offensive reactions. The perceived danger associated with a Pluto transit is the possibility of losing control over your own life. As combatants take a stance and stake out a claim, situations escalate and complications arise. *Complex scenarios* are the hallmark of the Pluto transit. Problems tend to be compounded by numerous subplots. There are no clear-cut answers to questions or perfect solutions to problems, and one can easily become emotionally overwhelmed by their circumstances.

To gain power and move forward during a Pluto transit, you must understand the Path to Empowerment. This includes the extent and source of your personal power, how best to use or expand it, and where you are headed. Once these parameters are set, you can move forward decisively by anticipating the next step toward growth and having the courage to take it. You cannot begin to do this until you understand where power needs to be applied. This is a crucial point for understanding the Pluto transit. The path splits here. There are only two broad choices, only two points of reference: either you apply power internally, intent on maintaining and acquiring inner strength and knowledge, or you apply power externally, intent on fulfilling your personal or professional ambitions in the world arena.

Although both orientations might be connected or follow one another in the final analysis, your reactions or goals during this transit and your effectiveness in the end are determined by your ability to discern the most powerful and appropriate action at any given time. The nature of the transit is that you must choose, and choose well, to progress. You cannot be wishy-washy. The longer you delay the decision, the more complex the situation becomes. Vacillation leads to complications and power leakages since definitive action does not take place and you undermine yourself. It is only when you come down firmly on one path or the other that your course of action becomes clear, no matter how complicated the situation itself becomes. Under these circumstances you will progress steadily. Incorrect choices will be obvious, since all actions in keeping with an inappropriate path will lead to failure and frustration.

The problem with the Pluto transit is that many people automatically assume a defensive or offensive position before they have considered using power in a positive and transformative manner. Fear speaks louder than insight with this transit and it is easy to lose your way and overreact. One engages the enemy without fully understanding the root nature of the threat or choosing an appropriate course of action.

Path of Internal Empowerment

What does it mean to choose internal empowerment? It means that who you are is more important than what you do, and what you understand is more important than what others think. It means you practice personal wholeness, a process by which individual integrity is maintained regardless of the external situation.

What do you gain from the process of internal empowerment? You gain freedom of personal action. Since all decisions are based on your personal value system, the possibility of interference is removed. You are not dependent on external criteria or results. What is important is not what you do, but *who you are* in the processing of doing or not doing. You maintain a goal of trueness to self. Inner calmness sets in and you are able to focus and not lose momentum. There is an efficiency of thought and deed. Power is not split between two courses of action, but used in a consistent manner. Emotional over-reactions are eliminated and therefore complications based on fear are kept to a minimum. You easily release counterproductive situations and personality traits. You control yourself internally and remain fearless. You influence others indirectly through the power of your calm presence and example. Issues are handled rationally by all parties. De-escalation occurs. Power is conserved.

Techniques for Gaining and Maintaining Internal Power

For internal empowerment to occur, growth and inner transformation must be emphasized over external results. Those who are sensitive to inner transitions understand the movement taking place regardless of external circumstances. You detach from what others think. You accept conditions as they are. This is the way of no resistance and there is minimal pain when it is followed. If two people fight over a rubber band, the one who lets go first doesn't get hurt. To practice the path of internal empowerment you must know when to let go and then do it with great regularity. The way of no resistance is the course of action to choose when there is nothing you can do that will make a difference in the long run. Matters are out of your hands. Any attempts at controlling outcomes lead to frustration and lost power. This is also the course of action to take when you are in a very weakened state and have no more to give. You must focus inward on recovery.

It is natural to want to fix things. But sometimes we try to fix things that are not our responsibility. It might be better not to take action and allow situations to develop on their own. This conserves energy and power.

Internal Loss of Power

For some, gaining power starts with preventing the loss of power. Certain character traits can erode personal strength. Reactionary blind spots get you into trouble. Psychological buttons bring forth an immediate response of a less than intellectual nature. As you get out of control, fears arise, tempers flare, and conflicts escalate. Weaknesses must be recognized and corrected before someone uses them for advantage against you.

You can also lose power by remaining in circumstances that are nonproductive and draining. These situations have no sustaining power of their own and are only preserved through the force and power of your own will or someone else's. I am speaking specifically of relationships and positions that are passé. Healthy circumstances will be sustained naturally and will not require extraordinary methods or effort.

Some people use psychological insights to control and block their own growth. They set up a negative pattern of stagnation wherein information is not accepted, but twisted to fit previously conceived notions about life and self. Insights become weapons against growth and understanding. Contradictory realizations are suppressed or misinterpreted by the ego. A fixed mind-set is imposed on all information. In a very negative situation such as this, the power associated with increased Plutonian awareness and its creative potential is never realized.

Misuse of the inner Plutonian process creates an inability to continue on the life path until issues are resolved and lessons are learned. Stagnation occurs when the individual is afraid to progress to the next level of comprehension and misinterprets all available information.

Path of External Empowerment

What does it mean to choose external empowerment? It means to take action. If you have an idea that can make the world a better place, you implement it. The emphasis is not on what you think or know internally, but the application of knowledge to an external situation with a specific purpose in mind. Results are important and sometimes the ends do justify the means. *What you accomplish* is more important even than who you are. You establish a goal and go for it, holding to the highest good for all those involved. Personal power is used to make things happen and, if it is done correctly, empowerment occurs.

What do you gain from the process of external empowerment? You gain results, confidence, and position. The environment changes because you directly influence others and situations. You gain freedom of action since you are the one in control. In the best of circumstances, many of the participating parties become stronger because of the empowerment process.

Techniques for Gaining and Maintaining External Power

One way to gain external power while also conserving energy is to anticipate and circumvent problems before they occur. Energy follows thought. There is a natural progression to every chain of events. Those who are perceptive can anticipate the next move and stay one step ahead of the game by using de-escalation techniques to defuse explosive situations. Respond to anger with calmness and intelligent insight. Create alternatives and negotiate compromises that are win-win situations. Provide avenues for the release of tension before things get out of hand.

To gain the most empowerment from this path, kinetic (lively, dynamic, on-going) interactions must occur. This leads to the creation of power for all those involved. The Dalai Lama, for example, who is an exile from his own country, preaches and practices non-violence in all things. Others have been drawn to his teachings and he has gained a following. He is a Nobel Peace Prize winner, and the year 1991 was called "The Year of Tibet." Many people are being empowered by his insights, but he is also gaining external empowerment from the kinetic interaction. Anytime anyone establishes a goal that is clearly good for all those involved, it catches fire and is embraced. Kinetic interactions create power for all those involved. To walk this path you must be as concerned with the welfare of others as you are with your own gratification. When others realize your good intentions, all fears recede and creative solutions arise. In daily living, seek out those situations of heightened power and kinetic interchange.

External Loss of Power

One reason for losing external power is the lack of concern for others. There is no respect for the highest good of anyone. You defend your territory only and do not care about the implications to others. Others perceive a threat to their position, and barriers go up. Fears magnify and defensive and offensive attacks begin. Power struggles ensue. No one is totally right and no one is totally wrong. Everyone is caught in a cycle of reactionary responses that only complicate issues. Always be aware of the interactive process and the role you play in any battle. Blaming others for your problems distorts perceptions of self.

The other reason you lose power is a lack of concern for self. You undermine your own position or surrender power to others. A world without struggle is an ideal, and not reality. At some point in your life, it may be essential to take a stand. Certain injustices must be corrected for everyone to progress. Sometimes the only viable option is to fight back. Always be aware of the struggle you take on. Go for the simplest task that gets the job done. It is usually easier to correct a situation than to convince your opponent he or she is wrong. It is easier to get forgiveness after the fact than permission before. Seek the quickest solution. Do not get locked into unnecessary long drawn out struggles. Do it up right and get the job done. Power struggles are expensive in terms of time and energy. Some are essential to growth, others are self-inflicted. Know the difference and don't waste your time on unnecessary or nonproductive conflicts.

The most efficient use of power exists on the internal plane. It is much easier to use energy to control your own reactions than to seek power externally. However, there are times when you *must* take action. In these instances, wield power wisely.

Pluto Transiting the Sun

When Pluto transits the Sun, empowerment can occur either through awareness of self or struggle with others. The more attuned you are to your own personal power and any lacks you might have, the more likely you are to grow through awareness. Insights into power are heightened. You become acutely perceptive and you easily observe how people get, maintain, use, and abuse power for personal gain or loss and for control of others. Power usage in everyday situations becomes more obvious, but even subtle shifts in power are evident as you learn to recognize psychological motivations and manipulations. It is only when you identify the manipulative tactics aimed at you personally that you begin to dismantle the controlling influences of others. This process by itself is very empowering.

Experiencing an upsurge in personal power or the lack thereof can also occur through conflict. You might have to defend yourself from attack by a controlling or angry person. These situations are more likely to occur to victim-personalities and those who do not know how to defend themselves. You need not be swayed by guilt, fear, or irrational accusations. Learn to neutralize these negative influences. Awareness of manipulative tactics is particularly helpful in deflecting blows and dealing with attacks on your character.

Some individuals study psychology during this transit. Others enter therapy or consciousness raising groups. Psychological awareness breeds power. Regardless of the educational background, many people notice examples of obsessive, compulsive, phobic, neurotic, or manipulative behaviors in themselves or others. Unconscious needs are intensified. You see your own shadow reflected in the people you meet and the situations you encounter. A cleansing of negative behavior patterns can take place in those who are introspective about their actions.

Professional ambition is one of the more positive and noticeable manifestations of this transit. You are more likely to start your own business and become self-employed. The desire for power and self-control can reach into any area of life. Learning to deal effectively with power on many levels is the hallmark of the Plutonian transit.

> *Sun at 16 degrees Scorpio in the 10th House opposed Jupiter at 15 degrees Taurus in the 4th House and square the North Node at 16 degrees Aquarius in the 1st House. Midheaven is 7 degrees Scorpio squared by the Moon at 6 degrees Leo in the 7th house.*

Marilyn was married and had one teen-aged son. She had been an agoraphobic for years. She would never leave the house and was afraid of open spaces. As Pluto began to make the conjunction with Marilyn's Sun, she decided to seek therapy for her problem. While in counseling, she realized how powerless she was. She had no financial security. Her husband had put them on the brink of financial disaster by gambling and spending money extravagantly. They were deeply in debt.

As the months passed, Marilyn went on outings with her therapy group and began to leave the house on her own. She grew stronger mentally and became more assertive in her relationship with her husband. When he was about to leave on a week-long golfing trip they couldn't afford, she confronted him with their unpaid bills and financial problems. She demanded to know what he intended to do about them. He patted her on the head and said, "You'll think of something." Then he left.

Marilyn did think of something, and it only took her one week to do it. She decided she had progressed as far as she could internally. Thanks to her therapy group and therapist, she had made numerous inner changes, but now she needed to make some *external* changes to have power over her life. It took her two days to find a full-time job. She wrote all the credit card companies and disavowed any responsibility for her husband's bills. She established her own credit and separate bank accounts. Then she saw a lawyer, filed for a legal separation and had all the locks changed on the house. When her husband came home after one week, his clothes were packed and on the porch along with a note that said, "I thought of something."

Marilyn had empowered herself internally as much as she could. When the time came to shift gears to the external process, she was able to do so. She chose to use her personal power swiftly and in the most efficient way.

Pluto Transiting the Moon

When Pluto transits the Moon, the emotional makeup is complicated by unconscious influences. Emotions are tainted by events or complexes from the past, and you relive a former happening in an immediate and present situation. The garbage can of your own mind opens up so you can survey the contents and eliminate the trash. Feelings seem more volatile, intense, and even overwhelming. Reasoning becomes based on emotional factors and sometimes defies logic.

Relationships are likely to be affected and unconscious influences can distort communications. You or someone close might need counseling. If the other person is less than rational, you must deal with issues in an insightful way. This is a good time to become more aware of how psychological games affect you emotionally. You may merely observe these influences or you may be directly involved, playing either manipulator or manipulated. If you are feeling insecure, you might cling to others and try controlling them.

At their worst, Pluto transits to the Moon imply a major emotional power struggle. Though you may think you are struggling with another, you are also struggling with yourself. For example, suppose you have limited means, but are married to a wealthy person who is very tight with money. Since you resent this person's power over your economic situation, you withhold sexual relations. You have now gained some power over your spouse's life, and the two of you have established a power struggle which complicates your relationship.

Although you have succeeded in controlling your spouse's behavior to some extent, *you have not gained any power over your own existence.* Your situation has not improved much and you are still without financial recourse. There are more positive ways to handle this situation. Either one or both of you could decide to enter counseling to resolve this problem. Or you could get a job, earn your own money and totally frustrate your spouse's attempts to control you. Emotional blackmail and manipulation are consistent with this transit, but they only work if you allow another person to have control over some portion of your life. As soon as you begin to control yourself and take responsibility for your own well-being, manipulators lose all power.

Not all Pluto-Moon transits involve difficult circumstances. Writers, counselors, psychology students, poets, artists, and those whose work depend on their ability to understand human nature use this transit to gain insight. It is the awareness that is significant, and not the struggle itself.

Knowledge brings power. Use this period of time to become aware of how unconscious drives affect your life. A very pleasant reason for being so emotional is an involvement in a new and exciting romantic relationship. All relationships, even those which are established, are subject to transformation.

Domestic situations can also change. You can move, renovate, add on, or tear down. Roommates might come or go. The changes occurring in the physical home are symbolic of the internal emotional changes taking place. (See the example for Pluto transiting Mercury.)

Pluto Aspecting Mercury

Pluto transits to Mercury indicate a time when the conscious mind is more apt to be aware of unconscious material and psychological complexes. This awareness may originate from naturally occurring insights into human behavior or educational pursuits. You are better able to perceive what is unspoken or hidden. Mind games and motivations will be clear to you even when they are not verbally stated. Awareness is not all one-sided. You will be as aware of your own unconscious nature as you are of the complexes of others. Being aware of these psychological forces can be stressful, especially if you know more than you are capable of handling or the realizations come too quickly. In these cases, seek counseling.

You might be involved in a verbal battle over ideology, religion, or the truth. Others might doubt what you say, or push you to defend what you know or think on a given subject matter. The implication here is that knowledge is power and it is not taken for granted that you speak the truth. You must stick with your story to be heard. If you would convey wisdom and insight, you must make your words relevant and understandable to others.

A passion for learning is associated with this transit. Obsession with any topic is likely, but certainly an obsession with any occult practice is common. All forms of information are valuable whether they come from a book or the observation of life. Great insights can be gained from journal-keeping and creative writing. This is a time meant for those who wish to know more.

The Moon at 15 degrees Scorpio in the 1st House square Mercury at 11 degrees Aquarius in the 4th. Jupiter trines the Moon from the 9th House at 15 degrees Cancer.

Laura was a young housewife and mother. She could not remember much of her childhood and she did not know why. As Pluto squared her Mercury and conjuncted her Moon she began to have horrible flashbacks to a time long ago. She thought she remembered being raped at a very young age by a family friend. She went into therapy to help her cope with the memories and also to bring them to the surface. Gradually the age interval between 3 and 12 years began to be filled in; it was not a happy time.

Laura spent many days crying alone after the children went to school. She smashed empty bottles on the basement walls trying to release her rage. Image after image rose and haunted her. It was particularly upsetting that her parents were still best friends with her attacker. She could not face another holiday with this person around. After harboring the secret for many months, she finally began to tell others. Not everyone believed her and this was hard on Laura emotionally.

She stuck to her story and one day sent a certified letter to her rapist, telling him of her memories and accusing him of the attacks. He denied the accusations, but Laura did not back down. Next she decided to visit her parents and personally tell them of the trauma. She and her therapist rehearsed the meeting many times, and ultimately, Laura was able to tell her parents about the various incidents. She was not sure they would believe her, but she had to have some semblance of power after such a long time of powerlessness. She knew the truth even if they could not accept it. As it turned out, they supported her 100 percent and shunned their long-time friend. It was very important that they believe her. This calmed Laura's nerves. She knew her children and the other grandchildren would be protected from this man.

Pluto Transiting Venus

Pluto transits to Venus indicate intense emotional involvements. New relationships begun at this time are especially compelling and kinetic for reasons that are hard to understand. Unconscious forces play a major role in these attractions. Like a moth to a flame, you are drawn to a particular individual without understanding why. In the beginning, the perceived loss of control and diminished rationality is disconcerting. Enthusiasm is high and you might feel obsessed. Regardless of what you think or plan, you end up reacting to situations in a spontaneous and revealing manner. Your usual psychological defenses don't seem to work while all your unconscious complexes are laid bare for the world to see. A persistent sense of vulnerability becomes coupled with your growing need for intimacy. If you are able to keep your defenses lowered, a relationship begun at this time can be most rewarding.

Potential or existing partners might exhibit a new and troubling flaw (which may or may not be serious.) In all relationships, considerable emotional growth can occur if you work with each other's faults and become aware of the unconscious urges and psychological games played by both parties. These ploys are barriers to further intimacy and must be recognized. Learning to deal effectively with these influences affects the success of the relationship. It is a good time for counseling of any kind, especially marriage or relationship counseling.

Situational barriers include attraction to married, gay, or bisexual partners, those living in a different locality, or those who cannot be fully present or involved for one reason or another. These pre-existing impediments to intimacy were probably known or suspected before the relationship began.

Psychological impediments to intimacy are those unconscious complexes that distort reality and destroy trust. These include, but are not limited to, possessiveness, obsessive thinking, sexual fantasies, compulsive behaviors, and controlling attitudes.

Power is an issue in both intimate and casual relationships. Individuals who learn to trust, compromise, and share power see their relationships deepen and transform. Accommodating the emotional needs of others breeds increased understanding as long as you do not compromise selfhood and surrender too much power. Those who are unable to reach compromises should let go of passé relationships before they become locked in power struggles. Combatants view their fates as dependent on the whims of others. They feel powerless to control their own destiny until they have resolved some issue to their personal satisfaction. They resort to controlling behaviors as the only solution. Within this kind of power struggle, manipulative techniques are the main weapons; sex and money become the main issues.

Financially, Pluto transits to Venus indicate strong financial changes or complex monetary arrangements. Salary changes are common and may result from a career move, relocation, leave of absence without pay, cut-back in hours, or retirement. On the other hand, ambition can cause your salary to rise dramatically, especially if your earnings are based on commissions or profit-sharing. Those who are self-employed experience monetary ups and downs. If your financial status depends on another's resources, a struggle over shared money is likely.

The goal here is to experience personal power in relationships and power over your own financial situation. By gaining insight into your behavior and the behavior of others, you can master both areas of concern. (See the example for Pluto transiting Mars.)

Pluto Transiting Mars

When Pluto transits Mars, actions are not truly conscious or planned out. There is an acute awareness of the interplay between what appears to be purposeful activities and unconscious motivations. One does not just *set* career goals, one is *driven to succeed*. Compulsions and obsessions, healthy or not, are common since many psychological issues and complexes are intrinsic to the scenarios you are involved in. With very negative situations, fears arise and phobias develop. While the psychological influences affecting you spring unsolicited from your own unconscious, they frequently arise from your encounters with another. Generally, you must deal with this person regularly, and he or she may or may not be totally rational. Reacting from the gut level can become the standard mode of operation for those who do not work toward a greater understanding of these forces.

Control issues are likely during this time, and some individuals get locked into power struggles. In this type of situation, you are both able to manipulate others and subject to manipulation yourself. Surreptitious actions or underhanded maneuvers are also possible. Rather than battling with someone else, you can instead (or also) be locked into a power struggle with yourself. One man with Pluto transiting his Mars was seriously wounded by a past relationship. He recognized the need to deal with unconscious anger and develop a philosophy for handling anger-producing situations in the future. During this transit, he met and was compulsively drawn to a new relationship. The loss of control over the inhibitions to intimacy frightened him. Consequently, the scene was set, and the interplay between the unconscious obsession to resolve the anger issues and the fear of being hurt again dominated the involvement. Efforts to control yourself consciously will be thwarted until you gain insight into the problem at hand. The man was both irresistibly drawn and frightened by the attraction until he began to resolve issues from the *original* relationship. This cleared the way for a more meaningful interchange.

Understanding psychological forces and learning to work with rather than against them can lead to productive encounters. Use insight to break bad habits and negative attitudes. The ability to comprehend new knowledge fostered by the unconscious leads to new power over your own actions and the situations you are involved in. It is at this point that realistic control over behavior begins.

Mars at 16 degrees Leo conjunct Pluto at 17 degrees in the 10th House. Venus at 21 degrees Scorpio conjunct the 2nd House cusp.

Heather was married to a verbally abusive man for many years. She eventually left him and started a new life on her own in a distant state, but she never divorced her husband or sought a formal separation agreement. He still carried her on his health insurance policy and gave her a little money from time to time. Heather worked to support herself, but she always struggled with limited funds. During the years they were separated, without her knowing, her husband grew fairly wealthy. There was little contact between the two of them until Heather's husband decided to remarry and asked for a formal divorce. Transiting Pluto was squaring her natal Mars-Pluto conjunction, approaching conjunction with her Venus.

It was during the divorce proceedings that Heather learned how much her husband was worth and that she had been a fool not to get a separation agreement before she left. Many years had passed, and it was impossible to recover funds. The court's position was that since she left without anything, she was not entitled to much now. Her husband cut off all extra money. While Heather continued to struggle to feed and clothe herself, her husband's new love arrived at the courthouse decked out in jewels and fancy clothes.

The stress eventually wore on Heather's health, and she became seriously ill. When she submitted her medical bills to the insurance company, her husband received and cashed the health insurance refund checks, leaving her seriously in debt. Heather's anger grew and so did her chronic illness which became more and more debilitating. Eventually she could no longer work. She thought that the judge would recognize her disability and award her a fair amount of money plus permanent maintenance. He did not. Heather found it difficult to go to court and speak in her own defense though her husband told lies about their relationship. This hurt her case. In the end, Heather was given a small sum of money from the house they owned jointly, based on its value at the time of the separation.

Externally, Heather was not in a position of power at the beginning of the divorce proceedings. She had not anticipated the next step when she left her husband years ago. The choices she made proved disastrous. She was not internally powerful either. She vacillated between feeling like a victim of her husband's continuing abuse and feeling guilty about asking for money. She was as angry with herself as she was at her husband. The internal conflict wore on her body until eventually she was ill. She never took a definitive position and worked against herself in all matters. This left the door open for someone else to assume power.

Conclusion

As you read through the stories present here in this article, you cannot help but notice how dissimilar the people and situations are, and what diverse choices they all made. Some took the bull by the horns, while others choose a gentle route. Some tried to catch up from years of stagnation, others were ahead of their time. Personalized sensitivity to Uranian impulses, subtle Neptunian awareness, or Plutonian urges for power influenced the type of situation faced (internal or external) and the strength of the response (active or passive). Some choices were better than others, but there were never any clear-cut *wrong* decisions. The complexity of a Uranus, Neptune, or Pluto transit implies dilemma. It may be impossible to be right or wrong. But it is important that you learn. This you will do, willingly or not.

One cannot take these outer planets lightly. Taken individually, they represent tremendous growth potential. But taken as a group, as they presently are, the possibility for accelerated evolution exists. Now more than ever, we have ways to go beyond what is, if only we would choose.

Progressing the Outer Planets—Solar Arcs to the Rescue

Noel Tyl

Every astrologer has been frustrated in the system of Secondary Progressions by the slow movements of the planets Jupiter, Saturn, Uranus, Neptune, and Pluto. In the day-for-a-year system that takes us symbolically into the structure of future time, slow diurnal movement curtails the progressed "activity" of these planets drastically. Where the Progressed Moon will move some 13 to 15 degrees in one day/year, Jupiter will move only five minutes of a degree in one day/year, Saturn two minutes, Uranus 43 seconds, Neptune 24 seconds, and Pluto about 15 seconds. In short, nothing happens from these planets, the outer three especially, over a lifetime.

Indeed, the outer planets (and Jupiter and Saturn) do *receive* progressed aspects from the other planets that move more quickly on a daily average, and these aspects can be very telling. But the "heavies," so to speak, stay home on the range.

The Solar Arc System of Directions (the word "Directions" is used to echo Ptolemy's system of Primary Directions and to set the system apart from the Secondary and other "progressed" systems) evolved mainly over a period of about 200 years from the early 17th century (Antonius Maginus and Valentino Naboda) to the mid-19th century (W. J. Simmonite). The evolution was a simplification of the tortuous Ptolomeic Directions and, really, a common sensical application of symbology that related the Secondary Progressed Sun's arc to *all the planets and Angles of the natal horoscope*, bringing all planets and points of the natal horoscope forward into future time in the same relative positions, one to another, that were established at birth. The predictive "magic" occurred through aspects from the Solar Arc positions for any given day/year to the natal positions of the planets. Only the Sun's motion mattered, and all planets were active in this powerful system of time measurement.

Since the Sun's diurnal motion is the key to Solar Arc projection, we can generalize about Solar Arcs in terms of *one degree equals one year*. Rudhyar named these generalizations "rapport" measurements. When we get a bead on a significant Solar Arc aspect to a natal planet or point, we can then do some easy calculations (or the computer can) and we get exact positions.

To compute the Solar Arc to the birthday month of any given year, we simply compute the Secondary Progressed Sun position for that year and then subtract the natal Sun position from that Secondary Sun position. We get the arc the Sun has traveled to the birthday month in the given year after birth. Then we add this arc to every planet and point in the natal horoscope and place the planets around the natal wheel (or the computer lists them and their fixed aspects to natal planets).

When we see that a Solar Arc aspect to a natal position will be exact, say, in 22' of further arc after the birthday month reference point, we simply divide that extra distance by 5' (the average arc distance the Sun travels in one month; i.e., 60'/12 = 5') and get the number of months after the birthday month for the arc to be exact. In this case of 22', the interval is a bit over four months.

Here is Lyndon Johnson's horoscope. The birth time has been in use under study for many years, although it is not established by certification or biography. The natal horoscope has held up under much scrutiny. The Secondary Progressed positions around the natal wheel are for Johnson's 52nd year, set for his birthday month of August in 1960.

The computation of the Secondary Progressed horoscope simply entailed counting ahead in the ephemeris after Johnson's birth year of 1908 52 *calendar days*: four to end August 1908, 30 more in September 1908, and then 18 in October 1908 for a total of 52. The horoscope drawn for the birthtime in October 1908 at the birthplace co-ordinates establishes the Secondary Progressed portrait for Johnson's 52nd year, the year when, in November, he was elected Vice President in John F. Kennedy's presidential victory.

There is little here that is dramatic, but there are measurements that are auspicious: SP Mercury is hovering in opposition to the SP

Midheaven while sextile to Johnson's natal Uranus, ruler of his 7th House. Johnson's natal Uranus trines his Midheaven, so this Mercury reinforcement is significantly positive. Mercury rules Johnson's 11th House and his 2nd and is the dispositor of his Mars, Sun, and Moon in the natal Ascendant. Finally, Mercury, natally, is in its own sign, the final dispositor of the horoscope. Very strong.

Additionally, SP Venus is also trining the natal Midheaven and Uranus. The analysis certainly would be that this year would see the

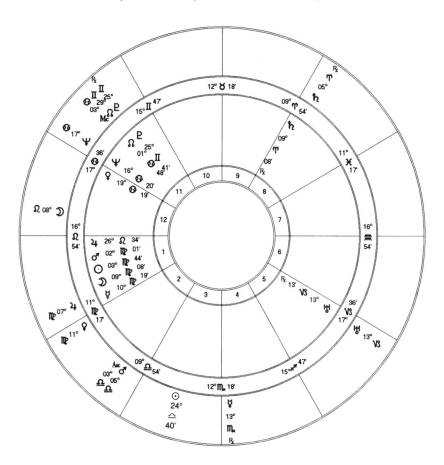

Lyndon Johnson
Secondary Progression: Aug. 27, 1960
Aug. 27, 1908, 4:52 a.m. CST
Gillespie County, TX
98W25 30N16
Placidus Houses

fulfillment of Johnson's plans and public popularity; also that his thinking would have a gifted, practical bent; that strategy would dominate successfully to put him forward, and soon he would come into his own, with the SP Moon crossing the Ascendant in April 1961 (one degree per month projection after the birthday month position at 8 Leo) and then conjoining the natal cluster in the Ascendant, all building trines with the natal Midheaven and Uranus.

Note: Lyndon Johnson's birth time is not sure, but has been refined throughout many years of observation and study. The Angles hold up well in the study of his life, set at an Ascendant of 16 Leo 54. Doris Chase Doane, in her *Horoscopes of the U.S. Presidents* (Professional Astrologers Incorporated, Hollywood CA, 1952) arrived at this Ascendant using a birthtime of 4:18 a.m., Local Mean Time. While the Angles do hold up, her time is incorrect because Texas adopted Central Standard Time (except for the far western region) on November 18, 1883.

The next step for rectification of Johnson's horoscope, to preserve the Angles as we have tested them so successfully, is to use the birthtime of 4:52 a.m., Central Standard Time. This preserves the horoscope exactly as Doane and others have created it while including clock time correctly.

When we add the transits of that time in Fall 1960 to the picture, we start to add a more significant framework upon the backdrop of auspicious trines shown in the Secondary Progressed picture: transiting Saturn was exactly conjunct natal Uranus, and, therefore, also trine Johnson's Midheaven in November 1960 at the election, when Johnson shifted strategically from his presidential bid to vice-presidential acceptance; transiting Uranus was conjoining natal Jupiter in the Ascendant; and transiting Jupiter at 2 Capricorn was trining Johnson's natal Mars and Sun. In November 1960, Johnson was "golden" in terms of all his plans and public projection; certainly to that date, one of the finest times of his life.—We know in hindsight now, that it was the beginning of an extraordinary series of happenings that would make history.

In studying the Secondary Progressed positions here, we see clearly that SP Uranus has remained in its birth position, exactly, after 52 years. We see that Neptune has advanced only 47 minutes, and Pluto only four. Experience and instinct suggest that these planets should have been involved in this momentous time in Johnson's life through our astrological system. Through Solar Arcs, they are brought into the picture dramatically.

Computation—In August 1960, the SP Sun was at 24 Libra 40. To compute the Solar Arc to that birthday month reference point in 1960, we subtract the natal Sun position from the SP Sun position:

24♎40 = 54♍40 = 53♍ 100′ Progressed Sun
$$\underline{-3\ ♍\ 44'\ \text{Natal Sun}}$$
50°　56′ Arc

The Solar Arc to August 1960 is 50°56′. To get the Solar Arc for November 1960, three months later, we simply add 15′ (3 x 5′) to the arc: 50°56′ + 15′ = 50°71′ or 51°11′.

Nowadays, the computer does all of this in a flash, of course. It is very simple to do by hand or calculator as well. Whatever way you compute Secondary Progressions will suffice to determine the SP Sun position. Then, the subtraction is simply a matter of five seconds of brain time.

Look again at Johnson's natal horoscope. Count the number of degrees between natal Pluto at 25 Gemini 41 and the 16 Leo 49 Ascendant. It's easy: five degrees to complete Gemini, 30 degrees in Cancer—that's 35 so far—and then 16 more into Leo for a total of 51 degrees, plus 8 minutes. Johnson was 52 in 1960. The arc generality that we've just computed with our eyes is close to Johnson's age, as we would expect.

The reason the rapport measurement, the generalized arc, is not *exactly* Johnson's age in 1960 is that he was born in the summertime when the Sun's diurnal motion is *slower* than one degree per day. The Sun is higher in our sky and takes more time to arc the heavens. In the winter, the Sun is lower in our sky and faster in our ephemeris.

With experience making rapport measurements, which then lead us to more accurate Solar Arc measurements, you learn that it takes more life time in years to fulfill a slow Solar Arc born in the Summer. You learn to add on an extra year to the rapport degree total in such cases after the age of 30. Here then, with a summer birth and an arc of 51 degrees, SA Pluto to the Ascendant, we can anticipate its occurrence in Johnson's 52nd year.

Let's see: Johnson's Solar Arc to November 1960 is exactly 51°11′. We add this arc to his natal Pluto position of 25 Gemini 41 and we get 76 Gemini 52 or 16 Leo 52. *SA Pluto was exactly conjunct Johnson's Ascendant in November 1960!* This is the measurement for a whole new perspective in life. This is history for a big-time politician. It is notable almost in a flash, when looking at the natal horoscope...at any time in Johnson's life. It would have been easy to predict such a momentous time.

Let's try another Solar Arc projection, more quickly. Look at Johnson's natal Uranus at 13 Capricorn 13 and add the birthday month Solar Arc to it for 1960. Add 50°56'...or just 51°...to 13 Capricorn; you get 64 Capricorn or 4 Pisces. This rapport projection of Uranus —ruler of Johnson's 7th House—puts SA Uranus in the 7th and in opposition with his natal Sun!

When was the opposition exact?—about 20' of arc before the birthday month of August. That comes out to be four months earlier: April 1960, precisely when the primary bids and election campaigns go into high gear. This is a measurement of enormous self-awareness and tremendous personal projection to the public. Johnson was running for the Presidency of the United States.

Solar Arc Neptune was at 7 Virgo (16 Cancer plus 51°), about to conjoin Johnson's Moon and then, *in 1963 in September/October*, to conjoin the very important Mercury. We must note that Neptune is the ruler of Johnson's 8th House where we see circumstances about matters of death.

Solar Arc Directions bring the outer planets dramatically into the action of life development and future time.

Look at Your Own Chart!

Focus on one of the outer planets in your horoscope, especially one that may be in a Cadent House and can be easily directed counter-clockwise to the next Angle. For example, from the 9th House to the Midheaven, from the 5th or 6th House to the 7th House, from the 2nd or 3rd to the fourth cusp, or out of the 11th or 12th to the Ascendant. Just count the number of degrees, relate that number to years (add one year if a summer birth and over age 30), and think of the changes in your life at that time in relation to the planetary symbology.

Uranus will suggest the potential for sudden, sharp change; intensification, recklessness, even calamity. If you were very young and experienced SA Uranus conjunct one of the Angles, the significance was probably absorbed by your parents and filtered down to you through their activities and their lot in life. Remember, your 7th cusp is the Midheaven of the parent represented by your 10th House; your Ascendant relates similarly to your 4th House parent.

Neptune arcs to conjunctions with Angles will suggest the potential of losing ego presence, questioning identity, getting off the track, having the sense of individuality blotted out, feeling lost; peculiar states, high sensitivity; scandal.

Pluto arcs to Angles usually correspond to extremely dramatic changes of life perspective; major milestone adjustments.

These Solar Arcs to conjunction with an Angle (or square to an Angle) are the basis for rectification in astrology. Along with major transits *involving Angles*, Solar Arcs are absolutely indispensable when trying to rectify a birth time from events in a life.

Of course, Solar Arcs involve aspects among planets—not just with Angles. The Solar Arc of the Sun to conjunction with Venus or Venus conjunct Sun; Mars conjunct or square Venus usually correspond to romance, marriage, conception, birth, love affairs, *if they occur at the time of life when such an occurrence is possible or practicable*. But our study here is concentrated on the outer planets, to bring them into predictive time frameworks through the use of Solar Arcs.

With a little experience, using your own horoscope, you should quickly be at home with rapport measurements. You might even reverse the process by thinking first of a singularly important time of your life, and translating that year into an arc distance, seeking out the planet(s) and aspect(s) that you feel would have been involved symbolically, and then measuring the arcs that may have been present. For example, if you were divorced at age 33, you may find that SA Uranus made a square with your natal Sun 33 degrees into the future from your year of birth. In this case—and perhaps your Sun rules your 7th or Uranus does—the symbols suggest the intensification of individuality jarring the life energy, probably in an effort to build more selfhood, to gain more prominence; and such egocentrism upsets the togetherness of relationship. Separation and/or divorce can follow.

Another Example

The horoscope on page 201 belongs to Senator Edward (Ted) Kennedy. The birth data are recorded and reliable. Kennedy has had a most trying life by anyone's evaluation. Tragedy has again resurfaced in scandals and public outrage against him from 1989 through 1992: transiting Saturn and Neptune have slowly crossed his Ascendant, and transiting Uranus was conjunct that same point in 10 Capricorn for the entire year of 1991. The public media have sensationalized Kennedy's trials in life.

The Secondary Progression positions in the outer ring of the horoscope drawing are for Kennedy's 60th year, beginning February 1992 (Ephemeris date, April 22, 1932). We see SP Mars closing into conjunction with natal Uranus, suggesting for the period of about four years that there will be much anger, upset, self-worth attack (Uranus rules the 2nd), possible financial drain, and even harsh retaliatory communication (Uranus in the 3rd). SP Uranus in 60 years will have moved some four degrees, intensifying the natal square with Pluto in the 7th House of the Public, Pluto ruling Kennedy's Midheaven. This suggests great upset with the public and the public with him, and a threat to his position, to his job throughout his whole career, but intensifying in the last years of it.

That simply does not seem to be enough of the picture. I know what the Solar Arc picture looks like and, looking back over my shoulder at the Secondary Progressed portrait, I am not seeing the entire panorama of anticipated scandal and upset. Look again at the natal horoscope. Look at that dominant Moon-Neptune conjunction, with the Moon ruling the 7th House so vitally important to a politician. Look at that conjunction's natal opposition with the Sun. The Moon-Neptune conjunction is also semi-square the 7th House Pluto.

This conjunction flashes at us in purple neon lights! NOW: *look at its distance to the Midheaven:* very close to a sextile, 60 degrees, Kennedy's 60th year; i.e., in his 60th year, SA Neptune-Moon will conjoin his Midheaven. This is a potential wipe-out of personality, a loss of ego strength, being off the track, even scandal. And this Solar Arc movement can be seen in a flash, it could have been predicted 5, 10, 15, 20 years ago easily. And, with the involvement of the 7th House through the Moon's rulership, there could be a new marriage.

With the Progressed Sun in 2 Taurus 01 in February, the birthday month in 1992, we find an accumulated Solar Arc of 59°29' from the natal Sun position of 2 Pisces 32. Adding the Solar Arc to Neptune and to the Moon, we (or the computer) get an arc 37' short of Neptune's conjunction with the Midheaven, i.e., 7 more months to go to be exact, which is October, one month before national elections in 1992; 56' or 11 months, January-February 1993, for the Moon.

These are very difficult measurements for Ted Kennedy. The Solar Arcs for this outer planet bring Neptune into action. This is a major indication that Kennedy may not run for re-election in 1994.

The public will turn on him; he has gone off the course; his image will be wiped out somehow. A redemption time is offered in February 1993, through the Solar Arc of the Moon conjunct the Midheaven. Then Kennedy will know what he is supposed to do in this life. The chances are high that what he decides to do, if it is away from the government, will be emotionally very important to him and will still be in public service (Moon; ruler of the 7th House). At best, he will adopt an extremely low profile. At the same time, remarriage is a strong possibility.

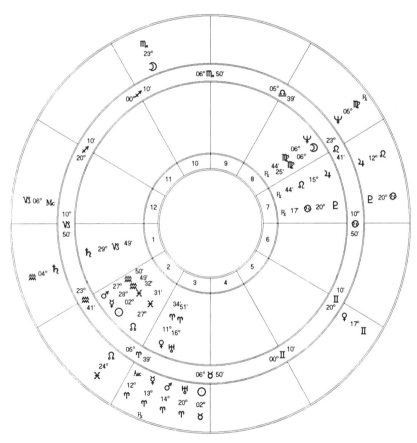

Ted Kennedy
Secondary Progression, Feb. 22, 1992
Feb. 22, 1932, 3:58 a.m. EST
Dorchester, MA
71W04 42N17
Placidus Houses

Anticipating Arcs

Anticipation is the key to prediction. Without anticipation, a baseball player cannot home in on a fly-ball to the outfield; a bridesmaid cannot position herself best to catch the wedding bouquet; an astrologer cannot find the way among myriad measurements.

Every symbol in astrology is in some kind of relationship, some kind of aspect, with every other symbol. That is holistic verity; no human can see the back of the neck directly, but we are definitely related to it. A loved one is far away, yet we can feel the attachment.

One of the major problems facing the astrological analyst is the enormous number of measurements that *are* possible, the systems of measurement that abound, and where to begin the process of making sense of them all. Anticipation helps to lead the astrologer to the telling measurement, *the* major punctuations within time that are beacons of development.

Anticipation comes from knowing about life and, indeed, from as much correlative astrological observation as it is possible to have. Anticipation is deduction from the past and projection to the future: "this batter, 80 percent of the time when batting left-handed, pokes the ball to right center; play in on him, especially when he's up on the count; and, remember, throw to second right away." *Anticipation works with time to make the future happen.*

Anticipation is also common sense: "After all the talks we've had about my being next, I know she intends for me to catch the bouquet. If I catch her eye, she'll spot me." And the astrologer: "This man's job came to him when transiting Uranus conjoined Jupiter, ruler of his Midheaven. And now, with Solar Arc Uranus about to cross that Midheaven, we've got to anticipate a major change, especially with the Midheaven squared by natal Saturn."

If we do not use our head, if we do not think in terms of past performance, projected intent, and common sense, we cannot make any sense out of astrological observation. The measurements become just so many bits of confetti falling from the sky onto our horoscopes. We must think before we measure.

Along with Saturn, the outer planets are the major symbols of life change. Where Saturn is a master timer, Uranus, Neptune, and Pluto are allied with extraordinary substantive adjustment, in presence, focus, and perspective, respectively. Using the rapport measurements we see so easily within the natal configuration, we can begin to anticipate major substantive development in the life. We do not have to go through reams of measurements to see what can catch the eye; we do not need all the confetti. Rather, we need to sight major arc movements that will reveal potential developments of real importance. Beginning with these milestone arc relationships, we can build an architecture of advance. In order to fulfill astrology the best we can, not only *can* we anticipate, we *must*.

• This portion of a woman's horoscope is as clear as a bell: two of the outer planets are obviously due to cross two of her Angles at key times in her life: Uranus across the seventh cusp at about age 22—and immediately, the astrologer's understanding about American society, relationship experience, female intent, and common sense suggest *a time for marriage*. Indeed, this arc could also suggest a time for upset or separation; but at age 22, the chances are that it is the first marriage.

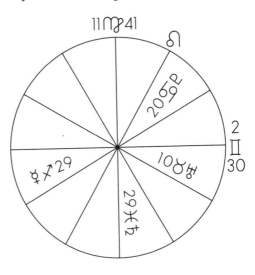

The second rapport measurement observation is Pluto arced to the Midheaven at about age 42. This would be the time for a major change of perspective, quite possibly in professional life as well as in personal life.

Both these times certainly deserve more careful measurement. The computer reveals the month when these Solar Arcs are exact, and then transit triggers active within three or four months of these major arc milestones focus the energy of change more specifically. For this woman, just before SA Uranus crossed her seventh cusp, transiting Saturn conjoined her natal Mercury and squared its own natal position. With natal Mercury ruling the 7th and the 10, Mercury is extremely important. At the time of the Saturn transit, this woman broke up with a major love of her early life and, a year later, "perhaps on the rebound, I don't know," married someone else. That marriage time is shown by the Uranus arc.

At age 42, this woman, with a partner, opened an astrology

bookstore in a sizable city. Business has been good and has become the major focus of her life and study. Eleven years later, she has bought out her partner and is now sole owner. The new perspective established at age 42 endured and is still going strong!

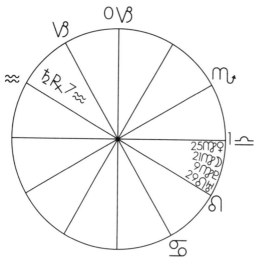

• This next horoscope portion is from a young woman's horoscope. She has chosen a lesbian lifestyle. After keying in on the Saturn retrograde phenomenon and the Saturn placement in the 11th House (father concerns, probably a breakup in the early home, and a very strong need for love), our eyes are drawn to the 6th House which holds two outer planets. Enroute to crossing the seventh cusp —the fulcrum for public self-presentation and relationships—we see a developmental scenario involving the Moon and Venus, the rulers of the 5th and 7th, respectively.

In consultation, dialogue would have to be devoted to age 12+ when SA Pluto conjoined the Moon, age 16+ when SA Pluto conjoined Venus, and finally, age 21-22 when SA Pluto crossed the seventh cusp while squaring the Midheaven. At these times, new perspectives would have have been put before this young woman, which could be seen as molding not only 10 years of her life, but most of her life thereafter, as well. At 13 her father left the family and the homelife was disrupted; at 16-17, there was sexual experimentation and confused relationship tensions; and at 21-22 a confirmation of homosexual lifestyle.

As so often is the case, *several* Solar Arc situations present themselves simultaneously at key times of life development. Notice that Solar Arc Uranus conjoined the Moon, ruler of the 5th, at age 22 as SA Pluto was at the seventh cusp. When SA Uranus conjoined Venus, ruler of the 7th, there were protracted tensions within the live-together relationship the woman was maintaining with another woman.

We can look ahead out of this Solar Arc development structure and note that SA Uranus conjoins the seventh cusp and squares the Midheaven at about age 33 (summer birth, slow arc). And, note: at the same time, SA Saturn (add 32 degrees to Saturn's natal position) will oppose natal Pluto, a time of great challenge and possible loss. There is every indication that, at that time, perspectives in relationship, and perhaps sexual preference, will change dramatically for this woman.

These rapport measurements are so clear, they can be grasped so quickly. Of course, more careful measurements would be made for the arcs ahead, and a rich dialogue between astrologer and client would be well supported.

Exact Solar Arc measurement would set up a superstructure for change, and strong transit activity near those times would suggest the catalysts for development. For example, at the time of SA Saturn opposed Pluto and SA Uranus conjunct the seventh cusp and square the Midheaven, transiting Pluto squares natal Uranus. There will be a tremendous challenge to the woman's value system, who she is as an individual, what her goals are, how she may look afresh at her need for love, and how her professional perspective may change for her adult life.

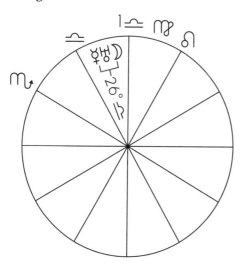

• This young doctor is eager to expand his health services. He is consulting with you when he is 34 years old. When would you begin to anticipate such a new perspective for him?

Of course: at age 35, the very next year, with SA Pluto crossing the Midheaven That is the very reason the doctor has come to you for a consultation. He may not be able to articulate this sense of imminent fulfillment, but he senses this development that is presented to the astrologer through the horoscope.

Interestingly, while the doctor was determined to make the development happen, he required an *extra year* to make it a reality. Perhaps this would be a point of departure for rectification of his horoscope. But, in that interim year, he made all the plans and then embarked on some spiritual studies (Mercury, Neptune, Moon conjunction; Pluto in the 9th) as if to reinforce his decisions to make the big move. Finally, plans came together and, with the transit triggers Pluto conjunct Venus, ruler of his Midheaven, and Pluto semi-square the Sun, which is at the Midheaven, the doctor opened a clinic four times the size of of his former facility, with expanded staff and grand new perspectives ahead.

In our first example, we anticipated developments in the past. In our second example, we did the same; but then, with common sense, we were able to press development forward into time. In our third example, we could immediately zero in on imminent development for the future.

In all these examples, we are co-participants. We are personalizing the outer planets and establishing a superstructure of development for the client. The great bonus of the superb system of Solar Arcs is that they reveal themselves so simply within the natal configuration. Measurements are not needed to give birth to potentials; instead, measurements *refine* the potentials that already speak eloquently from the birthright revealed in the natal horoscope.

Meanings for Solar Arcs

It is well known in astrology that the slower the movement of a planet, the more impact it has in analysis and in life manifestation. This variable of intrinsic motion—the average speed a planet in its orbit has around the Sun—is the key consideration that determines astrological significance. We say that the outer planets are the "heavy" planets, not because of their size or their distance from the Sun, but because of their significance in analysis, their importance in life development, which is related to their slow orbital speeds.

The speed of a planet tells us that the planet in transit will spend a longer time applying, conjoining, and separating from an aspect with another planet or an Angle, in real time as a transit, or in symbolic progression systems. In other words, the symbological import of the particular transit aspect is protracted in time and magnified in importance. With the outer planets moving so slowly, they are associated with weighty, long-term developments in life and mighty turns of events.

In Solar Arc Directions, while advance is determined by the Sun's day-for-a-year movement, the outer planets still carry with them their intrinsic speed-determined spectra of importance. Their slow orbital speed has in great part determined their astrological character. Mythology and empirical observation join orbital speed in filling out the planetary profiles.

For Alan Leo, Uranus was "The Awakener," a marvelously appropriate start in understanding the intensification dynamics of Uranus. Modern astrologers know Uranus as a jolt, a shock, a sudden alert, a "happening"; invigorating, adventurous, startling; self-aware, existential, pressured, individualized; aberrant, rebellious, anxious. Uranus seems to *underline* any need, any cause, hope, dream, or philosophy, elevating a quiet aside to a stage scream. Uranus is a blazing splash of orange paint.

With such energies transferred to the sensitive angular points of development and to the needs and behavioral faculties represented by the planets, we expect from Uranian contact—by natal aspect, by transit, and by Solar Arc Direction—an intensification of self-awareness, a tie-in with events that compel us to feel, think, and act differently; to separate ourselves from the norm; to upset the applecart; to be ourselves more perhaps than we've been before. If we have no say in the matter, as when we are very young and under-developed as an individual, events around us, through family and the social group, challenge us to assimilate change, upset, and new directions, all in a thrust to develop more quickly and substantively.

Solar Arc Uranus in conjunction with or square to the natal Ascendant usually suggests a new start for personal self-projection. Along with intensification of individuation, there is a high probability of geographic relocation. The individual wants to do something new and will go to extremes to make that something new happen.

When Solar Arc Uranus contacts the Ascendant by conjunction or square when the person is very young, the Ascendant should also be viewed as the Midheaven of the parent symbolized by the 4th House (i.e, starting from the 4th House as a new Ascendant, we count around the wheel counter-clockwise and see that the natal Ascendant is the 10th House from the 4th) and the 4th House derived from the 10th. This is the young person's tie-in with family happenings: there is usually a move or a change of social status through the parent's employment, and this change is important to the young person because of a change of friends, locale, future benefits, etc.

Solar Arc Uranus in conjunction or square with the fourth cusp usually suggests another time of new start. Again, through the fourth cusp, we can easily anticipate the tie-in with family when the person is very young. When this arc takes place in adult life, it is extremely important: while it suggests a new start in terms of home (4th House), it also suggests the time for a new start in terms of job or profession since the fourth cusp opposes the Midheaven.

When Solar Arc Uranus conjoins the seventh cusp, it opposes the Ascendant (and in some horoscopes squares the Midheaven axis at about the same time, suggesting extraordinary development protracted over perhaps a year or two, i.e., one or two degrees). The effects are very dramatic. Usually the focus of individuation is intensified so strongly that relationship ties break down under the tension. The way one presents oneself to the world changes. There is new status, new self-awareness; even a sense of tremendous freedom. The intensification of selfhood is such that a new image is created for public show.

When this Uranus arc occurs during childhood, the manifestations are usually through the parents. Once again, we see the seventh cusp as the Midheaven of the parent symbolized in the 10th House and as the fourth cusp of new beginnings for the parent symbolized in the 4th.

Solar Arc Uranus in conjunction or square to the Midheaven usually corresponds to an extraordinary time of life: probably reorganization of family life in the early home; dramatic adjustment of job status as an adult, with a change of profession entirely possible. We can expect a sudden change of direction in practically every department of life.

In relation to the natal planets, Solar Arc Uranus, by conjunction, square, or opposition, awakens extraordinary individualistic intensity. With the Sun, we can expect a nervous, even impetuous, burst of independence, a breaking away, a freeing from limitations. If this drive for change is frustrated or thwarted in some way, we often see an enormous amount of stress manifested. Even problematic behavior can ensue—anything to get attention; the radical emerges to assert a person's specialness.

In Solar Arc theory, only aspects within the fourth harmonic are used: (360°/4 = 90) the conjunction, square, semi-square, sesquiquadrate, and opposition. These are the aspects of action and change (sextiles and trines tend to keep things as they are). The conjunction, square, and opposition appear stronger in manifestation than do the semi-square and sesqui-quadrate.

SA Uranus in strong aspect with the Moon brings strong emotional tensions to the foreground. There's an impulsivity to fulfill one's strongest needs no matter what the cost. This arc corresponds to times when someone sets sights on very special goals. Again, if there is frustration, there is stress.

With Mercury, the Uranus arc stirs up impulsive action, provocative ideas, even inspiration. Here we can anticipate inventiveness; plans for personal freedom. There is an intensification of the nervous system. Often, there are very important travel plans made to put the person forward in development.

With Venus, there is a great desire to be appreciated as special, and there is an intensification of love desire and emotional excitement. Contact between SA Uranus and natal Venus so very often corresponds with the excitement of intense love experience, marriage, an affair, or sexual experimentation.

With Mars, there is intense self-awareness, a tremendous urge to action, even a test of nerves. There can be a sudden application of great energy, an exertion of will upon any circumstances that may be getting in the way of individual fulfillment.

When Solar Arc Uranus contacts natal Jupiter, we can anticipate an intensification of the reward potentials symbolized by Jupiter: there is often the big break, there is success, or the person goes off to greener pastures. This is a time when optimism usually leads the way for the individual.

In relation to Saturn, Uranus always sets up a clash between the avant garde and the traditional; between the pressure to do things in a new way and the caution to remain conventional and predictable. In short, there is a developmental tension between the new and the old. If a sense of confinement or control is present, rebellion is sure to raise its head. Under the best of circumstances, there can be an invigoration of ambition, a boost to one's plans, and a sudden awareness of new ways to improve one's lot.

When SA Uranus connects with Neptune within the fourth harmonic, individuation is explored through imagination, through speculation, and through creativity. With Pluto, there is often a dramatic overturning of the status quo; a whole new perspective is established—or is trying to be—for ego-recognition.

In 1912, when Alan Leo's *The Art of Synthesis* was first published, Neptune was the end of the line. Neptune was 66 years old, almost the age Pluto is for us now in the early 1990s. Leo and the other great astrologers who flourished in turn-of-the-century England had had a good long look at this outermost planet.

Leo wrote, "Neptune is supposed to be the planet of Chaos, representing a state of things undifferentiated, disordered, without shape or definite form; it is therefore the planet of confusion . . ." He suggested ideas about Neptune and masquerading, about the love of mysticism, the involvement with drugs, and about dreams and visions and deceptions. Most startlingly, in my opinion, Leo wrote, "Neptune allows the soul to leave the body."

As many theorists have put forward, Uranus is the higher octave of Mercury and Neptune is the higher octave of Venus. Leo affirmed this and named Neptune "The Mystic." Even though we recognize that Leo was an adept and entrenched esoteric astrologer, deeply involved with the spiritual movements of his time, we would be hard pressed to find a better title for Neptune. But in the arena of demands on self-development that are anything but spiritual for the most part in our society, what can the soul's leaving the body mean? What everyday use is that dimension of ourselves which can be called "The Mystic"?

This is where astrology introduces the concept of *not* doing what we should with what we have: if we don't pay attention to our soul, our spirit, our awareness of the mystical, we are losing out on an echelon of development. The proclivities of behavior into those directions take on different forms: we get camouflage, substitution, subterfuge, escape addictions, dementia. In short, we act differently than we normally do to express something we don't understand. Things are other than they seem. We lose ego definition in the real world. The body retreats from the soul.

I realize that this introduction to the Solar Arcs of Neptune is itself decidedly Neptunian. It just comes out that way. I am still concerned—ten or twelve pages later—about Ted Kennedy taking on Solar Arc Neptune in conjunction with his natal Midheaven in the Fall of 1992. This directed aspect always signifies a very important time in life: there is usually a sense of ego disappearance; the personal identity somehow gets lost in situations through disregard, or through drugs or alcohol in emotional defensiveness. The "up" side of the potential here is for extreme imagination, success in the arts;

not necessarily as a creator but, say, as a philanthropist. With SA Neptune conjoining the Midheaven, if one *is* a spiritualist, one *understands* and benefits. If not, one may feel lost.

Because the Midheaven is strategically the symbol of one's place in the Sun, one's profession, there can be peculiar employment concerns, false claims, bogus promises. In the early home, peculiar goings on in the homelife through the parents can affect the young person deeply.

With SA Neptune conjoining or square the Ascendant, there usually is a high sensitivity, a high impressionability for better or for worse. There can be a spiritual projection, the soul far away from the body, a loss of self-awareness or self-respect, or no understanding of why one is alive.

With SA Neptune in fourth harmonic relationship with the fourth cusp, we can anticipate much the same as when SA Neptune is in relationship with the Midheaven by conjunction or square.

With SA Neptune conjunct the seventh cusp and opposed the Ascendant, there is often deception from without, a misleading by others, a dissolution of relationship ties.

As the outer planets were discovered, all the demanding and painful dimensions of life were shifted out and away from Saturn (and Mars) onto Uranus—which was so astoundingly new in terms of independence and revolution and invention—and Neptune— which was so captivatingly amorphous, self-absorbing, and catching of all or anything.

When SA Neptune aspects the natal Sun, there definitely is the sense of ego loss at worst and creative inspiration at best. Usually there is befuddlement, potential spiritual rationalization, and even deception and illegality. The world accosts the sense of self in ways that are very hard to understand and assimilate.

In aspect with the Moon, SA Neptune arouses very special sensitivities for refinement or bewilderment. With Mercury, the fantasy becomes very active for inspiration or escape. With Venus, love becomes a swoon of the sensibilities; there are erotic imaginings beyond the norm; there is the fear of being alone, without relationship. With life circumstances and personality potentials that function well in terms of highly focused aesthetics, imagination, conceptualization, creativity, love, and spirituality, Neptune's contact with the Moon, Mercury, and Venus can mark periods of enlightenment, growth, and fulfillment.

When SA Neptune makes conjunction, square, opposition, semi-square, or sesquiquadrate contact with natal Mars, there usually is a change of the course of action due to dissatisfaction; there is the idea of going to where the grass seems greener. The focus of applied energy somehow becomes diffused.

When SA Neptune makes contact with Jupiter, two planets that echo one another meld symbolically. Historically, both planets are co-rulers of Pisces. We can expect an emphasis on things spiritual, philosophical, religious, extrasensory. There can be a show of benevolence, all in the spirit of idealism. On the "down" side, there can be strong self-indulgences, escape actions, rationalization, or self-pity. The potential for tricky legalisms should not be overlooked, should one's reality-situation present that possibility.

In Solar Arc aspect with Saturn, Neptune seems to undermine the directness, the thrust of ambition. One feels depressed, feels wronged; waiting for rescue. As well, there can be the inclination to give up under stress, to play the martyr.

When SA Neptune aspects natal Uranus, a loss of ego-focus is possible; the spiritual world is awakened. If these potentials do not seem evident, there usually is an underlying irritability; one feels blunted somehow, having no effect.

In aspect with Pluto, if a registration of these planets' potential together will occur, we can anticipate an awakening of things supernatural; there are unusual problems to be solved, peculiar experiences to be assimilated. There very well may be concerns about death matters. On the "up" side, if one's reality supports the possibility, there can be a considerable thrust of creative enterprise.

Within the legacy of richly developed insights and innovation-provided us by Alan Leo, there is nothing about Pluto, of course, discovered 12 years after Leo's death. I have often wondered, with Leo's marvelously apt turns of phrase, what would *he* have named Pluto? How would he have captured what we know today about this small, slow, erratic, distant planet that now marks our end of the line?

Maybe Leo would have come up with the title "The Extremist." Indeed, extremism *is* a dimension of the Pluto portrait as we have come to paint it. Leo would have been welcoming the newest planet from a turn-of-the-century spirit of adventure, expansion, and exploration; Pluto would take all of that further, to an extreme. The world was opening up. Society was revolutionizing itself industrially, politically, and in terms of personal conduct. So much more was being expected of modern individuals. In my opinion, though, "The Extremist," while close to the mark, carries with it too much sociometric editorialization. Understandably, from a vantage point in the 1930s, it does not capture the whole picture.

From our vantage point today, I have suggested another concept, another name: "Perspective." I think this keyword captures the sense of outer frontier and, at the same time, the invitation to or challenge of extremes. "Perspective" suggests the *adverbial* dimension of Pluto in our lives: how much, how far, how strong. To me, Pluto can not yet be anthropomorphized; it can not become a "person" like the Awakener or the Mystic. Pluto is still very much a *principle*, an indication of open-ended potential, a projection of self to new levels, into new directions, into whatever is beyond the norm.

In the natal horoscope, when Pluto is configured with Venus, for example, by fourth harmonic, by demanding aspect, we can expect a waste of emotions to be part of the behavioral pattern. An extreme is aroused by the sense of unlimited perspective. The same concept applies to aspects with Mercury, within the perceptions, communication, and/or nervous system. With Mars, in relation to the application of energy, reactionism to the world can go "off the charts," so to speak. "How much" becomes a response to how far one needs to go.

Within Solar Arc measurements, the manifestations of Pluto's contacts with natal Angles and planets are usually profoundly important. New perspectives challenge, confront, invite, or fulfill the person within the developmental process.

SA Pluto in contact with the Ascendant, especially by conjunction or square, almost always accompanies dramatic changes of perspective: identity transformation; geographic relocation; taking command of things. It is often a life-milestone period involved with personal power, persuasion, strategic change, and, if the reality supports the potential, concerns with death matters. As with all three of the outer planets, when such a powerful arc takes place in the early life before the individual is free of the home situation, effects will manifest through the parents and the structure of the homelife. Again, we must remember that the Ascendant is also the Midheaven of one of the parents.

We have seen on page 195 that Lyndon Johnson's SA Pluto conjunction with his natal Ascendant occurred in November 1960 when he was elected Vice President, his beginning of nine years in the White House.

SA Pluto crossing the fourth cusp signals a powerful new start in life, where one lives, how one plans the next grand period of life. As well, since SA Pluto at the fourth cusp is opposed the Midheaven, we can anticipate major job adjustment.

SA Pluto crossing the seventh cusp and opposing the Ascendant usually accompanies major changes in relationship ties or, in early life, some major adjustment of the family in relation to one parent's job or life crisis.

SA Pluto at the Midheaven corresponds to an extremely important time of life. Job or professional upset and change are almost sure. These changes are life-significant. Parental adjustments in the early home are personally significant. There are separations and changes brought about throughout one's life and environment to alter the direction of development to a new perspective.

When SA Pluto is in touch with the natal Sun, a powerful force is usually set up to catalyze a major change in life. Identity may be altered. There can be sudden prominence, even exhibitionism. The ego is thrust forward powerfully.

With the Moon, SA Pluto brings forward extreme emotional intensity for upheaval and/or exaggerated new plans. The thrust is to finally pay attention to one's own needs and fulfill them at any cost.

In aspect with natal Mercury, SA Pluto usually manifests in the ability to persuade, to demand new perspectives for self-fulfillment. With Venus, there is an intensification of love desires, affairs, compulsiveness with relationship needs. And with Mars, extreme force can be manifested, even brutality, as energy is applied within excessive efforts of all kinds.

When SA Pluto makes an aspect with natal Jupiter, we usually encounter a tremendous optimism, a thrust for leadership and power.

When SA Pluto relates by aspect in the fourth harmonic with natal Saturn, we have a very difficult outlook: there is the threat of loss in any area of life; potential self-destruction; hard work. This is one of the most difficult progression measurements in astrology.

In aspect relationship with natal Uranus, SA Pluto calls forth tremendous intensification of ego-awareness and the possible attainment of great goals through great effort. And with Neptune, we can expect great intensification of sensory sensitivity. There is even a threat to losing the reality dimensions of life situations. There is the possibility of subterfuge and the introduction of drugs or alcohol dysfunctionally.

Extra Notes and Advanced Arcs

As we have learned, Solar Arcs are timed by the Progressed Sun's day-for-a-year advance. All planets and points of the natal horoscope are directed uniformly so that their relative positions one to another never vary from the relativity of the natal configuration. With the outer planets, however, the intrinsic heftiness of importance determined by their slow orbital speed is carried over to Solar Arc measurement with considerable impact. The Solar Arc aspects formed by the outer planets with the natal planets and sensitive points are formidable.

As with any major event or attitude change in life, there is usually a build-up of circumstances and then an adjustment to a new status quo. Major change usually *takes time* to focus itself, happen, and stabilize. Such a reality period is covered by the approach of the directed planet to the aspect with the natal planet and then by the separation of the directed planet from the aspect. An orb of application and separation of one degree extends the arc of importance of a major Solar Arc to about two years, with the climax of change expected near the middle of that time (usually just before, on the early side).

Especially with the outer planets, the Solar Arc sets up the background of expectancy for developments, and a major series of transits brings the potential into being. The transits appear to trigger what is anticipated from the Solar Arc measurement. A major Solar Arc involving the outer planets can "reach out" from the time of partile three to six months into the past or into the future in order to "pick up" the transit catalyst, the support needed to gel. In my presentation of Solar Arcs in *Prediction in Astrology* (Llewellyn Publications, 1991), I call this outreach into time the "Time Orb" of any Solar Arc. Through the concept of a Time Orb, astrology imitates life.

No measurement in astrology manifests in life every time it occurs. Measurements often go by without a ripple in life development. This is due to several considerations, several verities: the person's reality does not support or embrace the potential the arc suggests; the person's plans, resources, or talents do not support the potential; the potential of the arc does not fit the person's environmental circumstance; the level of consideration suggested by the arc is simply foreign to the make-up of the person. For example, tremendous aesthetic awakening or arousal of creativity may find no audience or medium for expression in someone living a routine life at a mechanical job with no special artistic hobbies. The person may be very happy and fulfilled, but the talents of aesthetics and creativity are not called for in his or her millieu. The measurement may adopt another level of expression or disappear. If one's parents are both dead, no parent can die; but an in-law may; or someone extremely important to one's life perspective. Job changes probably may not occur if one is truly content with one's job; relocation can not occur unless there is the potential for it financially, resourcefully in many related departments of life; but there may be a raise, a change of responsibilities, even a relocation to a new workplace.

In short, common sense and practicality are prime considerations which must precede application of any Solar Arc—especially those involving the outer planets—to a life situation. What *is* happening is the best clue to what *can* happen.

A great help in identifying the specific substance of a major Solar Arc can come from the House ruled by the arcing planet first and then second, from the House where the arcing planet is positioned natally. For Lyndon Johnson (see page 199) arcing Pluto ruled his 4th House, new starts. This is an obvious companion-concept to the "perspective" symbolism of Pluto. Pluto was positioned in the 11th House natally, the House of hopes, wishes, objectives, values from the profession (second of the 10th).

For Ted Kennedy (see page 202) for his Solar Arc Neptune conjunction with the Midheaven, through which we can expect conspicuous loss of ego definition and status, there are connotations we can take from the 2nd House of self-worth, holding Pisces ruled by Neptune. Neptune's position in the 8th suggests the values of society (second of the 7th). Additionally, the Moon, following right behind Neptune to Solar Arc conjunction with the Midheaven, rules the 7th and refers directly to Kennedy's potential redemption of himself in further public service professionally after his crisis. The Moon and Neptune are a little over one degree apart; with the application of one degree for Neptune to the Midheaven (i.e., the latter half of 1991, the scandal attending Kennedy's nephew), the one degree for the Moon to reach the Midheaven, and then one more degree for settling into a new status quo, we see a three-year period of deep upset and change that, through Time Orb consideration, can pick up many key transits to punctuate metamorphosis in real time.

Solar Arc theory and practice also relates arcing planets to fourth harmonic aspects with the *midpoints* between planets and the midpoints between planets and Angles. For example, in July 1969, when Ted Kennedy faced the crisis with the death of Mary Jo Kopechne (July 18), he was "protected," if you will, by the Solar Arc midpoint picture Uranus conjunct the Midpoint of Sun-Jupiter. This is a good luck symbolism; it suggests circumstantial extrication from difficulty.

In February 1992, strongly within the Time Orb buildup of his Solar Arc Neptune conjunction with the Midheaven, Ted Kennedy has the Solar Arc midpoint picture of Pluto opposed the midpoint of Venus-Mars, a measurement with very strong sexual connotations. On February 4 and 5, 1992, transiting Mars in Capricorn makes an opposition with Kennedy's natal Pluto in the 7th House. Pluto is making the Solar Arc aspect, rules Kennedy's 10th House and has come from Kennedy's 7th. As is typical with major lifetime change keyed by much Solar Arc activity, the picture keeps repeating itself over and over again: echoes of scandal and possible remarriage.

Publishers Note: This Chapter on the Solar Arc aspects of the outer planets is necessarily only an introduction to Solar Arc theory and practice. In Noel Tyl's *Prediction in Astrology* (Llewellyn Publications, St. Paul MN, 1991), the author presents the entire field of Solar Arcs and Midpoint pictures. It is the most complete presentation written in English and includes an Appendix describing the potential of all 1,014 Arcs and Midpoint configurations.

Jeffrey Green

Jeffrey Green has been a professional astrologer in Seattle, Washington since 1976. He has lectured at all the major astrological conferences in the United States, Canada, and Europe, including AFA, UAC, SWAC, NORWAC, WRAC, SEAC, the Canadian National and Regional Conferences, the 3rd World Astrological Conference in Zurich, Switzerland, Astrolgical Forum in The Hague, Holland, etc. He has authored numerous astrological articles published in the United States, Canada and Europe, and two best selling books *Pluto: The Evolutionary Journey of the Soul*, and *Uranus: Freedom from the Known*, which have been translated into Dutch, German, Spanish, and Yugoslavian. Jeffrey spent two years in monastic association with the Vedanta Temple. His formal education is in philosophy and psychology. Jeffrey is a Viet-Nam Veteran.

Trauma and the Outer Planets

Jeffrey Green

I would like to thank Noel Tyl for inviting me to write to this topic, for it is a highly personal subject for me. The opportunity constitutes an act of personal therapy, since some of the material that follows will be autobiographical in nature. For those who have experienced me as an enigma over the years, the mask will be removed.

In this chapter, we will examine just exactly what is trauma; consider possible causes of it, and examine the effects that it produces. Specifically, we will examine trauma from the point of view of *types* of trauma: mental, emotional, spiritual, physical, and collective trauma. We will examine the astrological correlations (planets, signs, houses) to these types of trauma, and specific case histories in order to uncover possible astrological signatures in birth charts that reflect higher probability rates for trauma.

Also, in this section we will include Saturn, even though it is not considered to be an outer planet. Saturn correlates to the outer threshold of our conscious awareness, the boundary defining the interface between conscious awareness and the unconscious. Because Saturn also correlates to the psychological function of repression or suppression, which is based in the act of denial of some dynamic or experience, its presence as a causal factor in certain types of trauma is implicated. Saturn will also be included because of its correlation to the inner and outer structure of the physical body; thus it has a linkage to physical trauma of the body.

So, what is trauma? A succinct definition will suffice: trauma is an intense mental, emotional, physical, or spiritual/psychic disturbance resulting from stress or shock that can have a lasting psychic or psychological effect. *An intense disturbance caused by shock or stress*

219

that can have a lasting effect. Yes, this statement can probably describe the state of affairs for the entire planet right now because of what psychologists have termed the Delayed Stress Syndrome. Astrologically, this is a function of Saturn, Capricorn, or the 10th House. Delayed stress infers some dynamic or event that has been suppressed, repressed, or ignored.

All one has to do, in this country for example, is tune into one of the talk shows to witness yet another person, or set of people, talking about some horrible event: rape, sexual or psychological abuse, etc., to understand the effects of delayed stress caused by trauma. Or the Viet-Nam veteran's problems, or the collective (Neptune) search for the inner, wounded child. The wounded child syndrome infers "origin issues" and how these issues define one's sense of identity.

When Saturn, Uranus, and Neptune began their transits through Capricorn, the delayed stress of childhood surfaced into the collective consciousness of many within the Western World. Because Capricorn is a Cardinal Archetype there has been and is a need to go backwards, in the sense of recovering the inner child, by bringing to light the nature of the psychological and emotional imprinting that occurred in childhood. This must occur in order to go forward, by becoming free or liberated (Uranus) from these early conditioning (Saturn) patterns.

On a larger level, there is a collective need all over the planet to politically, economically, and philosophically restructure (Uranus transiting Capricorn) the internal nature of each society/country in order to be free (Uranus) from outmoded or crystallized (Capricorn, Saturn) political, economic, and philosophic structures that are impeding the evolutionary growth (Pluto) and needs of the planet, and each nation on the planet as a whole. The revolutions within Eastern Europe, the Soviet Union, the restructuring of the Middle East, the "new world order," the progressive enforcement powers extended to the United Nations, the rebellion within the Canadian Provinces, the replacement of dictators in South America with freely elected officials, the soon-to-be social revolution within the United States—all attest to individual and collective stress and trauma that will have lasting effects.

Delayed stress is implied in all of this because we are living in very transitional times in which everything has to change. The old ways of doing things do not work anymore, yet to confront new and unknown ways of doing things creates fear of the unknown. Fear of the unknown creates an individual and collective insecurity. The essence of feeling secure lies in our need for self or collective consistency. So the tension or stress between the old and the new, the transition therein, leads to the delayed stress syndrome because the resistance (Pluto) to necessary change generates a suppression or ignoring of the "signs" that change is necessary. When evolutionary needs are ignored or suppressed, then the need to change, now suppressed or ignored, compresses and intensifies, like the increasing friction in a fault line, until change can no longer be avoided. This resistance can lead to cataclysmic change, which produces intense forms of individual or collective trauma.

The gaia of the Earth (our planet as an integrated biosphere) has been generating many such signs for many years now. The breakdown in the ozone layer, the greenhouse effect, the contamination of the water, the contamination of the food chain, the alteration of weather patterns—all attest to a trauma within Nature that will have powerful and enduring effects. The signs have been and are many, and yet the necessary changes to adjust to the scientific and empirical facts have been and are still too slow. The delayed stress in the gaia of our planet will mushroom into possible cataclysmic events that will have long range consequences leading to irrevocable change.

This may occur in many ways, including the accelerated (Uranus) mutation (Pluto) within the the genetic structure and coding of many forms of life within Nature, as all forms of life seek to adapt and adjust to the increasing trauma within the biosphere of Earth. This includes the forms of life called viruses and bacteria, as they attempt to sustain their own lives through accelerated mutation within their own genetic structures. Uncontrolled disease is the result, the AIDS virus but the first manifestation of this planetary trauma.

This is interesting to consider from the point of view of the gaia. Astrologically, Neptune correlates to the overall functioning of the immune system, and specifically to the pineal and thymus glands. Saturn or Capricorn correlates to the overall structural integrity of the human body. Uranus correlates to the overall atmosphere of the planet, and, among other anatomical and physiological correlations, to the respiratory system of the human body: specifically, the lining of the lungs. Pluto, again, correlates to the phenomena of evolution, metamorphosis, mutation, and the genetic coding in all forms of life.

So what do we have here? The delayed stress within the gaia of the biosphere is now manifesting as an acceleration within the breakdown of the atmosphere; Uranus transiting Capricorn. This breakdown is fundamentally and radically altering the nature and quality of "light" within the atmosphere of Earth. The functioning of the pineal gland within the brain is determined by the quality and nature of light entering the retina of the eyes in all living organisms. By altering the quality of light entering the biosphere there is the simultaneous altering of the pineal gland and immune system within all living organisms. In effect, this alteration will initially weaken or depress (Capricorn) the immune system as it seeks to adjust to these new conditions (Uranus in Capricorn).

In conjunction with this, there are mutations of the various forms of viruses and bacterias as *they* seek to adjust to these new conditions as well (Pluto in Scorpio). Thus, we have the AIDS virus which is known as a retrograde virus, a function of delayed stress, which has the capacity to merge (Scorpio) itself within the RNA/DNA genetic structure and coding in such a way as to turn the immune system in upon itself (lupis in its worst form) to the point of killing the organism (the human body) that it has invaded.

This condition is but the first warning to mankind that the gaia is out of balance due to the activities of humankind. With Neptune leading Uranus (as of this writing) through Capricorn, the immune system is that which suffers first from the effect of the delayed stress within the gaia. As Uranus catches up to Neptune, the next major disease that will likely occur will be specific to the respiratory system. By way of viruses which will have mutated through evolutionary necessities, this will probably manifest as a multi-drug (Neptune) resistant (Pluto) form of tuberculosis which will be spread through casual contact; by simply sharing the same air or atmosphere with other human beings. In conjunction with immune systems that are being altered or weakened, the impact of such disease has incredible implications for the planet. And, from the point of view of the gaia, this just may be a way that Nature adapts to the imbalanced state that it is in. Maybe this is Nature's way of culling organisms in to order rebalance itself into a state of structural integrity.

On a collective psychological/emotional level, the breakdown (Uranus) and dissolution (Neptune) of societal beliefs and values

(Saturn/Capricorn), i.e. the American Dream, have begun to generate an ever-increasing collective futility, depression, anxiety, Angst, and hopelessness that have potentially far-reaching socio/political/economic implications to radically (Uranus) alter "the system" as currently structured. This kind of collective trauma is necessary because it forces the collective and individual consciousness to invert (Saturn/Capricorn), to withdraw from the individual and collective "system" so that new ideas, realizations, and directions can be realized to reflect and symbolize the new and necessary way. A quick glimpse into modern history when Uranus and Neptune were transiting through Capricorn the last time they were together, in the 1820s, reveals this dynamic relative to the Industrial Revolution of that time. The Industrial Revolution totally altered and restructured western societies. We live with that imprint still today. And it is this imprint or structure that is once again demanding radical change.

The point of citing delayed stress as an example of trauma is that it is one of the most common forms of trauma; it generates an individual or collective reality that is defined (Saturn/Capricorn) by the effects of the trauma itself. Yet, the behavioral effects that are generated are not recognized as being caused by the trauma itself because of the suppression or repression within the individual and/or the collective. And, of course, the reasons for the suppression or repression are that the natures of the specific trauma are so severe that the individual or collective can not accept that the trauma has or is occurring in the first place.

Yet, the suppressed trauma continues to dictate behavior, the dictation of the behavior operating at a subconscious level (Uranus). Operating in this way, the effects of the trauma produce many "signs" within the behavioral patterns at any level of reality, i.e., the breakdown in the ozone layer, irrational rage in individual behavioral patterns, economic structures that produce increasing homelessness, bankruptcy, mergers of corporations, insane budget deficits, etc.—all telling us that something is amiss. As of this writing in late 1991, one out of ten Americans is currently on Food Stamps. One out of ten!

If we focus on the individual, such signs can be classified as (1) personality disorders of various types such as agoraphobia, pathological lying, extreme forms of masochistic or sadistic behavior, intense or irrational rage that permeates an individual's behavior, and all forms of pathological or repetitive compulsive behavior, (2) sociopathic behavior (3) multi or split personalities, and (4) neurosis or psychosis. And even though these "signs" of behavioral disorder define the nature of one's identity, the individual typically does not recognize or "own" the behavior until the nature of the specific trauma is unlocked. Once unlocked within the individual, it becomes imperative that treatment or therapy work to reintegrate the personality.

Therapy does not necessarily mean that the effects of the trauma can be permanently erased as if the trauma never happened, but it can mean that the affect of the trauma is changed because it has been brought up from the unconscious into the full light of consciousness. In this way, a perpetual awareness of the effects relative to the cause can be sustained, and over time the individual can consciously change his or her behavior, the repetitive compulsion syndrome linked with traumatic behavior fundamentally altered.

The delayed stress syndrome caused by specific trauma is but one type of reaction to trauma, even though the most common and pervasive. Behavioral reactions to it are not dependent on suppression of a specific trauma. This means an individual can experience trauma and *not* suppress it, and yet the effects of that trauma will alter the individual's behavior anyway. This alteration can continue on for a potentially indefinite amount of time, until the affect of the trauma is worked out in some way. The behavioral alteration is a function of the stress associated with the trauma even though the trauma is not suppressed.

Trauma occurs, again, to the mental, emotional, physical, and spiritual or psychic bodies. And, as we will see, these bodies, when trauma occurs, can interact in a chain reaction, i.e., severe physical trauma causing a trauma to the mental, emotional, or spiritual bodies. Let us examine in detail, through case studies, the types of trauma associated with these different bodies and provide the appropriate astrological associations for them.

The Mental Body correlates with Uranus as the primary significator, and with Mercury, its lower octave, as secondary significator. The types of trauma associated with the mental body are stroke, various types of psychological or psychiatric disorders, epilepsy, various diseases of the brain, and sudden, unexpected life changes that alter the psychological reality of the individual and the external structures of personal reality that have defined the sense of identity up until the unexpected changes began to occur.

The Emotional Body correlates with Pluto as primary ruler, and the Moon and Neptune as secondary rulers. The types of trauma associated with the emotional body are violations in trust associated with betrayal, abandonment and gross misuse through misapplied trust, psychological and sexual abuse, sudden loss, the experiencing of cataclysmic events of an individual or collective nature, anticipation of events that appear to be fated or beyond the control of the individual.

The Physical Body correlates with Saturn. The types of trauma associated with the physical body are various physical traumas such as severe injuries of various types, rape, torture, intense physical illness, degeneration of the body through various causes such as disease, birth disorders such as cerebral palsy, spinal bifida, etc.

The Spiritual Body correlates with Neptune. The types of trauma associated with the spiritual body are loss of faith, loss of beliefs, loss of values, massive disillusionment, and, in rare cases, being possessed by an unwanted spirit.

Again, a key point to remember is that when trauma occurs in one of the specific bodies, there is almost always a chain reaction effect that impacts the *entire* organism, the other bodies, in a variety of ways.

Let us now examine two case histories, from an astrological view, to help illustrate these ideas. In these cases, you will notice the presence of stressful aspects to the relevant astrological dynamics or archetypes. In my work with over 15,000 clients, I have observed that stressful aspects do indeed correlate with a higher probability rate for traumatic experiences than to the non-stressful aspects. Natal charts that have stressful aspects to the planets that correlate with the various traumas thus have a higher probability rate for trauma than those that do not. When these natal planets experience stressful aspects through transits or progressions, the probability of some kind of trauma becomes quite high.

Case #1: Physical Trauma

This is a case history of a girl born with a genetic disorder called Turner's Syndrome. This syndrome is a genetic condition in which 45 of the 48 double Y chromosomes in a female child are damaged or split. The causes of this condition are not known by western medicine. Turner's Syndrome essentially is a growth disorder, because these girls are born with no ovaries, or severely damaged ones. This does not allow them to have their own biological children, as well as having a lack of estrogen in their physiology which impacts the ability of the receptor cells within the bone marrow to absorb the growth hormones produced through the pituitary and thyroid glands. Maximum height is generally 4'4" to 4'8". In addition, generally half of Turner's girls have malformed kidneys and hearts which can cause death. These girls also have difficulty with their motor skills and left-brain logical organization of information, and with spatial relationships.

Western medicine typically treats this syndrome with anabolic steroids, estrogen, and testosterone in order to induce growth larger than genetically prescribed. The anabolic steroids, in particular, have been demonstrated to damage the liver and thyroid, and testosterone to produce an abnormally sized clitoris. Around 13 or 14 these girls must be given estrogen in order for them to develop secondary sexual characteristics, allowing for psychological and emotional maturing into adulthood. If left untreated, these girls will reach their genetically prescribed height around 30 years of age. Western medicine claims that these girls can not grow more than one inch a year if left untreated. Turner's babies are also typically born premature which creates its own set of traumatic conditions.

Pluto correlates with the RNA/DNA genetic coding in all forms of life. Saturn correlates with the physical structure of the body. Saturn also correlates with the pituitary gland, as does Jupiter. Venus correlates with the kidneys, as well as estrogen and the receptor cells within the bone marrow. The 5th House, Sun, and Leo correlate with the heart. The 3rd House, Gemini, and Mercury correlate with the motor skills and the logical left-brain organizational skills. Pluto, Scorpio, and the 8th House correlate with the hormones that the baby emits within the womb (Moon) to trigger birth.

In the horoscope on the next page, this girl has Pluto conjunct Saturn at the point of a T-square with the Moon and Mars which are opposed. The Moon is inconjunct Venus, and Venus is in a semi-square with the Saturn/Pluto conjunction. This girl was indeed premature, being born one month early. The T-square which involves Pluto, Moon, and Mars suggests the early triggering of the birth hormone by the baby. She was diagnosed with Turner's Syndrome at five years of age. This diagnosis was triggered because this girl had stopped growing for a period of about one year. The physical trauma is certainly obvious in this astrological signature. In fact, the entire Turner's Syndrome is within this astrological pattern. With Jupiter in the 6th House (overall health) trining the Moon, and sextile Mars, the more severe conditions causing or leading to premature (Mars) death (Pluto) were not genetically programmed: Jupiter in Scorpio in the 6th House. She did not have a malformed heart or kidneys.

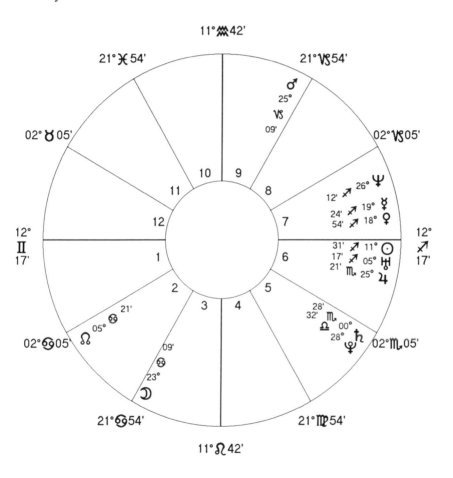

Case #1, Female

Even though western medicine does not know the causes of Turner's Syndrome, it may be interesting to note that the father of this girl served in Viet-Nam and was heavily exposed to Agent Orange. This is a dioxin that accumulates in the liver, and has been demonstrated to cause genetic disorders in laboratory animals. This girl's father also has Jupiter (liver) in Scorpio conjunct his daughter's Jupiter in her 6th House. And the girl's Jupiter, Saturn, and Pluto fall in his 12th House (the 12th House often being an indicator of genetic problems). Since this girl has Saturn conjunct Pluto in her 5th House square Mars in Capricorn, and the Moon in Cancer, a linkage to the father as a possible cause could be inferred.

This genetically programmed physical condition (trauma) could also trigger trauma in the mental, emotional, and spiritual bodies: the mental body because of the breakdown in the left brain that controls the motor skills and the ability to logically structure or organize spatial relationships and information; the emotional body because of the physical conditions that she is unable to change or control; and the spiritual or psychic body because of a psychology that would be based on feeling victimized or punished by forces (God?) larger than herself.

In this girl's case, the role of the parents (the planetary rulers of her 4th and 10th Houses are conjunct in her 6th House) becomes paramount to her sense of identity within this genetically programmed condition. With her Sun conjunct Uranus in the 6th House, the parents' roles as teachers generating a positive self-image are critical. In addition, the parents rebelled (Uranus) and rejected (6th House) the medical establishment methods of treatment (6th House). They sought out alternative methods (Uranus in the 6th) of treatment involving certain nutritional supplements that enhanced the ability of the receptor cells to absorb the growth hormones. They taught the girl the power within her own mind, the power of thought, to create her own reality (Sun conjunct Uranus). Uranus at this level correlates with the creation (Sun) of dendrites (Uranus) within the brain (Uranus) that allows it to evolve (Pluto). The teaching had the affect of returning power (empowerment) to the girl (Pluto conjunct Saturn in the Fifth House). As a result of these two remediations, the girl grew four inches within the first year after diagnosis, two inches in the second year, and two inches and counting within the third year.

This sense of empowerment led to a positive self-image. In her own words this positive self-image is stated best: " I may be small in body, but I am big in heart and soul." The psychological attitude has allowed her to withstand negative peer-group feedback because she is "different."

In addition, her parents helped her to develop her motor skills and logical ordering by simply teaching her to work with making jewelry out of beads *every day*. This was very difficult at first, but through persistence and determination she evolved new dendrites within the brain that bypassed the brain's normal structure relative to this function. She now has perfect motor skills and organizes information and spatial relationships like everyone else. Instead of feeling victimized by God she has learned to draw upon God as an ally, and to ask for God's help to grow. In essence, the affect of the physical trauma has now generated different effects that will allow a positive integration of the personality.

Case History #2. Emotional Trauma

This is a case history of a man who was severely sexually and psychologically abused by his mother. This abuse started right after birth; his first six months were spent black and blue, and this continued until he was placed in an orphanage at six years of age when his parents separated for a period of time. After they got back together, they brought him home. The sexual abuse then stopped, but the psychological abuse continued.

Without being explicit, suffice it to say that the sexual and psychological abuse were severe. And it began immediately after birth. This is called pre-verbal abuse. When this occurs one of the critical stages of an infant's development is not accomplished: the internalization of the mother. When that stage of development does not occur, the infant does not learn to feel safe or secure when the mother is not present.

The inner, feminine dynamic within a male is called the anima in Jungian psychology. When the anima is wounded through abuse, abandonment, violations of trust, and betrayal, it leads to emotional trauma and displaced emotions. When this man was a child, as a survival function he inwardly detached from his body and the immediate environment. He developed a life of total fantasy and illusion considered as reality. He blocked the body from all sensation. He was "visited" in the dark of the night by an "angel" called Mary whom he considered his real "mother" because this angel provided comfort and nourishment. He longed for the dark of the night; he feared the days when his mother was alone with him.

Because he learned to survive through detaching from his body and environment, through living in his inner world, he became a loner as he grew up. Acutely shy and sensitive, he felt alienated from his peers and the world. The memories of childhood were blocked; they were suppressed within the unconscious anima. He remained emotionally infantile and compensated, unconsciously, by a singular focus upon philosophical and spiritual development as he grew into adulthood. This was accomplished by being initiated into shamanistic practices via the Navaho peyote tradition, and by entering monasteries of an Eastern Tradition.

He shunned normal relationships with women, and the few that he engaged in were based on women who would aggressively pursue him. These women were *femme fatale* types who repeated the patterns of his mother: violations of trust, abandonment, betrayal, and abuse. Because the memories of his mother, the initial trauma, were suppressed, the effects generated by the trauma were repeated into adulthood through the function of emotional displacement. This function thus set him up to be re-victimized.

Astrologically, this man has the classic signature of sexual and psychological abuse and trauma associated with the mother. This pattern is reflected in his Pisces Moon in the 4th House being squared by Mars in the 2nd House, and Uranus in the 8th House, Mars and Uranus being in opposition. In addition, the Moon is at the apex of a Yod with Pluto and Neptune. Beyond the sexual abuse that this pattern demonstrates, the psychological abuse (Uranus in the 8th House) created an extremely inferior self-image (Moon in Pisces in the 4th House). This image was built upon messages that there must be something wrong with him, that he was "nothing," that he deserved pain and punishment even though he did not know why (Pluto). His inner compensation through fantasy and spiritual development allowed him to experience himself in a larger-than-life type way, but the subjective personality or ego (Moon in Pisces) was fractured, diffuse, and not integrated: it was weak and inferior. The emotional infant wanted to please others in order for some sense of personal approval to be given. When this combined with the unconscious anima which was defined by "there must be something wrong with me," an emotional masochist was produced who had no inner or outer sense of boundaries.

This masochistic emotional psychology generated a reality of wanting to help others, to be of service to a larger whole; of never saying no. He became a very successful counselor, teacher/lecturer, and writer. The archetype of masochism is one of surrendering the ego, to sacrifice and crucify it, to a larger purpose, goal, or good.

Astrologically, by the way, the archetype of masochism is reflected in Pisces and Virgo, the 6th or 12th Houses.) With this man having his Moon in Pisces at the apex of a Yod with Neptune and Pluto, and at the apex of a T-square with the Mars and Uranus, the masochistic archetype defines his sense of ego or personality. Even though he became very successful in his work role, *inwardly* he could not personally relate to his success or the acclaim heaped upon him because of messages that defined his wounded anima: "there must be something wrong with me, I am nothing." And, yet, he learned that it was safe to hide behind the outer persona or animus so that the wounded anima, his "real" self, would not be seen.

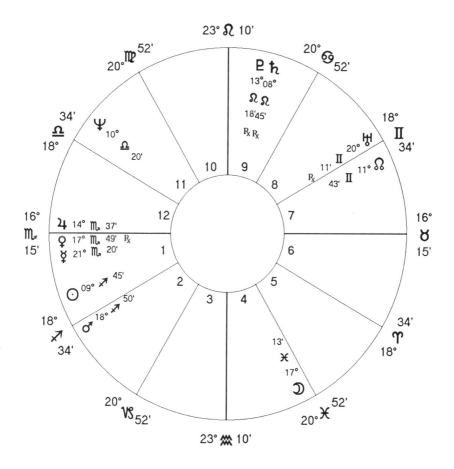

Case #2, Male

The emotional trauma of childhood finally became unblocked in his 44th year. At this point he was married to what he was sure was his soul mate: a woman who appeared through words and actions to be everything he had ever wanted, a woman who was the ultimate embodiment of his wounded anima in both forms: the angel Mary who offered relief from his suffering, and the actual mother who created it within him in the first place. After three years of marriage in which she appeared as the angel Mary, she became, almost overnight, the actual mother. She abandoned him and his children from a previous marriage through behavior and actions that could only be judged as evil and sadistic.

Through synastry, her natal Pluto-Mars opposition landed in his 10th and 4th Houses: her Pluto in the 10th House opposing his Moon, and her Mars in his 4th House conjunct his Moon. (As an aside, individuals who have Mars in opposition to Pluto often have what psychologists call "split personalities," or the Jekyl and Hyde syndrome.) By attracting this type of women into his life, another *femme fatale* type, it seems as though a fated life experience unfolded in such a way as to unlock the effects of the initial emotional trauma of childhood because of the effects of the immediate trauma that she created through her actions toward him and his children.

This trauma occurred when the transit of Pluto in 20 Scorpio was exactly inconjunct his natal Uranus in the 8th House. Overnight, he was separated from his wife and children. This occurred when the other side of his wife's personality suddenly, without warning or provocation, manifested. Without going into detail, suffice it to say that her actions and the allegations she asserted to others about him had the temporary effect of displacing him from his children and permanently from her.

In addition, astrologically the Pluto transit was also squaring his Midheaven axis, conjuncting his natal retrograde Venus (recovering something from the past), Mercury, and Ascendant, and trining his natal Moon in the 4th. If this were not enough, the transits of Uranus and Neptune at 13 and 16 Capricorn, respectively, were inconjuncting in his natal Pluto and Saturn in his 9th House, and inconjuncting his natal North Node in his 7th House.

The emotional trauma set in motion via the Pluto transit also triggered a psychological or mental (Uranus) trauma, a spiritual or psyche (Neptune) trauma, and a physical (Saturn) trauma. Physically, he experienced heart problems (natal Saturn in Leo), spiritually he lost all his beliefs, and psychologically he was blown to pieces, which required intense therapy. With the Neptune and Uranus transit occurring within his 2nd House, he also became bankrupt in that he ended up having to spend a tremendous amount of money on lawyers, defending himself legally against the allegations that were made.

The truth (9th House) finally prevailed, and all allegations were dismissed. The one non-stressful aspect, the Pluto transit trining his Moon, not only allowed him to recover his children, but also to uncover the initial emotional trauma of childhood in such a way as to help him understand the dynamics within himself that were serving as the causal factors in dictating the types of adult women with whom he formed relationships. The long buried memories finally surfaced through the assistance of a professional therapist. He began the long process of integration between the Soul (Pluto), and the personality or ego (Moon): the little picture within the big picture. These transits created a total identity crisis that is now producing a *new* individual who is more fully integrated than ever before—the mask is now removed from my story.

Hopefully, these two case studies have helped you understand the ideas and dynamics concerning trauma. At this point I would like to take Saturn, Uranus, Neptune, and Pluto through the Houses in order to illustrate where and how the various traumas can manifest when they do. As in all astrological work, an entire horoscope must be evaluated to determine the exact application to any given individual. The following statements and descriptions are only relative to *one* factor: a planet in a House. These statements are not presented as if they are fated. They are suggestive of what kind of traumas can begin to be defined by astrology.

Physical Trauma and Saturn

Saturn in the 1st House or Aries: physical trauma that can occur includes severe injury to the head, stunted growth of the skeletal system, imbalance of the white and red blood cells that can cause various problems, malformed genitals, various forms of arthritis due to dehydration of the soluvial fluids, osteoporosis in females after menopause, severe anemia, and prostate problems in men.

Saturn in the 2nd House or Taurus: physical trauma that can occur includes severe injury to the lower back, blockage of the ducts within the kidneys, kidney disease, build up of deposits within the veins or arteries leading to a variety of problems such as phlebitis, imbalance in the white and red blood cells that could lead to leukemia, ovarian cysts or cancer, tipped wombs in females impacting on the ability to conceive, disease linked to the cervix, womb, or vagina, problems within the inner ear that can cause vertigo and unexplained dizziness.

Saturn in the 3rd House or Gemini: physical trauma that can occur includes severe accidents to the hands or arms, nerve damage impacting on motor skills, problems impacting on the autonomous nervous system, various degrees of hearing loss associated with the nerves being diseased or dying within the ear, disease within the larynx, tumors on the left side of the brain, synapse dysfunction on the left side of the brain.

Saturn in the 4th House or Cancer: physical trauma that can occur includes diseases of the lymphatic system, ulcerations within the stomach or duodedum, cancer of the stomach or intestinal tract, gall stones, chronic constipation leading to progressive infusion of toxins throughout the system, glaucoma, cataracts and diseases associated with the eyes, prolapsed wombs, and chronic fatigue syndrome generated through yeast infections.

Saturn in the 5th House or Leo: physical trauma that can occur includes malformed hearts, disease of the heart, heart murmurs, high or low blood pressure, circulatory problems, retinal detachment, progressive degeneration of the nerves within the eyes, night blindness, stroke, heart attacks, angina, anemia and general constitutional weakness of the life force available to the entire system.

Saturn in the 6th House or Virgo: physical trauma that can occur includes breakdowns in various magnitudes within the immune system leading to uncontrolled infections of all kinds, various forms of arthritis, motor skill dysfunction, dysfunction of the cognitive skills controlled by the brain, dysfunction or disease with the throat or larynx, skeletal diseases and breakdowns within the bone marrow's ability to produce healthy, functional B and T cells.

Saturn in the 7th House or Libra: same as the Second House.

Saturn in the 8th House or Scorpio: physical trauma that can occur includes disease of dysfunction of the pancreas, colon, intestine, stomach, liver, duodenum, various cancers, prostatitus, cervical, uterine, or ovarian growths, cysts, or cancer, genetic birth defects, disease or dysfunction of the endocrine or lymphatic systems, candida or yeast infections, improper levels of enzymes regulated through the pancreas and liver, problems associated with the spine such as curvature of the spine, disintegrating spinal discs, fusion of the vertebra, etc.

Saturn in the 9th House or Sagittarius: physical trauma that can occur includes dysfunction or disease of the thyroid and pituitary glands, insufficient constitutional strength through a lack of zinc and/or silica, natural accident-proneness because of an general absentmindedness which can lead to physical injuries of various magnitudes, restrictions within the sciatic nerves that then impairs circulation within the legs, causing a state of chronic muscular tension in the legs and feet, liver dysfunction generating toxic conditions throughout the system, and digestive problems associated with enzyme levels controlled by the liver.

Saturn in the 10th House or Capricorn: physical trauma that can occur includes various forms of arthritis, osteoporosis, breakdowns within the B and T cells emanating from the bone marrow that then implicates the integrity of the immune system, disease or dysfunction of the pituitary or thyroid glands, severe problems with the skin, cancer or dysfunction within the digestive tract, growth disorders, skeletal disorders.

Saturn in the 11th House or Aquarius: physical trauma that can occur includes stroke, all manner of dysfunction or disease of the brain, damage to the brain leading to various conditions such as cerebral palsy, respiratory disease or dysfunction, inherent or genetic weakness in the lining of the lungs, dysfunction or disease of the hypothalamus and thalamus glands, dysfunction or disease within the overall nervous system.

Saturn in the 12th House or Pisces: physical trauma that can occur includes auto-immune syndrome, any manner of disease or dysfunction of the immune system, endocrine and lymphatic systems disease or dysfunction, abnormalities linked with the feet, severe water retention, and apparently unresolved or wrongly diagnosed chronic systemic issues that create the effect of never being really well, or truly healthy.

Mental Trauma and Uranus

Uranus in the 1st House or Aries: mental trauma can occur within these individuals because of an inability to accept physical, psychological, or karmically prescribed limitations that create the effect of blocking them from achieving their inner sense of special destiny, of not being able to do anything or everything that they feel they could do. Typically, these individuals have a "superhuman" complex that requires circumstantial restraint in order to realign the ego into a state of balance or equality with other individuals. The natural power of leadership and breaking new ground exists within these people, yet they must learn how to integrate this capacity within the "system" as it is currently defined so that these intrinsic abilities can be actualized.

Subconsciously, many of these individuals will have memories of premature or early life-endings from other lives. This can create irrational fears of loosing control, or of going too far from their immediate environment in which they feel safe.

Uranus in transit through the 1st House, forming a stressful aspect through transit to the planetary ruler of the 1st House, Mars, or to natal planets in the 1st House can generate this type of trauma.

Uranus in the 2nd House or Taurus: mental trauma can occur when these individuals are forced to change the nature of their value systems, values that have defined their identity and overall reality for a long time. Everything that has been held dear and cherished becomes lost: this can include material loss as well. Because of this trauma these individuals must realign themselves with a new set of values, or at least adjust or modify the existing ones, which will allow them to relate to themselves and others in a totally different way.

Many of these individuals will have subconscious memories of physical or emotional destitution which can create the effect of desperately hanging on to what they have, as well as a fixity of values that have defined their sense of meaning in life.

The transit of Uranus in the 2nd House, through transit forming a stressful aspect to the planetary ruler of the Second House, Venus, or to planets within the 2nd House, can generate this type of trauma.

Uranus in the 3rd House or Gemini: mental trauma can occur when these people experience life situations that directly confront the way in which they understand life via their ideas, opinions, and mental constructions. The intensity of the confrontations or experiences forces them to question and restructure their mental constructions so that a new ideational system occurs. The transition between the new and the old systems is the period of greatest trauma and psychological instability.

Subconsciously, many of these individuals can have memories of a knowledge base or understandings that is not present in, or part of, the current life reality as reflected in other people or society in general. The frustration of trying to communicate or relate such knowledge creates a state of psychological confinement because of the "differentness" or wide gap that they experience within themselves in contrast to those around them. This frustration can generate its own mental trauma that is defined by a state of alienation from others and society.

When Uranus transits the 3rd House, forms a stressful aspect through transit to the planetary ruler of the 3rd House, Mercury, or to natal planets in the 3rd House, it can generate this type of trauma.

Uranus in the 4th House or Cancer: mental trauma can occur when these individuals experience an intense lack of emotional understanding, and a lack of nurturing, related to their biological parents. Through extension, this same lack is experienced in adulthood because of the displaced emotions of childhood. This creates a core insecurity, and an unresolved inner child, that can project emotional demands onto others in an effort to recover or experience the emotional nurturing they desire. This can generate quite erratic and unpredictable emotional states and moods that hurt themselves and others. These individuals will continue to generate environmental or circumstantial experiences that have the affect of throwing them back in upon themselves until they understand that the nurturing and security that they are seeking is wholly *within themselves.* This will occur because Uranus here will cyclically remove or radically change their life conditions to the extent that these people are finally forced to learn this lesson. This can clearly generate psychological trauma.

Subconsciously, many of these individuals have memories of many other lifetimes in which this same dynamic has been operative. This only adds too and intensifies the projected emotional demands and needs which in turn only intensifies the effect of not having these needs met at the most crucial of times.

When Uranus transits the 4th House, forms stressful aspects through transit to the planetary ruler of the 4th House, Moon, or to planets in the natal 4th House, it can generate this type of trauma.

Uranus in the 5th House or Leo: mental trauma can occur when these individuals experience an indifference or non-acknowledgment from from society or others. This is so because these people have a need to be acknowledged as special, to be acclaimed and validated as a Zarathustra or superhuman as measured against others. This experience of indifference or non-acknowledgment can occur throughout life, or it can occur cyclically, since these individuals may indeed achieve relatively great heights or achievement for a time, only to experience a fall from grace. Thus, there is the onset of periods of time of no acclaim or achievement. This effect can also appear when Uranus transits the Sun in any chart or begins a transit of the 5th House, or forms a stressful aspect through transit to the planetary ruler of the 5th House. Typically this generates the evolutionary need to almost totally change, restructure, or redefine how an individual's sense of purpose in life has been actualized, and how the individual has understood the very meaning of his or her life in relation to that purpose. This period of disassociation, and the consequent need to reassociate one's sense of purpose and meaning in new ways, can be truly psychologically traumatic. This is because the very core of the individual's beingness seems to have changed so radically. The period of disassociation can fracture the ego or personality in potentially horrendous ways. A bomb has gone off, and the pieces that are falling back to earth are doing so in a new way. Being responsive to this *necessary* change, as opposed to trying to maintain what was, is the key leading to psychological stability and reintegration.

Many of these individuals will have subconscious memories of achieving great fame, acclaim or heights from other lifetimes, some having memories of being part of some royal family. This can only fuel the frustration of not be acknowledged as special in this life.

Uranus in the 6th House or Virgo: Mental trauma can occur when these individuals focus upon and experience a sense of psychological separation or isolation, from their immediate environment. Within this isolation or separation they can interpret their overall environment as being unduly critical toward, or persecuting them.

Other people seem to be conspiring against them in one way or another. In addition, these people can experience trauma with respect to the type of work in which they find themselves, because they typically feel that they have a very different approach to work in general, and a very different ability or capacity that remains unactualized specifically.

The underlying or subconscious memories that these individuals have suggest that they are not good enough or ready to actualize their sense of larger capacity. This creates its own trauma because of the implied crisis of not actualization what the individual senses to be possible. This sense of inner and outer containment creates a dynamic of rebellion in which these people can create one crisis condition after another. Each crisis, large and small, creates the effect of being in an almost perpetual state of trauma in one way or another.

Many of these individuals will have subconscious memories from other lifetimes of intense, irrational persecution and ridicule. This creates the effect of not only feeling victimized, but also one of trying to appear normal in their lives, even though they do not *feel* normal. This form of compensation creates the sense of frustration and isolation.

When Uranus transits the 6th House, when through transit it forms a stressful aspect t0 the planetary ruler of the 6th House, Mercury, or to planets in the 6th House, it can generate these types of trauma.

Uranus in the 7th House or Libra: mental trauma can occur to these individuals when they experience sudden, unexpected disruptions, fracturing, or outright termination within their relationships, intimate and otherwise. This can occur by another person or persons projecting their own subconscious dynamics upon these individuals, or because of these individuals projecting their own stuff upon other people. In both scenarios this type of projection creates a high degree of irrationality into the composite effect of the relationship(s) that can lead to psychological instability or trauma.

In addition, these individuals have an intrinsic sense of fair play, of justice, and of equality. When these principles are consistently violated in relationship, the cumulative stress can induce a psychologically traumatic state. When this occurs these individuals must reevaluate themselves in terms of their expectations about reality in general, and relationship dynamics specifically. And because these individuals will rebel against the feeling of being overly confined or enmeshed in a relationship, they can create trauma for themselves and their partners when they begin to look for the exit sign.

Many of these individuals will have subconscious memories of sudden losses within relationships that intensify a core detachment from people in general, and those that they are intimate with specifically. This inner, subconscious vibration can thus attract others who seem to be just as detached at a core level as they are. This can create trauma for both, because neither will have the feeling of being totally connected to the other.

When Uranus transits the 7th House, or forms stressful aspects through transit to Venus, planets with the natal 7th House, or to the planetary ruler of the 7th House, these types of trauma can occur.

Uranus in the 8th House or Scorpio: mental trauma can occur to these individuals when absolute betrayals of trust occur. This can occur when an individual(s) to whom they have extended trust ends up violating this trust to the extent of becoming totally different than they had seemed or appeared to the individual when the trust was initially extended. This violation of trust thus generates the experience of abandonment and intense loss that can lead to psychologically cataclysmic states. By experiencing others "turning upon them," they can endure intense states of psychological abuse that can appear sadistic. The abuse dynamic linked with violations of trust can also include sexual abuse in a variety of ways. The sudden loss linked with partnerships wherein a merging of resources and realities had occurred can create fundamental psychological trauma that impacts on their ability to trust ever again.

In many ways Uranus in the 8th House is an intensification of Uranus in the 7th House. This is so because these people can project psychological intentions, motives, or agendas onto others, and have others project the same upon them. This is problematic in that these individuals have very keen and accurate perception about how others are motivated and psychologically structured on the one hand, and on the other hand they can mix up and project their own subconscious dynamics onto others. This produces intense psychological confrontations and tests of will between these people and others that can generate its own set of traumatic conditions.

In addition, many of these people will have subconscious

memories concerning these dynamics which can only intensify these problems in this life. Also, these individuals commonly had, and still have, desires to experience and know the different uses and forms of sexual energy that go beyond normal procreational or conventional expressions. The potential for misuse of sexual desire and experience can create karmic conditions wherein others can misuse or abuse these individuals sexually as a result. Conversely, some of these individuals, through evolutionary development, may have known, or come to know, the highest forms and right use of sexual energy that is possible.

When Uranus transits the 8th House, or forms stressful aspects through transit to Pluto, natal planets in the 8th House, or to the planetary ruler of the 8th House, these types of trauma can occur.

Uranus in the 9th House or Sagittarius: mental trauma can occur to these individuals by the very nature of their beliefs because those beliefs are typically at odds with consensus. The trauma occurs through others who isolate these people because of their beliefs, this isolation occurring through ridicule, persecution, or outright attack. In turn, these individuals can create traumatic affects for others as they challenge and rebel against the belief structures of anyone who is not in sympathy with, or supportive of, their own beliefs.

Trauma can also occur for these individuals when traumatic experiences occur at such a level as to make them question the nature of what they believe in. This type of trauma generates an incomprehensibility as to why the trauma or traumas have occurred in the first place, because their existing beliefs can not account for or explain why the trauma could occur. An example of this could be an individual who fervently believed in a Christian God who, while in Viet-Nam, experienced his friend being blown to bits while reading the Bible in his bunker during a rocket attack. The shreds of a blood-stained Bible were all that remained, the bloodied pulp of his friend staining the sand. This person could then find himself in a theological/existential void of despair which will alter his beliefs forever.

When Uranus transits the 9th House, forms a stressful aspect through transit to the planetary ruler or the 9th House, Jupiter, or to planets in the 9th House, it can generate these types of trauma.

Uranus in the 10th House or Capricorn: mental trauma can occur to these people by way of their family of origin, wherein one or both parents are dysfunctional in some way, absent, emotionally unavailable, or who were suddenly lost. Trauma can also occur through not being validated or acknowledged for who they are by the parents. As adults, these same dynamics can occur through non-acceptance by mainstream people or society, of being severely misjudged by those in their career field, by sudden loss of social position or career, and through feeling psychologically misplaced in their overall environment.

In addition, these individuals can suffer from severe forms of depression and psychologically self-defeating attitudes toward life in general. These states are created because of the experience of feeling blocked or thwarted by the environment. This can generate a feeling that it is pointless to work towards any goal or objective because it does not mean anything. These attitudes reflect subconscious memories that reflect other lifetimes of being "defeated" by forces that they can not control, of memories that reflect lifetimes in which the promised rewards linked with goals that were pursued but never materialized. A permeating sarcasm and pessimism underlies these individuals' very way of being.

When Uranus transits the 10th House, forms stressful aspects to the planetary ruler of the 10th House through transit, Saturn, or planets in the natal 10th House, it can generate these types of trauma.

Uranus in the 11th House or Aquarius: mental trauma can occur when these individual realize that they have been living a lie. This lie is one wherein they have not actualized a life or lifestyle that is reflective of their inner self. This inner self is one wherein the individual feels fundamentally different than the consensus reality that constitutes the environment in which these individuals find themselves. And yet, because of this fundamentally different inner self, these individuals will compensate by adopting the external appearance of normalcy. The act of compensation is that which generates the lie. Psychological trauma occurs relative to this realization and the need to radically alter their life. There is a need to rebel against the normal, "consensus life," yet there is also a fear in doing just that. This fear can implode on these individuals in such a way as to not act toward change, this implosion similar to the famous Dutch Boy putting his fingers in the leaking dike. This creates its own state of instability. To fully act upon the impulse to cast off the consensus life also creates a period of instability that may be undetectable to the observer until there is a sudden, unannounced rebellion; the husband or wife who simply did not come home one night.

Trauma can also occur via a myriad of social connections and relationships that suddenly turn ugly, disruptive, or simply terminate almost overnight. Friendships suddenly go astray, unforeseen dynamics and issues suddenly and irrationally appear.

Many of these individuals will have subconscious memories that they have been persecuted or criticized for being different by others, which can only fuel the psychology to compensate by adopting the appearance of normalcy.

When Uranus transits the 11th House, through transit forms stressful aspects to the planetary ruler of the 11th House, forms stressful aspects to itself, or when it forms stressful aspects through transit to planets in the natal 11th House, it can generate these types of trauma.

Uranus in the 12th House or Pisces: mental trauma can occur to these individuals when their ego or personality begins to fracture, disintegrate, or dissolve due to externally experienced stress, or through an inner stress emanating from the unconscious. This inner stress is couched in thoughts or impulsive desire to escape or run away from the mundane conditions that define life. Anatomically and physiologically, this impulse is rooted in the pineal gland within the brain. Uranus correlates to the electricity within the brain, thus a high degree of electrical impulse impacting on the pineal gland. This gland secrets a protein called melatonin which is responsible for what we call dreams, sleep, and the need for transcendence; to embrace a more holistic, inclusive, ultimate or spiritual reality. Failing to understand the right actualization of this impulse, i.e., to embrace spiritual realities, the individual becomes quite "crazy"' at a subconscious level, which can manifest in any manner of psychosis, phobias, neurosis, personality disorders, split or multi-personalities, addictions and escapes of all kinds. Consider that Uranus was transiting Pisces for most of the 1920s and, in the United States, this decade became known as the "Roaring 20s" with respect to rampant alcoholism, drug use, the invention of credit spending, and other excesses.

Many of these individuals will have subconscious memories of being imprisoned or incarcerated, and of being severely persecuted by many people. This type of memory generates a fear that translates into "hiding" from people.

When Uranus transits the 12th House, forms stressful aspects through transit to the planetary ruler of the 12th House, Neptune, or to natal planets in the 12th House, it can generate these types of trauma.

Neptune: Spiritual or Psyche Trauma

Neptune in the 1st House or Aries: idealistic expectations about self-potential that generate a sense of having something special to do, yet the awareness and experience of self seems so small as unconsciously compared to the Universe, God, or the Other. This awareness makes it seem as though the idealistic expectations about self are impossible to achieve. A disillusionment within the self generates a disillusionment with the All, or Other: the Universal. The trauma is one of identity confusion, and how to actualize or make real that which is instinctually sensed as possible.

When Neptune transits the Ascendant, forms stressful aspects through transit to the planetary ruler of the 1st House, Mars, or to planets in the natal 1st House, it can generate these issues and subsequent traumas.

Neptune in the 2nd House or Taurus: idealistic expectations about sharing, exchanging and giving that which constitutes the substance of life itself, a substance that allows for life to be sustained. This is the famous example of individuals who would give you the shirt off their back. Thus, these individuals by nature own nothing in the sense of egocentric identification with whatever constitutes substance. Disillusionment through loss of natural values and beliefs occurs through and because of others who take advantage of these people. This is done by taking away what is naturally shared and given freely without returning equally to the individuals whatever constitutes their own substance of life, whatever it may be. Disillusioned, these individuals can unconsciously react by way of hoarding and taking because of a psychology that now feels that he or she is owed everything, by everyone! Irrational fear of destitution at all levels results from this. The psychic or spiritual trauma is one wherein God is not a giving, loving God, but an avenging, cruel God. It is one in which people are not inherently good, but inherently evil.

When Neptune transits the 2nd House, forms stressful aspects through transits to the planetary ruler of the 2nd House, Venus, or to planets in the natal 2nd House, it can generate these issues and subsequent traumas.

Neptune in the 3rd House or Gemini: an idealistic expectation linked with an inherent knowingness that there is a much larger reality than what is perceived or known by the logical, rational mind, and that others should understand and know this too. A frustration can exist between the inner expectation to be able to intellectualize or put into logical mental sequence what is inwardly sensed and the ability to do so. The experience of a limited language as spoken by most of the people around them is that which frustrates their efforts to communicate that which is essentially incommunicable. It is as if these individuals are tuned into a radio station that no one else can hear. Disillusioned by their efforts to communicate in ways and about things that no one else seems to understand can generate a spiritual or psychic trauma. These people can simply give up all efforts at communicating, to withdraw to the point of total reclusion from the world.

When Neptune transits the 3rd House, forms stressful aspects to the planetary ruler of the 3rd House through transit, Mercury, or to planets in the natal 3rd House, it can generate these issues and subsequent traumas.

Neptune in the 4th House or Cancer: an idealistic expectation that the world, the universe, the origin of all things, the home, and the family are but a universal womb of purity, simplicity, of love, and of nurturing for all. This expectation produces a natural emotional empathy for all, a compassion linked to the common suffering of all. Disillusionment and spiritual trauma occurs to these people through the experience and perception of a natural innocence that exists within themselves, which, becomes violated, abused, destroyed, or contaminated. This experience is based on the ugly realization that impurity exists in others, that others can have malevolent intentions, that the world in not good, and that the soul can be corrupted. The natural child of innocence becomes lost, confused, and alienated within an impure world. An existential void of a godless world now haunts their souls.

When Neptune transits the 4th House, forms stressful aspects through transits to the Moon, planetary ruler of the 4th House, or to planets in the natal 4th House, these traumas can occur.

Neptune in the 5th House or Leo: an idealistic expectation that the eternal Spring and dynamic of Creativity are unlimited and un-bound, that this principle and dynamic are at one's disposal, and that Creation should be perfect and beautiful. Disillusionment and psychic trauma occur when one realizes that one is not God, that the ego can not create in and of itself. This realization occurs when the apparent well of Creativity runs dry, appears blocked, when these individuals are not acknowledged as special and godlike by others in the way that is idealistically and unconsciously expected. Trauma occurs when what is being created appears to be insignificant in re-lation to what is ultimately or idealistically sensed as possible, when what others achieve or create seems more spectacular and grand than what these individuals create for themselves, and when others are acknowledged or treated more specially than they are.

When Neptune transits the 5th House, forms stressful aspects through transit to the planetary ruler of the 5th House, Sun, or to planets in the natal 5th House, it can generate these issues and sub-sequent traumas.

Neptune in the 6th House or Virgo: an idealistic expectation of collective and individual purity and perfection in all things, of right action. These expectations are judged against some ultimate stan-dard of conduct. For these people, purity and perfection are uncon-sciously linked to the desire to sacrifice oneself, the ego, to the prin-ciple of service to another, others, or the Whole. These people carry an unconscious, yet pervasive, undefined guilt that needs to be atoned for. This leads to the creation of personal crisis and maso-chistic behavior, a behavior defined by the unconscious that leads to personal crucifixion to that which is impure and unholy. Psychic or spiritual trauma occurs through creating a life of suffering in a vari-ety of ways, including physical illnesses that can not be explained, cured or properly diagnosed. Trauma occurs via an inability to un-derstand why their suffering persists despite every effort to purify and atone for themselves through personal sacrifice.

When Neptune transits the 6th House, forms stressful aspects through transit to natal Mercury, planets within the natal 6th House, or to the planetary ruler of the 6th House, it can generate these issues and subsequent traumas.

Neptune in the 7th House or Libra: an idealistic expectation that all people are essentially pure and good in general, and specifically those with whom they form intimate relationships. There can be an unconscious desire to rescue or save people through masochistic self-sacrifice, a desire to heal the hurts of their intimate partners, and to have their own sufferings and hurts healed by others as well, and especially by their intimate partners. These individuals "see" the potential and spirit in all people, their partners in particular, and expect that potential to be actualized. Through identifying another's inner spirit, these individuals can experience disillusionment and great pain when the other's actual reality prevails in ways that seems contradictory to what he or she wants to see or believe. Disillusionment and trauma can occur when these individuals realize that they have given themselves away to another, and that they have nothing to show for it but pain and needs that have gone unfulfilled. In addition, these individuals idealistically expect that the dynamics of giving and receiving, of equality, of justice, and of fair play do prevail in all human interactions, and especially between themselves and their intimate other. When these expectations go unfulfilled, when life experience teaches them that these ideals rarely occur, tremendous disillusionment and trauma can occur.

When Neptune transits the 7th House, forms stressful aspects through transits to Venus, natal planets in the 7th House, or the planetary ruler of the 7th House, it can generate these issues and subsequent traumas.

Neptune in the 8th House or Scorpio: this can be one of the most problematic positions for Neptune in that these people can unconsciously project a complex of fears, motives, or intentions onto other people that creates the effect within themselves of being unable to open up to life in general, and other people specifically, even though they desperately want to. There is a high level of intense suspicion that is projected onto people which is but a reflection of the impurity in themselves. This impurity reflects lifetimes of manipulating, using, and destroying others relative to their own purposes. When such behavior is pointed out, these people create a stance of absolute denial. Through such inner denial, they project that which they are onto others, the inner denial reflecting their own unconscious idealistic expectations of how they want to be, of how they want to see themselves. Psychic or spiritual trauma occurs when the holy mask that they create for themselves shatters into the nightmare of their actual reality, and when they realize that what they have projected onto others is but a reflection of themselves. The struggle between good and evil, masochistic and sadistic behavior is most emphasized when Neptune is in the 8th House or Scorpio.

In addition, these individuals can have unconscious fascination with "taboo" forms of sexual expression, a need to be dominated or to dominate, a desire to dissolve the ego through consuming forms of sensation of a sexual nature, and at the same time denying all of this to themselves and others. Some, by way of denial, will even pretend that they have no sexual desire at all, or that sex is a function of evil. Others can develop a superstructure of fancy words reflecting high-minded intentions that only mask where they are actually coming from. A few will understand and experience the metamorphic and transcendent nature of sexual energy properly used.

When Neptune transits the 8th House, forms stressful aspects through transits to Pluto or Mars, the planetary ruler of the 8th House, or natal planets in the 8th House, it can generate these issues and subsequent traumas.

Neptune in the 9th House or Sagittarius: an idealistic expectation that the way in which these individuals view the world in general, and whatever specific views that they hold about the nature of some dynamic or experience that is occurring in their or another's life, is understood and shared by others. It is as if their 'truth' must be the general truth for all. Disillusionment and trauma occur when they are forced to see that their truth or vision is but one among many other truths and visions.

In addition, many of these individuals have a core feeling of inadequacy and impurity which can generate the need to compensate. This compensation can take the form of becoming incredible liars, the thrust of the lies being to create an illusion that makes them appear holy, grand, sincere, and much 'larger' than they actually are within themselves. These lies can also be created to maneuver or manipulate others to do something that they want done for some devious and dishonest purpose. Disillusionment and trauma occur when their lies are revealed, and when the actual reality of who they are becomes exposed and in their face.

Some will have unconscious expectations that all people should be or are essentially honest. This is because this type of person is inwardly defined by this noble dynamic. Some are the very essence of unwavering honesty in all that they do, in the very nature of their beingness. Disillusionment and trauma occur when they experience the pain of dishonesty through others, when they become victimized by an unprincipled world.

When Neptune transits the 9th House, forms stressful aspects through transits to Jupiter, planets within the natal 9th House, or to the planetary ruler of the 9th House, it can generate these issues and subsequent trauma.

Neptune in the 10th House or Capricorn: idealistic expectations about the nature of family structures, societal structures, and the structure of the world itself. The essence of these expectations is based on the principle of sacrificing oneself, the ego, for a larger good. The principle of sacrifice can take many forms, have many applications. There is an unconscious expectation that purity and right action should define and prevail in any activity, large or small.

These individuals are typically defined by an unconscious and uneasy feeling of guilt; that they have done something wrong, or that there is something wrong with them. Thus, there is a need to correct or atone for that guilt. As a result, life experiences can be generated in which unconscious ideals of purity and right action, of egocentric self-sacrifice to the Other are violated: the abusive father, the emotionally unavailable parent, the narcissistic husband or wife, the needy of this world who latch onto these people for dear life and abuse what is offered, the imperfect world that violates the expectation of purity and right action, etc.

Over time, these kinds of experiences then can generate a horrible, depressive disillusionment and trauma that can create severe bouts of depression. This trauma can lead to a life in which these people struggle to throw off the undermining feelings of being continually defeated by life itself. In addition, disillusionment and trauma can occur through the experience that what is considered "real" becomes "unreal." Nothing seems to be permanent, nothing seems to last; the very nature of "reality" is comprised merely of transitory images that come and go; what is "real" is only real for the time that it actually exists.

Accordingly, cycles of despair, of fighting off an inner feeling of being consumed by a dark, bottomless pit, define the inner world for these individuals. As a result, these individuals conjure up a fundamental fear of losing control and, yet, longing to do so. Paradoxically, many of these people will seem like beacons of salvation's light to others *because of* this inner world. This is because these people know their inner pain so well that it serves to motivate them to heal the suffering of others. This symbol, Neptune in Capricorn, or the 10th House, is the ultimate symbol of crucifixion of the ego. If you doubt this, consider that Jesus was put on the Cross when Neptune transited Capricorn in His time.

When Neptune transits the 10th House, forms stressful aspects through transits to Saturn, the planetary ruler of the 10th House, or to planets within the natal 10th House, it can generate these issues and subsequent traumas.

Neptune in the 11th House or Aquarius: idealistic expectations that all people everywhere should be treated equally and with justice. Expectations that all artificial barriers of caste, race, and wealth should not exist, and that all social, political, and economic systems should be defined in ways that are equitable for all.

These people have idealistic expectations and a vision that each member within a group has an important and equal function that contributes to the well being of the whole group. In addition, these individuals intrinsically expect that people should approach group activities with the spirit of how each person can add to the purposes of the group, versus what the group can do for the individual.

Disillusionment and trauma occur when all of these expectations are crushed by reality, when, through experience, these people realize that most people do *not* live or think as they do. Trauma and disillusionment occur when they experience that one group dominates and takes advantage of another group; when they experience the horrible collective pain of people turning upon other people, when the awareness of so many people seems to be limited to the tip of their own noses.

This trauma can thus generate a total detachment from all external reality. This can create the effect of being extreme loneliness, removed from the fray that so many call life. Eccentric and iconoclastic, these people can experience a general uneasiness around other people, and others can also feel a vague uneasiness around them. They seem so "different" to most people, and most people seem so different to them. This creates the "plexiglass" effect wherein these people can be seen but not touched. And, for these people, they can observe life but never really experience it. Somehow they are always on the outside looking in.

When Neptune transits the 11th House, forms stressful aspects through transits to Uranus, the planetary ruler of the 11th House, or to planets within the natal 11th House, these issues can be generated with the subsequent traumas.

Neptune in the 12th House or Pisces: this archetype symbolizes the sum total of all the astrological archetypes combined. Thus, issues concerning disillusionment and trauma as defined in this section on Neptune can occur in all the ways descibed for these individuals.

Pluto and Emotional Trauma

Pluto in the 1st House or Aries: emotional trauma can occur for these individuals for the following causes:

(1) When the need to balance their desire for independence and relationships generates a reality of feeling trapped by the needs and demands of others, blocking or restraining their desire to do what they need to do in order to be. Then, being forced to make choices to change the conditions of the entrapment creates yet more trauma. That occurs because to consider termination of the relationship that he or she is feeling trapped within creates a feeling of emotional death. Not considering this choice of termination which will allow for the freedom of self-discovery, also creates a feeling of death because it leads to sustaining the reality of entrapment.

(2) Emotional trauma can occur when these individuals create circumstances that reinforce the awareness of egocentric limitations in order to counteract the underlying feeling of "superhuman" potential. In essence, the constraints that these people experience or create to reign in the ego leads to an emotional shock that generates a limitation trauma at all levels of reality.

When Pluto transits the 1st House, forms stressful aspects through transits to Mars, the planetary ruler of the 1st House, or to planets in the natal 1st House, it can generate these issues and subsequent traumas.

Pluto in the 2nd House or Taurus: emotional trauma can occur to these individuals for the following causes:

(1) When life conditions are created that have the effect of forcing these individuals to inspect their value system and how the

value system defines their sense of individual identity and meaning. Cyclically forced to reevaluate their meaning and values, these people discover ever deeper levels of resources within themselves creating new or refined values that allow them to relate differently to themselves and others. The will to survive is strong here, and intense emotional trauma can occur when this will to survive and carry on becomes weakened. Yet, the survival instinct is so strong in these people that it does enforce the deepening of an inner awareness so that new values and ways of relating can emerge.

(2) When their will to dominate others is met with equal or stronger wills, there is the effect of intense confrontations that require the individuals to grow beyond existing reality. These confrontations call into play the nature of the individuals motives, intentions, and emotional agendas in such a way that the light of honesty creates harsh, necessary realizations about the truth of emotional reality and dynamics.

When Pluto transits the 2nd House, forms stressful aspects through transits to Venus, the planetary ruler of the 2nd House, or planets within the natal 2nd House, these issues and subsequent traumas can occur.

Pluto in the 3rd House or Gemini: emotional trauma can occur for the following causes:

(1) When watertight intellectual constructions that define reality in general, and as well, the very core of emotional security become unraveled through intense, cataclysmic life experiences. The nature of these cataclysmic events forces them to change their way of thinking, of how they have understood the nature of things.

(2) Emotional trauma can also occur when these people experience intense intellectual confrontations with others who poke holes in the waterbag in such a way that there is no choice but to question underlying assumptions about the nature of reality. Once those assumptions are questioned and changed, the rest of their complex intellectual network also falls and changes. The emotional trauma is defined by a core instability and insecurity because of the need to change their intellectual framework and how to communicate ideas and opinions. The period of insecurity or trauma is defined by the amount of time it takes for these individuals to evolve into new ways of understanding.

When Pluto transits the 3rd House, forms stressful aspects

through transits to natal Mercury, to the planetary ruler of the 3rd House, or to planets in the natal 3rd House, these issues can be generated with the subsequent trauma.

Pluto in the 4th House or Cancer: emotional trauma can occur to these individuals for the following causes:

(1) Intense emotional, psychological and/or sexual abuse with their family of origin. This can generate a deeply wounded child who has not failed to learn how to internalize the mother and/or father in such a way that, when they are not present, the individual's sense of safety and security does not exist. This displaced emotional dynamic manifests in adult life in such a way as to recreate the early family dynamics in adult relationships. This effectively creates a reality in which intense emotional demands are projected upon their partners. Such partners will not be consistently available to them Emotional trauma can thus reoccur as the emotional demands and needs of the displaced inner child go cyclically unfulfilled.

(2) When the very nature of their overall reality, how they have structured their lives, is threatened or destroyed, taken away against their will. When this happens, these individuals will experience a sense of emotional death, an experience that is so total because the very essence of their emotional security and sense of identity is removed.

When Pluto transits the 4th House, forms stressful aspects through transits to the Moon, the the planetary ruler of the 4th House, or to planets within the natal 4th House, it can generate these issues and subsequent traumas.

Pluto in the 5th House or Leo: emotional shocks or trauma can occur to these individuals for the following causes:

(1) When life conditions occur to defeat egocentric delusions of grandeur totally. This deflation of the ego creates an inner sense of loss, and this loss is based on not being allowed on life's center stage, of not being the self-appointed star of the play.

(2) When life conditions occur with which these individuals feel a deep absolute powerlessness to change or alter them. The awareness of "forces larger than themselves" creates the sense of an ego-death until these individuals incorporate and align their egos *with* those forces at work. When this occurs, creative change begins in very positive ways. These changes can lead to very creative expansions of the overall life purpose.

When Pluto transits the 5th House, or forms stressful aspects through transits to the Sun, the planetary ruler of the 5th House, or to planets within the natal 5th House, these issues and subsequent traumas can occur.

Pluto in the 6th House or Virgo: emotional trauma can occur to these individuals for the following causes:

(1) When life conditions occur in which the individual experiences an intense lack of meaning or when life conditions themselves become meaningless. This sense of lack, of an existential void generates a total state of crisis. This crisis is one of feeling totally displaced in the environment, and a sense of acute inner aloneness, feeling victimized by the life conditions that they are experiencing.

(2) When life conditions occur in which the individual feels intense persecution or criticism of an unjust nature. Not being able to understand why these conditions are contracted generates the trauma.

When Pluto transits the 6th House, forms stressful aspects with Mercury, the planetary ruler of the 6th House, or to planets in the natal 6th House, these issues and subsequent traumas can occur.

Pluto in the 7th House or Libra: emotional trauma can occur to these individuals for the following cause:

(1) When life conditions occur in which they are forced to realize that the sense of purpose and meaning that they are looking for is *not* embodied in another person, but within themselves. Their core sense of identity and security is bound up, linked with, the need to be in intimate relationships. At key points in their lives, these individuals will experience fundamental breakdowns, confrontations, or cataclysmic loss within their existing relationship. This has the effect of forcing them in on themselves in order to learn to grown from within, not through and because of another person. The compulsion of co-dependency is shattered.

When Pluto transits the 7th House, forms stressful aspects through transits to Venus, the planetary ruler of the 7th House, or to planets within the natal 7th House, it can generate such conditions within existing partnerships with the subsequent trauma.

Pluto in the 8th House or Scorpio: emotional trauma can occur to these individuals for the following causes:

(1) When life conditions are created in which they experience severe and intense betrayal, and violations of trust.

(2) When they experience being intensely used and manipulated by another.

(3) When they experience intense sexual violations and misuse of such energy.

(4) When they experience intense loss of those who are closest to them.

(5) When life conditions are created in which they are forced to examine their own motives, intentions, and emotional agendas. This examination, at some point, will uncover the subtle and not so subtle ways in which they have manipulated others or situations in order to gain something that they need or want. The light of emotional honesty creates a cruel glare that exposes the inner lies that they create for themselves and others.

When Pluto transits the 8th House, forms stressful aspects to Mars and/or Pluto through transit, to the planetary ruler of the 8th House, or to planets within the natal 8th House, it can generate these issues and subsequent traumas.

Pluto in the 9th House or Sagittarius: emotional trauma can occur to these individuals for the following causes:

(1) By experiencing a core alienation relative to their country and culture or origin.

(2) By experiencing intense belief-system confrontations with others, or a society, in which their beliefs are fundamentally at odds, or contradictory too, the beliefs of most others.

(3) When cataclysmic life events occur that force them to examine the nature of their beliefs and underlying principles that generate those beliefs.

(4) When they experience intense violations of truth, honesty, and the principle of justice relative to the truth of any given situation.

When Pluto transits the 9th House, forms stressful aspects through transits to Jupiter, the planetary ruler of the 9th House, or planets within the natal 9th House, these issues and subsequent traumas can occur.

Pluto in the 10th House or Capricorn: emotional trauma can occur for these individuals for the following causes:

(1) When they experience a total "fall from grace," or from positions of power and/or social position. This can be extremely intense because these individuals are inwardly defined by their social

position or role. The fall or loss of position requires an intense inner reformulation or metamorphosis of identity, an identity that is not defined by social power or position. (The trauma of former President Nixon is an example of this dynamic.)

(2) When they are born into a family in which one or both parents are emotional dictators who expect the child to conform to their sense of reality. The children are thus not acknowledged for their own innate individuality. This type of trauma creates an adult who is emotionally closed and rigid because he or she has learned as a child to shut down emotionally in order not to be hurt. The delayed stress of childhood then manifests in adulthood when they try to control or shape the emotional lives of those with whom *they* interact. This is done through confrontational judgments projected onto others.

When Pluto transits the 10th House, forms stressful aspects through transits to Saturn, planets within the natal 10th House, or to the planetary ruler of the 10th House, it can generate these issues and subsequent traumas.

Pluto in the 11th House or Aquarius: emotional trauma can occur for these individuals for the following causes:

(1) When they realize that their lifestyle does not reflect their actual nature, or when their lifestyle is radically altered through cataclysmic events which they can not alter.

(2) When they experience being intensely used and manipulated by others who have been considered friends or lovers, or when their friends or lovers seem to turn against them for no apparent or legitimate reason.

(3) When the overall culture treats these people as iconoclastic threats, in such a way as to create the reality for them of always being on the outside looking in.

When Pluto transits the 11th House, forms stressful aspects through transit1 to Uranus, to planets within the natal 11th House, or to the planetary ruler of the 11th House, these issues and subsequent traumas can occur.

Pluto in the 12th House or Pisces: emotional trauma can occur to these individuals for the following causes:

(1) When their innate sense of ideals is so severely crushed through life conditions that they become lost souls; souls who become utterly aimless, ungrounded, and who simply wander the

alley ways of life.

(2) When these individuals create a reality that seems to be the embodiment of all that they have ever dreamed of, only to have that reality destroyed. The degree of disillusionment can create a state of absolute emotional devastation in which the will to continue living can become weakened, if not extinguished.

(3) When their innate need to rescue, save, or help those in need, or those who are unstable, weird, or fractured, becomes over-extended to the point of feeling all used up. The trauma is one of total emotional exhaustion wherein they begin to wall themselves off from life, to enclose themselves in order to create a protection from the emotional demands of those around them.

When Pluto transits the 12th House, forms stressful aspects through transits to Neptune, the planetary ruler of the 12th House, or to planets within the natal 12th House, these issues and subsequent traumas may occur.

Conclusion

I would like to mention that traumatic conditions are, of course, difficult situations that can be very hard to deal with as they are occurring. But, such conditions always have a way of being resolved, and there is always some leap in our growth *because of them.* Once we understand the reasons or causes of the various types of traumas, the solutions and ways of resolving them become apparent or known. The remedial key is in the understanding of the causes of any given trauma; and then, in the resolve to take the positive actions necessary *for growth and change to occur.*

STAY IN TOUCH

On the following pages you will find listed, with their current prices, some of the books and tapes now available on related subjects. Your book dealer stocks most of these, and will stock new titles in the Llewellyn series as they become available. We urge your patronage.However, to obtain our full catalog, to keep informed of new titles as they are released and to benefit from informative articles and helpful news, you are invited to write for our bi-monthly news magazine/catalog. A sample copy is free, and it will continue coming to you at no cost as long as you are an active mail customer. Or you may keep it coming for a full year with a donation of just $7.00 in U.S.A. and Canada ($20.00 overseas, first class mail). Many bookstores also have *The Llewellyn New Times* available to their customers. Ask for it.

Stay in touch! In *The Llewellyn New Times'* pages you will find news and reviews of new books, tapes and services, announcements of meetings and seminars, articles helpful to our readers, news of authors, advertising of products and services, special money-making opportunities, and much more.

The Llewellyn New Times
P.O. Box 64383-Dept. 389, St. Paul, MN 55164-0383, U.S.A.
• • •
TO ORDER BOOKS AND TAPES

If your book dealer does not have the books and tapes described on the following pages readily available, you may order them directly from the publisher by sending full price in U.S. funds, plus $3.00 for postage and handling for orders *under* $10.00; $4.00 for orders *over* $10.00. There are no postage and handling charges for orders over $50.00. UPS Delivery: We ship UPS whenever possible. Delivery guaranteed. Provide your street address as UPS does not deliver to P.O. Boxes. UPS to Canada requires a $50.00 minimum order. Allow 4-6 weeks for delivery. Orders outside the U.S.A. and Canada: Airmail—add retail price of book; add $5.00 for each non-book item (tapes, etc.); add $1.00 per item for surface mail.

FOR GROUP STUDY AND PURCHASE

Because there is a great deal of interest in group discussion and study of the subject matter of this book, we feel that we should encourage the adoption and use of this particular book by such groups by offering a special "quantity" price to group leaders or "agents."

Our Special Quantity Price for a minimum order of five copies of *How to Personalize the Outer Planets* is $44.85 cash-with-order. This price includes postage and handling within the United States. Minnesota residents must add 6.5% sales tax. For additional quantities, please order in multiples of five. For Canadian and foreign orders, add postage and handling charges as above. Credit card (VISA, Master Card, American Express) orders are accepted. Charge card orders only may be phoned free ($15.00 minimum order) within the U.S.A. or Canada by dialing 1-800-THE-MOON. Customer service calls dial 1-612-291-1970. Mail Orders to:
LLEWELLYN PUBLICATIONS
P.O. Box 64383-Dept. 389 / St. Paul, MN 55164-0383, U.S.A.

Prices subject to change without notice.

FINANCIAL ASTROLOGY
edited by Joan McEvers

Favorably reviewed in the *Wall Street Journal* by financial expert Stanley W. Angrist! This third book in Llewellyn's anthology series edited by well-known astrologer Joan McEvers explores the relatively new field of financial astrology. Nine respected astrologers share their wisdom and good fortune with you.

Learn about the various types of analysis and how astrology fine-tunes these methods. Covered cycles include the Lunar Cycle, the Mars/Vesta Cycle, the 4-1/2-year Martian Cycle, the 500-year Civilization Cycle used by Nostradamus, the Kondratieff Wave and the Elliott Wave.

Included topics are: Michael Munkasey: A Primer on Market Forecasting. Pat Esclavon Hardy: Charting the U.S. and the NYSE. Jeanne Long: New Concepts for Commodities Trading Combining Astrology & Technical Analysis. Georgia Stathis: The Real Estate Process. Mary B. Downing: An Investor's Guide to Financial Astrology. Judy Johns: The Gann Technique. Carol S. Mull: Predicting the Dow. Bill Meridian: The Effect of Planetary Stations on U.S. Stock Prices. Georgia Stathis: Delineating the Corporation. Robert Cole: The Predictable Economy.
0-87542-382-5, 368 pgs., 5-1/4 x 8, illus., softcover   **$14.95**

THE HOUSES: POWER PLACES OF THE HOROSCOPE
edited by Joan McEvers

This volume combines the talents of 11 renowned astrologers in the fourth book of Llewellyn's anthology series.

Each house, an area of activity within the horoscope, is explained with clarity and depth by the following authors: Peter Damian: The 1st House and the Rising Sign and Planets. Ken Negus: The 7th House of Partnership. Noel Tyl: The 2nd House of Self-Worth and the 8th House of Values and Others. Spencer Grendahl: The 3rd House of Exploration & Communication. Dona Shaw: The 9th House of Truth and Abstract Thinking. Gloria Star: The 4th House of the Subconscious Matrix. Marwayne Leipzig: The 10th House of the Life's Imprint. Lina Accurso: The 5th House of Love. Sara Corbin Looms: The 11th House of Tomorrow. Michael Munkasey: The 6th House of Attitude and Service. Joan McEvers: The 12th House of Strength, Peace, Tranquillity
0-87542-383-3, 400 pgs., 5-1/4 x 8, charts, softcover   **$12.95**

THE ASTROLOGY OF THE MACROCOSM
edited by Joan McEvers

The fifth book in Llewellyn's New World Astrology Series, *The Astrology of the Macrocosm* contains charts and articles from some of the world's top astrologers, explaining various mundane, transpersonal, and worldly events through astrology. It will help you gain insights into the global arenas of politics, social organization, and cultural analysis. It is the perfect introduction to understanding the fate of nations, weather patterns, and other global movements.

Featured are noted astrologers Nick Campion, Carolyn W. Casey, Steve Cozzi, Jimm Erickson, Charles Harvey, Jim Lewis, Richard Nolle, Marc Penfield, Nancy Soller and Judy Johns. Topics include ingress charts, cycles, Astro*Carto*Graphy, cultural and mythological evolution, the chart of England, and weather forecasting
0-87542-384-1, 480 pgs., 5-1/4 x 8, softcover   **$14.95**

Prices subject to change without notice.

ASTROLOGICAL COUNSELING: The Path to Self-Actualization
edited by Joan McEvers

A prominent, yet rarely discussed astrological topic, is that of the role between the counselor and the counseled. *Astrological Counseling*, the sixth book in Llewellyn's New World Astrology series, explores the challenges for today's counselors, and guides those interested in seeking a counselor to help them with their personal challenges. Editor Joan McEvers and ten top astrologers to discuss this subject.

Bill Herbst, Donna Cunningham, Gray Keen, Donald L. Weston, Susan Dearborn Jackson, Ginger Chalford, Maritha Pottenger, David Pond, Doris A. Hebel and Eileen Nauman are this volume's featured astrologers. Their articles cover such topics as co-dependency, psychotherapy, reading the body, healing wounded spirits, personal counseling, business counseling, medical counseling, and more.

There are more people consulting with astrologers than there are devoted astrological students. This book helps both groups understand the client's needs.
0-87542-385-X, 368 pgs., 5-1/4 x 8, softcover   **$16.95**

SPIRITUAL, METAPHYSICAL & NEW TRENDS IN MODERN ASTROLOGY
edited by Joan McEvers

This is the first book in the Llewellyn New World Astrology Series. Edited by well-known astrologer, lecturer and writer Joan McEvers, this book pulls together the latest thoughts by the best astrologers in the field of Spiritual Astrology.

She put together this outstanding group of informative and exciting topics: Gray Keen: Perspective: The Ethereal Conclusion. Marion D. March: Some Insights into Esoteric Astrology. Kimberly McSherry: The Feminine Element of Astrology. Reframing the Darkness. Kathleen Burt: The Spiritual Rulers and Their Practical Role in the Transformation. Shirley Lyons Meier: The Secrets behind Carl Payne Tobey's Secondary Chart. Jeff Jawer: Astrodrama. Donna Van Toen: Alice Bailey Revisited. Philip Sedgwick: Galactic Studies. Myrna Lofthus: The Spiritual Programming within a Natal Chart. Angel Thompson: Transformational Astrology
0-87542-380-9, 288 pgs., 5-1/4 x 8, softcover   **$9.95**

PLANETS: THE ASTROLOGICAL TOOLS
edited by Joan McEvers

This is the second in the astrological anthology series edited by respected astrologer Joan McEvers, who provides a brief factual overview of the planets.

Then take off through the solar system with 10 professional astrologers as they bring their insights to the symbolism and influences of the planets: Toni Glover Sedgwick: The Sun as the life force and our ego. Joanne Wickenburg: The Moon as our emotional signal to change. Erin Sullivan-Seale: Mercury as the multi-faceted god, followed with an in-depth explanation of its retrogradation. Robert Glasscock: Venus as your inner value system and relationships. Johanna Mitchell: Mars as your cooperative, energizing inner warrior. Don Borkowski: Jupiter as expansion and preservation. Gina Ceaglio: Saturn as a source of freedom through self-discipline. Bil Tierney: Uranus, the original, growth-producing planet. Karma Welch: Neptune as selfless giving and compassionate love. Joan Negus: Pluto as a powerful personal force
0-87542-381-7, 380 pgs., 5-1/4 x 8, illus., softcover   **$12.95**

Prices subject to change without notice.

INTIMATE RELATIONSHIPS
edited by Joan McEvers

Explore the deeper meaning of intimate relationships with the knowledge and expertise of eight renowned astrologers. Dare to look into your own chart and confront your own vulnerabilities. Find the true meaning of love and its place in your life. Gain new insights into the astrology of marriage, dating, affairs and more!

In *Intimate Relationships*, the seventh book in Llewellyn's New World Astrology Series, eight astrologers discuss romance and the horoscope. The roles of Venus and the Moon, as well as the asteroids Sappho, Eros and Amor, are explored in our attitudes and actions toward potential mates. The theory of affinities is also presented wherein we are attracted to someone with similar planetary energies.

Is it a love that will last a lifetime, or mere animal lust that will burn itself out in a few months? The authors of *Intimate Relationships* help you discover your mate.
0-87542-386-8, 298 pgs., 6 x 9, softcover $14.95

THE WEB OF RELATIONSHIPS
edited by Joan McEvers

The astrology of intimacy has long been a popular subject among professional astrologers and psychologists. Many have wondered why some people have successful relationships with one another, while others struggle. *Web of Relationships* examines this topic not only in intimate affiliations, but also in families and friendships, in this eighth volume of the Llewellyn New World Astrology Series.

Editor Joan McEvers has brought together the wisdom and experience of eight astrology experts. Listen to what one author says about the mythological background of planets as they pertain to relationships. See how past life regression is illustrated in the chart. Consider the relationship of astrology and transactional analysis.

Web of Relationships explores the karmic and mystical connections between child and parent, how friends support and understand each other, the significance of the horoscope as it pertains to connections and much more. Each chapter will bring you closer to your own web of relationships and the astrology of intimacy.
0-87542-388-4, 240 pgs., 6 x 9, softcover $14.95

HOW TO USE VOCATIONAL ASTROLOGY
FOR SUCCESS IN THE WORKPLACE
edited by Noel Tyl

Improve your astrological skills with these revolutionary NEW tools for vocational and business analysis. Edited by Noel Tyl, seven respected astrologers provide well-seasoned modern views on that great issue of personal life—Work. Their expert advice will prepare you for those tricky questions clients often ask: "Am I in the right job?" "Will I get promoted?" or "When is the best time for a career move?"

This ninth volume in Llewellyn's New World Astrology Series features enlightening counsel from these experts: Jayj Jacobs, Transits of Experience/Career Cycles, Job Changes & Rewards; Gina Ceaglio, Money Patterns in the Horoscope; Donna Cunningham, Attitudes & Aptitudes in the Chart; Anthony Louis, Void of Course Moon Strategies for Doing Business, Retrograde Planets, & Electional Astrology; Noel Tyl, Special Measurements for Vocational Guidance, and How to Evaluate Personnel for Profit; Henry Weingarten, 12 Principles of Modern Astro-Vocational Guidance, Planetary Rulership & Career Guidance; Bob Mulligan, How to Advance *Your Own* Career as a Professional Astrologer. Includes the complete 1942 classic by Charles E. Luntz, *Vocational Guidance by Astrology*.
0–87542–387–6, 384 pgs., 6 x 9, illus., $14.95

Prices subject to change without notice.

Llewellyn's Astrological Services

There are many types of charts and many different ways to use astrological information. Llewellyn offers a wide variety of services which can help you with specific needs. Read through the descriptions that follow to help you choose the right service. All of our readings are done by professional astrologers. The computer services are set up on Matrix programs and the interpretations are tailored to your needs. Remember, astrology points out potentials and possibilities; it will serve as your resource guide. Only you can decide what is right. Astrology should help you guide your life, not control it.

If you have never had a chart reading done before, we suggest that you order the Complete Natal or the Detailed Natal Service. We encourage informative letters with your request so that our astrologers can address your needs more specifically. All information is held strictly confidential. Be sure to give accurate and complete birth data: exact time, date, year, place, county and country of birth. Check your birth certificate. *Accuracy of birth data is important.* We will not be responsible for mistakes made by you! An order form follows the descriptions of Llewellyn Astrological Services.

Personalized Astrology Readings

These chart readings are done by professional astrologers and focus on your particular concerns. Include descriptive letter.

APS03-119 Simple Natal: Your chart calculated by computer in whatever house system stated. It has all of the trimmings, including aspects, midpoints, Chiron and a glossary of symbols, plus a free book! We use Tropical/Placidus unless you state otherwise. Include full birth data. . . . $5.00

APS03-101 Complete Natal: Our most thorough reading. It not only gives you the computer chart and detailed reading, but also interpretation of the trends shown in your chart for the coming year. It is activated by transits and focuses on any issue you specify. Include full birth data and a descriptive letter. $125.00

APS03-500 (3 months) **APS03-501** (6 months) **APS03-502** (1 year) **Transit Forecasts:** These reports keep you abreast of positive trends and challenging periods. Our reports can be an invaluable aid for timing your actions and decision making. Reports begin the first day of the month you specify. . . . . $15 (3 months), $30 (6 months), $50 (1 year).

APS03-105 Progressed Chart With Transits: Your birth chart is progressed by techniques to determine what it says about you now. Use this reading to understand the evolution of your personal power. Provides interpretation of present and future conditions for a year's time with a special focus as stated by you. Include descriptive letter. $85.00

Prices subject to change without notice.

APS03-102 Detailed Natal: Complete natal chart plus inter-pretation with the focus on one specific question as stated by you. Learn about aspects of your chart and what they mean to you. $65.00

APS03-110 Horary Chart: Gives the answer to any specific question. This is divination at its best, Should you marry? Will you get a new job soon? Give precise time of writing letter. $50.00

APS03-503 Personality Profile Horoscope: Our most popular reading! This ten-part reading gives you a complete look at how the planets affect you. It is an excellent way to become acquainted with astrology and to learn about yourself. Very reasonable price! $20.00

APS03-114 Compatibility Reading: Determines compatibility of two peo-ple in an existing relationship. Give birth data for both. $75.00

Personal Services Order Form

Remember to include all birth data plus your full name for all reports. When you order the Simple Natal Chart, you'll receive a 25% discount on any one additional computer report, a 35% discount on any second report, and a 50% discount on any additional report.

Service name and number_____

Full name (1st person)_____

Time_____ ☐ a.m. ☐ p.m. Date _____Year_____

Birthplace (city, county, state, country)_____

_____

Full name (2nd person)_____

Time_____ ☐ a.m. ☐ p.m. Date_____Year_____

Birthplace (city, county, state, country)_____

_____

Astrological knowledge: ☐ Novice ☐ Student ☐ Advanced
Please include letter describing questions on separate sheet of paper.

Name_____

Address_____

City_____State_____Zip____

Make check or money order payable to Llewellyn Publications. To charge your order use ($15 min.) Visa, MC or Am. Exp. (circle one).

Account Number_____Exp. Date_____

Day Phone_____Signature_____

Mail this form and payment to:
Llewellyn's Personal Services, P.O. Box 64383-389, St. Paul, MN
55164-0383
Allow 4-6 weeks for delivery.

Prices subject to change without notice.